Delmarva Review

Evocative Prose & Poetry

Volume 12
2019

Delmarva Review

VOLUME 12

Wilson Wyatt, Jr.	Executive Editor
Bill Gourgey	Managing Editor
Anne Colwell	Poetry Editor
Wendy Elizabeth Ingersoll	Poetry Reader
Harold O. Wilson	Fiction Coeditor
James O'Sullivan	Fiction Coeditor
Cheryl Somers Aubin	Nonfiction Editor
Gerald F. Sweeney	Book Section Editor
Ellen Brown	Associate Editor
Jodie Littleton	Copy Editor

Cover Photograph: "Rough Water" by Jay Fleming

Delmarva Review is a national literary review with regional roots. It publishes annually in print and digital editions by the Delmarva Review Literary Fund Inc., a nonprofit organization encouraging writers and readers of the literary arts. Financial support is provided by sales, tax-deductible contributions, and a grant from the Talbot County Arts Council, with revenues provided by the Maryland State Arts Council.

The *Review* welcomes new prose and poetry submissions from all writers, regardless of residence. Editors consider only those manuscripts submitted according to the *Review's* guidelines during open submission periods, which are posted on the website: delmarvareview.org.

Send general correspondence to:
Delmarva Review
P.O. Box 544
St. Michaels, MD 21663
E-mail: editor@delmarvareview.org

PREFACE

As a culture, we celebrate great literature. The best only comes along on occasion, at wide intervals of time. But we would have nothing to celebrate, ever, without the dogged perseverance of dedicated writers who struggle every day to produce their best work. Those who aspire to be better...to be the best...are the ones who fill the pages of established literary journals. The best writers have accessed something special in the hearts and feelings of readers, free of boundaries over time. It is a privilege for literary journals to be among the first to present this writing.

Welcome to the twelfth annual edition of the Delmarva Review, our current contribution to discovering the best of new literary work. Our editors selected the original prose and poetry of fifty-three authors from thousands of submissions. Individually and collectively, the writing in this volume touches us as human beings. We can also enjoy the authors' craft and unique voice in the telling of stories and poetry.

Our editors selected 72 poems, 10 short stories, and nine nonfiction essays. We also reviewed six recent books of special interest, by regional writers. In all, the authors come from 17 states, the District of Columbia, and four other countries.

We are especially pleased to feature the poetry of Meredith Davies Hadaway. Poetry Editor Anne Colwell interviewed Meredith about her work, and six of her poems follow the interview.

While there is not one common theme emerging from this year's work, there is an existential darkness that embodies many of the stories and poems. Perhaps that is a sign of our times.

As our Fiction Editor Hal Wilson described it, "In this post-truth era laced with self-serving cynicism, each author has unearthed a note of truth. It is the affirmation of life that runs counter to the basic Western belief that human beings are fundamentally flawed." The authors face the reality of life; they find something of value through their writing, something worth nourishing in the heart of every human being.

The cover photograph, "Rough Water," by contributing photographer Jay P. Fleming, perfectly embodies the themes from this year's selections. Jay's photograph captures the feeling of nature's power and passion, which is expressed throughout this year's writing. Pay attention to James Norcliffe's poem, "The Man Who Turned Himself Into A Gun." Norcliffe, from Christchurch, New Zealand, sent his poem to the Review soon after the mosques' shootings in March.

As a journal, our focus is on the voice and literary qualities of authors' work to tell their stories. We are impressed by the courage and clarity of a writer to reveal skillfully a personal feeling or truth that will be remembered. They represent human challenges in a changing world. In most cases, the stories take on more than one meaning. In all cases, the voice is authentic.

Delmarva Review was created to offer writers a valued venue to publish literary writing in print at a time when many commercial publications were shutting down. We favor the permanence of the printed word, but we also publish an electronic edition to meet the digital preferences of many readers. Both print and electronic editions are immediately available at Amazon.com and other major online booksellers.

We welcome submissions from all authors who pursue literary writing. Our editors read each submission at least once. Since the first issue, we have published the new work of over 340 writers from 42 states, the District of Columbia, and 12 foreign countries. Fifty-one percent are from the tri-state Delmarva and Chesapeake Bay region. Sixty have been nominated for a Pushcart Prize, and others have received notable mentions in Best American Essays and other publications.

As a nonprofit literary journal, we exist for aspiring writers and discerning readers. We are greatly appreciative of the funding support we receive from individual tax-deductible contributions and from the Talbot County Arts Council, with revenues from the Maryland State Arts Council.

Wilson Wyatt, Jr.
Editor
Email: editor@delmarvareview.org

CONTENTS

FICTION

NONFICTION

Book Reviews

Delmarva
Review

Jacob M. Appel

THANKSGIVING ASSEMBLY

Only nine and so quickly called to glory:
Pseudo-Pilgrims sporting pasteboard capotains
With foil buckles, ersatz feather-bedizened
Indians proffering "howghs" and calico corn.
What a sorry love-triangle we must fashion—
You as fair Priscilla tripping over petticoats,
A cocktail doily passing for your linen coif;
And me, Captain Standish, rust-cotton beard,
Crêpe paper ruff; and backstage somewhere
Lank John Alden, wed to his cooper's barrel,
Underoos bulging beneath his baggy breeches.

We raise our voices to the blinding floodlights,
Above Mr. Campanaro's sweat-manic temples,
Mauve pocket square, methodical piano fingers;
Above Mrs. S—in her last year as principal—oh so
Grand those tailored pastels, that jade scarab brooch;
Above my mother, how young she would be then,
My first stepdad still in the picture; your baby sister,
Who will never see a third-grade pageant of her own.
We raise our voices in multiple, colliding keys:
Over the river and through the woods sweet land of
Liberty and spacious skies and amber waves of grain....

JACOB M. APPEL

Yes, those were our voices. Mayflower and Plymouth,
Squanto and Samoset. Doublets, fowling guns, venison.
Papier-mâché squash. Pretty Miss Wick and her fiancé,
Who later drowned, dancing a turkey jig; someone's
Toupeed grandpop snoring through the reenactment.
And you, resplendent, remote as ten thousand winter suns,
And Mama, a glass of pride, freezing time with her Polaroid,
And me, at my prime, never once thinking to be thankful.

JACOB M. APPEL

AUNT HILDA IN HOLLYWOOD

(after Frank O'Hara)

Oh how they fooled her, those gods of celluloid
Because she Believed (with a capital B)—
As her sister did in lovers and her mother in the priest—
Believed in Jimmy Stewart's decency
Believed in Fred and Ginger's simpatico
Believed in Liz Taylor's marriages
(Even to the mullet-tufted hardhat from AA)

How that lady swooned over Cary Grant
Sobbed for the loss of Tyrone Power
Envied Robert Taylor's flame for Barbara Stanwyck
And the whole lot of them queer as billy goats
Grazing on three-dollar bills

She'd have died standing to believe it

Modern Screen was her *New York Times*
Hedda Hopper her Water Lippmann
Bring up Negroes and she'd reference
Sidney Poitier in *Lilies of the Field*
And how she resented those chorus girls
Who framed poor Errol Flynn
And prayed for Loretta Young's health
During her nine-month recovery abroad

Once at Thanksgiving or Christmas
I mentioned a classmate called Ona
You'll like this, Aunt Hilda, I said
She's named after Ona Munson
An old-time star who committed suicide
And my aunt coughed out the word
"Accident" with whetted vehemence

But oh how she fooled them too!
For they never saw the swell of her heart
How her flesh flushed with Garbo's
How her lips seared with Bacall's
And how her fidelity never flagged
Watching from her hospice bed
Their glow dimmed on the small screen
Clinging to life even as her eyes flickered
Credits rolling until they ceased to be.

JACOB M. APPEL

THE GIRL NEXT DOOR

Okay, not next door exactly; three streets over.
And more raw peasant beauty than all-American sweetheart
With her deep-set olive eyes and child-bearing hips
Yet still the girl next door—
As distinguished from the figure skater
Who didn't accompany me to the junior prom,
That carhop who out-sashayed Veronica Lake
But not once across the cushions of my Buick—
How that girl fueled my hopeless adolescent hopes.

Her father was an outside director on the MGM board
With his own motion picture theater in his basement
And all summer long he flaunted archived classics
After block parties: The Wizard of Oz, Singin' in the Rain.
That's where we were one clement August eve—I can
Close my eyes and savor the scent of verbena, hear
Champagne flutes clinking poolside, Molly Pugh's stepdad
(Who later wrecked a DeLorean drunk and went to prison)
Belting out Volare over the yapping of twin spaniels.
I must have been sixteen, seventeen. All limbs
And yearning beside my bulked-up Yale-bound brother.
Mama was there too, svelte and giddy, looking
As if she might outlive us all—although, of course,
She didn't. And the girl next door, swinging alone,
In the arbor beyond the swale and horseshoe pits,
Nearly pleading for an adoring arm around her shoulders.
How easily I might have approached and offered mine.

Only now I'm glad my oaf feet held like anchors,
My arms dead weights at my sides. And that girl,
Spared the irk of refusal, will never bear the stings
Of resentment—not even in the silence of my heart.

◆

Sylvia Karman

WOULD IT CHANGE A THING

praying for someone past? Because God, a crone begging
coins tells her, has no need for time.

Imagine a kindness tossed behind us, stirring up winter's
leaves the year that spring stalled and fieldstone
caught the jaws of her father's plow.

Let it summon one gritty pause in his day of churning
rock from soil and furrows for seeds, debts creasing
his brow. Redeem him

and the burden of burlap tales trailing her still
with their upturned faces, hungry for chaste
morsels of regret.

Pray the sun through those spring shy limbs,
let moss and mud grin up between her toes.

What if some far future soul is praying for us now?

SYLVIA KARMAN

WAKEFUL

A shouting dream rips the door off sleep,
drops me blinking into the lightless hallway
of another blue-black night, the kind where
nothing nothing ever changes. I want to, but
too late and tired.

Then other sounds draw me out
to stand under whispering star gaze
where I hear trees bending boughs,
knock and hum, the metallurgic chant
of stones, and air rustling its wings—
each joining in singular voice
over all the world

as if they'd once been
where I am now
and had left all that
and their skin and bones
for their first forms.
Returned to themselves,
reborn.

And I wonder
what am I to do
with this new breath?

◆

Barbara Lockhart

LIRIOPE
Fiction

January 6, 2018

This morning it's all about the snow, how it covers the place where your ashes lie buried under the mulberry tree. You again, and yet again. There could never be enough snow.

Well, you're home now, after an absence of nearly thirty years, in the garden where loam and leafy shade keep you in all seasons. Dig down to plant a flower or two and your ashes, uncontained, mysteriously rise up and appear on the trowel. *I am here. I am home.* It is always a shock. Not the usual homecoming with gladness, hugs, and smiles. Those days are over.

But you are painfully, brutally, lovingly, frighteningly, desperately home.

You know how a brightness at the windows when you wake up on a January morning stirs a bit of excitement in your soul because you know, by the light, that there is snow? And with a silenced wind, there will be the gentle, peaceful drifting down of down that outlines every branch, twig, trunk, stem, and stone? Everything touched in white? From the upstairs window, I have new knowledge of the blended grey and brown scene of yesterday, drawn to a revelation of something I'd known was there but hadn't paid much attention to, like an epiphany or an extension of mind and life itself. The duplication of life's growth patterns appeared again and again, in their various stages.

In plain sight is the circle of liriope I'd planted to mark the place where your ashes are. The ring stands out as if it is some kind of statement against the vestiges of last year's haphazard gardens. All else lies dormant and frozen under the snow without design or color or any kind of order, except for the tight white ring of liriope. I hadn't thought much of it before. How large it is—about the size of a tractor tire—and it stands out markedly, as if some insistent spirit whispers, *hey, remember*?

Yes. Oh, yes. It was where the family gathered and wept for you as we poured the ashes into the ground, bewildered at the strange events of your life and our own.

You and I—we'd married young. Had the kids quickly, as if in a hurry—one right after the other in a joyous, noisy rush. We laughed a lot in the old days. In the end, none of that seemed to matter—all that history. I hope it lives in memories the kids keep. When the first grandchild was born, when you held her in your arms and looked from face to face, not smiling, the sadness of what we'd done and not done, understood and not understood, was written there, sinking back behind our eyes and settling in our throats like golf balls. There was so much to say, and so little opportunity to say it.

So, I write you letters. I write letters all the time—in my head—to people I'd really like to tell something or other, but I rarely send them. I've written a few amusing letters of complaint in my life that I thought were pretty good, where I poured out my concerns in a sarcastic way or fairly wittily—like the one I wrote to my lawyer and cut out some of the words with scissors, stating that his having to read fewer words might reduce his fees.

The grandchildren text now, or keep in touch on Facebook, but being of the pre-baby boomer generation, I would rather take my time with words and try to use them carefully, unhurriedly, as meaningfully as I can and without abbreviations. I worry about what is happening to our language. The world is changing faster than I can cope. For all the words that you thought would wind up in books at some point, there's no one to say, "This ought to be in print." There's only someone who'll say, "For a couple thousand dollars, we'll do it." It takes humility or a big ego. I don't know which.

Written letters may never reach a destination. Given to the wind in time, dispersed or lost. Mental letters disappear into thin air. But my notes are a different matter. My thoughts in one place, quiet, unassuming and undirected.

Yet I keep writing the grandchildren letters and telling them they don't need to answer, to get the pressure off them to write back. They text back. It doesn't matter. I have the memories, rich with episodes of early childhood. I took care of the children often, got down on the rug and played blocks, animals and trains for hours on end. There were towns and a zoo and the little train that wound around all of it, dropping little people off and picking them up. Once my grandson had a toy bow and arrow and we went out in the yard and I said, "Be careful with that. Don't shoot it at me!" And he said, "Of course not. You're my favorite woman." It makes me laugh to this day. And my granddaughters used to love to go for rides in the stroller and I'd sing to them all the old songs I could remember until they went to sleep. They'd sleep as long as I kept pushing the stroller and wake up rosy-cheeked with serious questions written on their faces, like *where am I?*—the beginning of many lifelong questions to follow.

Those memories are burned in my brain. Only death can erase them, so that's why I am writing them down. Maybe someday the words will be flung out there and hopefully read before they are burned and go up in smoke with the rest of my words. Just maybe they'll hit home somewhere. The bonds we have through the written word—you never know where or when they might be passed on, or how. It all amounts to the same thing anyway. An embrace of life. The thing it will be hardest to say goodbye to.

See what that circle of liriope does? Brings up all that history? All that wondering and remembering? Writing down the words seems to keep them at bay, or silenced, or used up—I don't know which—and they don't bother me as much in the nighttime. Today, I'll walk in that white fairyland down there. I need the whiteness this morning—the newness of it—it's wetness on my face like a christening.

The bad stuff is nothing, I tell you. Nothing at all in the face of the kind of wealth born of a rich inner life. Determinedly won. I beg the bad stuff to leave me. Or I'll get a lobotomy. I swear I will. Maybe these notes will quiet me since there is so much to say to you even now.

I hate to leave the relationship we've had with the cold, *Goodbye, Sweetie*, that you exited with after the heart surgery. I wonder if you remember how ill you were, how you called me from the ER, how I spent nights watching over you as you lay in the hospital, begged you to take your meds and eat, brought you food (which you rejected most of the time), paid your bills, did your laundry, ran back and forth trying to fulfill your needs on a daily basis, (get me glasses, get me cough drops) put on your socks and shoes for you, walked you in your wheelchair, sat with you and held your hand while you were in pain, talked with the doctors and tried to get you help. How you kept losing weight until I demanded your release and took you home.

I wonder, too, if you remember being half-carried into the house by our son, bathed by him, shaved by him, supported by him through it all, his arms around you when you were in the hospital screaming in terror—"Dad, I'm right here. It's okay."

I wonder if you remember how I'd walk you around the house with your hand on my shoulder to steady you, how I cooked for you, brought you tea, helped you regain your strength. But of course, you don't.

Most of your life you have walked away from the emotional stuff, as if that was a river too deep and wide to cross. I have my theories about the reasons for that. I understand you were always turned inward and that the turmoil in your mind made it so.

I realize how difficult it was for us to do any real talking. But then we never could. The shock of your first leaving—not a word—the closet empty of your clothes—unspeakable. Yet having you home again was okay, and it was because of our long history, the summer house, the winter house, the trips cross-country, Christmases, your mom and your brother and family around the table, our kids, the farm, and all the laughter. Those were the best of times, and the brightest years of my life. I always had a feeling I owed you something because you brought a lot of color into my life, to say nothing of this old house, which I adore. We were happy then. Warning signs not yet clearly detected. Only later. Much later.

What I never talked about was my litany of pain, anxiety, stress, and devastation at being abandoned, the bitter disappointment at the break up of family. It took me years to stop crying. In time, I landed on my feet, though. There are blessings in coming into one's own, a stark realization of self when the roles in family dissipate.

Then suddenly you reappeared, and there was my awakening concern and empathy at hearing how you were living out of your car and needed help. And I took you in. No regrets there. And then again, in your last year, the stress and worry over you as I watched you in your manic phase wreaking havoc in your life—then the heart attack and surgery, then your physical and psychological problems which I couldn't help but respond to and tried to alleviate, pushing you toward doctors, psychiatrists, dentist, eye doctor, hearing specialists, counselor, etc., etc. Maybe if I owed you anything, I'm paid up.

I know a lot of it had been hell for you. I can only think of a weather vane in the midst of a storm, spinning around and around. *Maybe this situation will fix it, maybe that woman will do it for me, maybe I'll just leave and start over, maybe I'll just say I'm sorry and she'll take me back.*

Vincent Van Gogh said, "As for me, you must know I shouldn't precisely have chosen madness if there had been any choice. What consoles me is that I am beginning to consider madness as an illness like any other, and that I accept it as such." That was the most difficult thing for you to do, accept it. You ignored it. You loved being Superman. You fought the meds. Who wants to sacrifice the chance to be Superman? And the depressions left you powerless to do anything about anything at all.

As for me, I've asked myself a million times, *how much do you forgive in the face of mental illness?* And the answer is, *a hell of a lot.*

Nonetheless, having you disappear from and reappear in my life time and time again confused me. It was wearing because in my own way, I still loved you. I don't think love ends, really, but it does change.

So there we were. You left us again. Yet in our hearts, we were still family. As always, I hoped the best for you. I hoped you'd find peace, no matter where you were.

As I turn from the window, I wish I could turn from the sight of that circle of liriope as easily. I wish I could say planting it brought me satisfaction or a sense of completeness. It didn't. I've wondered at the wisdom of having you right there in the yard. I pass the circle every day and think of you as I mow the lawn in summer, view the wall of thick vegetation on my daily walk to the pond or look out the window in search of a sign of spring where daffodils slowly appear in drifts among the pines. The only evidence of my having done anything in the garden at all, after all my scratchings on this earth, the circle is the only thing recognizable.

But then reminders are everywhere. The loblollies at the edge of the pond still stand in a row alongside the path. I can measure time by the size of those trees. You planted the seedlings along with blackberry and raspberry bushes and serviceberry to invite the birds, running the tractor over the ground in a path around the pond. Dreaming. Planning. Thinking this was your lifelong desire.

And it was, for a while. Until the pipes to the house froze. You chipped away at the frozen ground unsuccessfully and then threw the shovel into the air. You were finished. Done. The darkness had come back. You were lost in it. I'd thought waiting for the next phase would fix everything. It didn't. Neither did the pills.

To live a life with such anomalies, such contradictions, such 180-degree turns must be exhausting. That's where forgiveness must enter. And a patient understanding. But that took me a very long time. We were all confounded by your strangeness, by your keeping us in constant, unpleasant surprise, by your distance, by your demands on our conscience. That's what devastated us. None of this was, of course, intentional on your part. It comes from blindness, from that egocentric puzzle that you became.

But if I could speak to you one more time, I would ask your forgiveness. I was not the wife I intended to be, and the stranger you got, the colder I got. Understandable, yes, but why am I haunted by the thought that if I'd been a better wife, maybe you wouldn't have left? I want to believe it wouldn't have mattered.

I think we were unable to love each other in the way we each needed. Coming home again after twenty-seven years, you kept introducing me to doctors and counselors and salesmen as *my bride, my wife, my Mrs.* You wanted me along on every doctor visit, wanted me to visit and bring food, do laundry, bring supplies from your apartment. It was as though I was your assumed wife without the benefit of real closeness or intimacy. I don't mean physical here, only in the way of the sharing of oneself. Puzzling. By puzzle, I mean the pieces of a life that don't fit together, that are missing. Missing. That's it.

We went out a few times. There was this vast distance between us, too many unanswered questions, too many assumptions. There was no retracing of the steps one usually takes to come together. At dinner, you would be absorbed in the menu, in the arrival of a filled plate, in flirtations with the waitress. And I would tell myself, *I'm not doing this again.* But still…

The last diagnosis carried finality. It was proof that things have finality, a concept I find difficult even at this stage of life. What could I possibly want from you still? Maybe this would offer us both release, I thought. I was not quite finished with you yet. Or was I? What was it I still wanted from you? Why would I want anything? I could go for days not thinking of you or what was happening to you, now that you were under your second wife's care, but then in the early morning or at odd moments, it would come back to me with a stab. Could it really be that I was waiting for your death? Not so much your death but the true ending of a marriage gone wrong, and a time of enormous doubt, agonizing over what to do, watching you reach out for other women like you'd done for decades.

How much do I blame on bi-polar? I don't know. Was it because you had no insight into who you were? Maybe that's it. You were constantly changing. You got lost in the changes. Got lost in your own wildness, the swinging weather vane. I can see that. And I can forgive that. However, it is time for me not only to forgive, but also to forget. Not the early days together. Not your mom. Not your wit. But your devastating absence in our family, your half-hearted desire to come back after twenty-seven years, your unwillingness to declare love and meaning, your eliciting an array of mixed and confusing emotions in us all.

After your heart surgery, I remember you, now in your seventies, riding down the lane on your motorcycle. You were bent and very thin, still struggling to find a woman who suited you, arranging dates through social media, still full of great spirit. (Always the question hung in the air: was it the return of mania?) You rode to the farm, and I greeted you, *well look at you*! You arrived to tell me you were going back to the second wife whom you had just divorced.

A few months later, the tumor advanced, slowly eating away at your speech. *I'm stupid*, you announced, not able to get the words out properly. *No, you're not*! I was quick to reply.

Why didn't I know you were dying? Why didn't I know the problem was more than the lithium overdose that the tremor in your right hand had to do with something more insidious that any of us could have dreamed? But there was a pulling back. Not that there was anything to pull back from. Going back to your second wife was *one of the options,* you said. You wouldn't say more. I got the message.

After the surgery to remove the tumor, I went to the hospital to see you. I found you peering out of the doorframe. Your head was wrapped in a huge bandage that encased your head like a turban. My God, did my heart weep for you then. You had the look of a child, curious, eager, and irrepressible. You wanted to walk, so we did. Again and again, up and down and around the hall, holding hands to steady you. You wanted to do what you'd always done with your great energy. You had to keep moving. You were getting stronger. I read you the newspaper. I talked to you about how grateful I was for the years together.

In that moment, it was plain to see what a pleasure it was to have you back at the farm for that brief time when I was taking care of you. I have to admit it. I was happy then. It was a bit like the old days, if I could wipe out the twenty-seven years of being alone. I look back in disbelief at how happy I was to have you to take care of, how good it felt to see you regain strength. I thought of your mother and her kindness to me, how much I loved her. And how I had an opportunity for kindness to her son. It was a brief dream, however, and very Pollyanna-ish. Its impact on me was astonishing. Did I do it out of guilt for all the times I pushed you away? Was it because it felt so good to have someone in the house, someone I knew well, and didn't have to guess about? Was there a glimmer of hope that you would return? I can't answer that. The reality of it is I couldn't picture it happening for good. I'd been through too much, had accomplished hard-earned independence and toughness, a veneer no one could crack, least of all you. We could be friends, I told you at one point. I should have known better. But *friends* to me was safer than husband and wife, and I was afraid you would be thinking about that—about moving into this house which I have made my territory, my shelter house, not to be jeopardized or intruded upon.

I love the farm, you said at one point. Never *I love you*. Never *I'd like to try again*. Never *I've missed you and always dreamed of coming back*. You couldn't say it, although I believe to this day that was the truth. You could never give me what I needed and wanted. You just couldn't. I guess that situation goes both ways.

Goodbye, Sweetie. Poor lamb. May you at last know peace. We wept for the loss of you a long time ago, and we weep now for the end of an opportunity to understand and resolve the whys. We weep because we never really knew you, and because you never knew us. In fact, I wonder now if you ever saw us.

The ashes were sent by mail in a plastic bag, packed in a cardboard box. The second divorced wife was done. I pictured her wiping her hands after she'd nursed you to the end. She'd cleaned out your savings and disappeared. Still, bless her for opening her door to you. I admit her devotion was greater than mine. Or maybe it contained a lot less in terms of history and disappointment.

September 7, 2019

It's September now, a time when deep, dark green lies heavy on the trees like gloom at the foretold loss. All, all, will soon be given up to the earth as nature's mulch. Now a few leaves, the first of many, drift down in a flutter of gold flakes. The garden beds stand somewhat wild and uncultivated, as there are just too many of them. If a garden is the autobiography of a life, mine suffers from too many plantings. Too much of a hodgepodge, too many varieties here and there, unorganized and ill mannered. Surprises of pink phlox that had appeared in strange places, now lean in unassembled disarray. Admittedly, I am a scatterer. I fill in empty places with whatever happens to be in my hand at the time. The idea of making plans seems to be something I gave up long ago. It was the way we'd lived. I filled in with whatever was needed as your episodes grew deeper and higher.

But liriope is steadfast, which is why I love it. The root system is thick and massive and discourages digging up. It can be counted on to stay lush and green, watered or not, as it marks the edges of the garden paths and produces elongated stems of lavender blossoms in late August. It never dies. I've never seen a dead liriope. It rests in winter, grows grey and brown, but if you run over last year's leaves with the mower in February, it bursts with new shoots like Phoenix rising from the ashes and in a week or two turns into persistently hearty clumps of thick blades.

Walking among the beds in late afternoon, a habit I love to end the day with, the liriope now appears as a kind of wall, a container, a matrimonial ring charged with a sense of duty. Sentinel. An imprisonment. Both yours and mine. Yet a preservation of the sweet remembrances of our beginning lingers. I knew you as well as my own two hands. Father of my children. Part of me as much as they are. With it comes a flash of a bit of magic of those early days. The laughing.

I am bothered by the ring now. The coming night seems portentous, with its promise of the scatterings of my brain resulting in lack of sleep. The cicadas keep on, and the crickets join in. Bullfrogs down at the pond keep on with their deep-throated gulping. You led another life away from me for twenty-seven years. Married again. Led a city life that included a proper job and a new wife. You dyed your hair red, but the doubt in your eyes remained. We got together occasionally for lunch at a midpoint in the hundred miles between us. You'd call occasionally, too, using my name at the end of the conversation in a rather wistful way. This was harder to bear than most other things. I could say love continued in a distant forbearing way.

The ring of liriope is blooming now. Stems of small delicate violet blossoms appear among the surrounding hostas and ferns that are scattered beneath the mulberry tree. The liriope ring could be a wreath, a symbol of eternity or a celebration of what was. Could be. But it is not.

Ah, yes. It is time. I walk to the garden shed and pull out the old shovel, the same one that failed to find the frozen pipe. Old shovels last forever. I still have one that belonged to my father. I think that one could have chipped open the frozen earth that long-ago winter. *Oh, so it's about the shovel now, is it? How easily we turn from truth in order to bear reality.*

I begin digging at the ring's edge. The liriope is stubborn. It doesn't give way easily. Each plant needs a wide berth of disturbed earth in order to be uprooted. I dig and pull at the leaves, dig deeper, and stop to lean against the shovel to catch my breath. *Such stubbornness matches my own. Didn't I stay at the farm? Didn't I care for it as though my life depended on it? As though it was something that could be mended, become fulfilling as I pursued a life of my own? I will stay, I said. Damn it.* I had called the real estate agent years ago and never signed the papers. Friends said, *Sell it. Move while you still can. Don't stay out there alone.* But as something left undone, or a memorial perhaps, or a solace I had to work out, I stayed.

What I found was a language I began paying attention to. It was written in the soil and the tall trees and the moonlit nights, the pond and the old house, the fields of corn and the migration of blackbirds settling in the old trees. It is the way of life I was born to live. But it had taken a while for this to occur to me.

The first clump I manage to pull from its bed only encourages me. I wander around with it hanging off the shovel as I look for a good place for it. Far from the circle. Far from the ring. Out among your trees. In the woods. At the edge of the pond. Amongst the ferns. Two or three together for company.

Out of breath now and back aching, leaning on the shovel handle, I pause to look at the broken circle that has been scattered. Soon, nothing is left of it except for one hearty liriope, which still marks the spot. Its roots are thick, deep and widespread. It refuses to be moved.

LIRIOPE

I walk to the old swing where the kids spent hours on summer days. I can still hear them screaming and laughing, all three of them on top of each other doing tricks on the swing that caused me to shout out wasted words of caution. As I hold onto the old rope, my feet push my body into a slow rhythm. I survey the landscape. The scattering is good. In fact, it is grand. It is harmonious with the wildness of the place, with the planting of trees and the mowing of paths around the pond, in tune with the natural order of things. In the brief patches of sunlight, the wild flowers grow in abandon in these last days of summer, and the spread of wild clematis climbs some of the trees and spreads over the ground with its own white glory and scent. A different kind of white over everything. Nothing any longer needs my care or edging or raking or transplanting—my endless fruitless attempts to make manicured gardens. It is all right. I have a feeling of relief, of acceptance, the long-held grief dissipating. Out loud, I raise a benediction. *I did it. I finally let you go.*

Turning toward the house, I think I hear you laughing. It was the best part of you, but then, maybe it had been the only shield left to you.

◆

Judith Bowles

THREE AMAZING THINGS

The sky is a piercing blue but there is no sun.
The light is intense and sharpens the edge of each leaf.

My oldest daughter is busy with clothes.
She is wearing a sweater with a red rose appliqué
that rests on what looks like a long green tulip leaf.

Tiny stitches hold flower and leaf in place,
which expand and contract with each breath that she takes.

She is telling her sisters three amazing things she has done
since she has come for her visit. The first is the sweater.

She sits up on my side of the bed, tells them that somehow
she owns it. I wonder who made it with all of those stitches,

the sweater with the rose which seems to grow larger
in the piercing light. Her sisters understand the other things she says.
I do not. I think they don't notice the stitches that breathe.

There is a ladder leading out of the room which I know is there
if I need it. I stay, as do my daughters, who all look at me

as if they know me.

◆

Richard Stuecker

THE IDEA OF ORDER AT OCRACOKE
Nonfiction

Always the dull dread.

The war was there, of course. The University. The Draft. Marches on Washington. Dope. LSD. Sex without fucking. 1970. I would be leaving soon, graduated, going back home. Jon was heading for Germany to study Russian. We lay on our backs under a fat sun. The surf monotonous: the Outer Banks. Farther out, an undertow. Farther out still, the graveyard of the Atlantic. Ocracoke Island. A barrier island. A sandbar holding a village, motels, and wild ponies. Drifting constantly to its demise.

I had been on adventures with boys since I was seven. We killed the Krauts and the Japs on alternate days when we didn't pick up a ball game. The dirty Nips. Neighborhood bloodbaths and now the real possibility of killing Cong.

Two boys seeking sense under the old chaos of the sun.

Jon was from Ohio. Kettering. Outside Dayton. His dream had been to pitch for Columbia, but he roamed the outfield at Duke. He claimed to be a native New Yorker because he had been born on Manhattan, but his family moved when he was under a year. His mother carried Polish genes, so his eyes were deep set, blue, and piercing. Blond. He was shorter than me but he was a natural jock. Jon quarterbacked the Fairmont Firebirds but loved pitching.

The sun scorched us, but it was May and we didn't notice it until we crawled into an old Army tent we picked up at the Outing Club before we left West Campus and Durham and headed to the Carolina shore. The smell of military canvas in the night wind.

That spring, the U.S. had invaded Cambodia. The university closed down during a fit of conscience. We were free to once again descend on the Capital, but Jon and I turned right and headed for the coast.

I got to know Jon during the November March on Washington the previous fall. Not that he was political or full of righteous outrage and drawn to protest. I was. He said he was interested in writing, and that is where we connected. But Jon was all logic. He intended to major in philosophy. I was all emotion and majored in literature. The Romantics.

I had been born in DC. Garfield Memorial Hospital. How strange to descend again into my birth city as an invader, joining an army of youth the same age as those who were being maimed and killed in the rice paddies on the other side of the globe. We told ourselves we were protesting for them. But other than being about the same age, we were not much like them. Jon and I had student deferments. We were white and came from some privilege. And maybe we were protesting the war—in all our rightness that it was immoral and unnecessary and a mistake—for ourselves and our personal safety. There was the Draft Lottery coming in the spring, and the pull of a pill would decide my fate.

An Army of the Night Mailer had called us. We came over a hill, and stretching across the Memorial Bridge over the Potomac into the city were thousands of candle flames. Now along the streets and avenues and circles—L'Enfant's splendid boulevards—Jeeps and convoys moved, the soldiers holding rifles, and on the roofs at the edges of government buildings machine gun nests. Nixon was in the White House behind iron gates. Already I felt as though we were part of something that was huge, with the potential for violence or illumination or transformation.

Waiting to march in the morning down at the Lincoln Memorial, a rumor spread, a report that Nixon had come down among the marchers at about three in the morning, talked to some protesters who later reported that he mumbled somewhat incoherently, asked where they came from, and got back into a black limousine and drove off. Early in the morning, news reports reported this and then the report disappeared by the afternoon.

Jon and I snaked through a line and took a cup of joe and a powdered sugar donut from a woman my mom's age who smiled at us and asked us where we were from. The typicals were there. Bummed-out hippies brushing tangles out of their hair, bell bottoms, tie-dyed, a cigarette dangling from lips or fingers, starring off into the morning sun. Middle-aged and older, union organizers, maybe, and those who had been in Selma on the bridge and beaten. Blacks in fatigues and berets. Sergeant Peppers in Army/Navy store surplus jackets, other men's names on their chest. I saw a man and his son not much younger than me who belly bounced, danced a jittery dance together, hugging each other, happy to be there, and I wished his dad was mine. I guess Jon and I were typical, too, plebe shirts, blue jeans, a puka bead necklace tight around my neck, my hair long but brushed back. There were a lot of us.

After the weak coffee and donut, we got in line and obeyed a voice in a bullhorn. We were standing just in front of a banner that read Third World People Revolutionary Committee—a Marxist group. About a week later, Jon and I would pick up a copy of *Time* and see our faces on the cover with that banner behind us. Someone hung a cardboard sign around our necks with the name of a fallen American soldier and his serial number. We were to walk up to the fence facing the White House and shout out the soldier's name and number as an indictment of his death. The sign stretched across our chests as we marched, and as we neared the President's home, we could hear the names and numbers one after the other. We were photographed and the TV cameras documented our progress when Jon was pulled aside by a female reporter and questioned in front of a camera with the NBC peacock logo on its side.

"What did they ask you?"

"My name. Where I was from. Why was I marching?"

"What did you say?"

"Not much. I said I was from Ohio, but then I looked down at the sidewalk and stammered something and smiled at the woman and didn't say anything."

"Shit," I said. "I wish they would have picked me."

"Me, too. She was disappointed and told the cameraman to shut off the camera. I don't really know what I think. I came here 'cause you were coming and you were so passionate about it, and I just wanted to see."

"See what?"

"I wanted to see what you were so passionate about, and I wanted to go on a trip, and I dunno. Maybe I thought I would get into it. But I know guys from my team back home in Ohio who are over there, and I kinda don't know what I think about this."

Tossing our signs on a designated heap, we marched to the Mall, past the Mellon and the Smithsonian and all the sites my mom and dad took me to see when I was twelve, and the speeches began. I didn't much care about the speeches because I knew what I thought and just being in the crowd was enough. The fact that there were 100,000-plus of us was a statement in itself, and I didn't need to be revved up about it. I pulled out two tabs of psilocybin and gave one to Jon, and off we tripped. I felt like the two of us were isolated from the earthlings—except a couple of others were also tripping—who were surrounding us and we were talking to each other in English but an English only the two of us knew, and we had known each other from a very long time ago. Souls connecting.

We walked around the city when the march ended: little clumps and clusters of protesters on the sidewalks and in the cafes where we must have eaten. The drug pounded inside us, and it was speedy with flashes of insight and fear and strange faces coming out of the night. The next morning, on our way back to Durham, we stopped at a rest area and entered the men's room, where it looked like there were a thousand urinals lined up for an eternity. We sat on the floor and laughed our asses off.

Our friendship seemed natural from the start, as opposite as we were. I had played sports, too, but never as well as Jon had—without the grace, the poise, the knowing—and mostly on teams of individuals: tennis, swimming. I was an only child. Jon had brothers and sisters and buddies and a natural banter. He seemed to have knowledge of things that boys knew but I didn't. That knowledge and knowing drew me to him, and his easy acceptance of me made me feel a part of the boy world—though sometimes he would cock his head, look at me, and laugh in a rippling outburst and put a hand on my shoulder. Our opposite natures maybe were the glue to our friendship.

I would graduate in a few weeks. Returning home to the room where I grew up. No job. At least Jon was heading to Germany to study Russian.

"It's hard to make sense of where we are," he said.

"You know where we are, Ocracoke."

"Yeah." I guess he didn't find my answer funny.

We stayed quiet for a while. We had brought an old camp quilt my grandmother had patched together to sit on and sleep under.

He flipped back over, grabbed his t-shirt—a DUKE T-shirt he had ripped the sleeves off—pulled it over his head and down his chest, and lay on his back again. He closed his eyes.

"Of course, there is the natural order of things."

"Yes," I said, not knowing why but wondering where he was going with this.

"The Natural Laws of things, you mean."

"Yes, of course," he said quickly as though what I had said had no importance, or at least my comment was in the way of where his mind was going. I felt a little diminished.

"Everything fits, of course. The natural order. Newton. Einstein. Darwin. All here at the beach."

"Yes, I suppose it does. It would, wouldn't it?"

"That would be a constant, wouldn't it, like gravity sticking us to this beach?" he said.

"Yes, I suppose it would."

"And that could be its meaning, couldn't it?"

"Well . . ."

"But it isn't, is it?"

"Isn't it?" I asked.

"It doesn't tell us where we are."

"We are on . . ."

"Ocracoke," he finished my sentence. "You said that as though it has some sort of sense to it. As though it should mean something."

"Doesn't it?" I waited awhile and then I said, "Or do you mean where *we* are? You and me. As friends. We are friends, aren't we?"

He stayed still for a while and then sat up and looked at me.

"We need to cook."

We were living on Dinty Moore Beef Stew and Campbell's baked beans. We were camping at the Ocracoke National Seashore in a primitive campground. They let us build fires, and I lit the stack of dry wood we brought with my Zippo with the Duke coat of arms I carried to light cigarettes and joints. Waiting for the fire to get going, I lit a Marlboro. Jon didn't smoke. His body was his temple. I didn't care much about mine, as it was all rangy and didn't make any sense to me. Jon opened the cans with a kitchen can opener. We ate out of the cans. He sat next to me on one of the logs that surrounded the fire pit.

"It got a little strange a while ago, didn't it?" he said.

"Yeah, kinda."

"It's okay. I'm sorry it did."

"It's okay."

"I like being here. With you. It's okay," he said.

"Yeah, it's okay with me, too."

"Okay, then."

Night gauzed over us. I felt bruised inside for a while as the darkness spread. We had brought some dope and some tabs of acid, and I wondered if we should drop it before it got too dark or if we should drop it at all. The moon rose and the night was splendid, the firmament spectacular with a racing Milky Way.

"Come on," Jon said.

He tore down across the beach, pulled off his shorts, and ran naked into the water. I pulled up the quilt and wrapped it around me. Maybe I was cold from the sunburn, but also the wind had blown up, no longer a breeze but a strong wind off the waves. I walked in the direction he had run.

"There's an undertow!" I shouted and I heard "I know!" shouted back at me.

I looked up at the tilting stars and stood where the water flowed onto the sand. I could not see him for some time. Up the beach and down, one by one, people I didn't know were there putting up portable tables. On the tables, which seemed to be equidistant up and down the beach, they lit hurricane lamps so that the sand was marked off in parcels, as though the people were laying claim. I could see Jon, finally, swimming parallel to the shore, then stopping, jumping up, and plunging back in the opposite direction. I could hear talk and laughter at the tables. Someone played a guitar, but I could not make out the song.

At last, Jon splashed out of the sea and bolted toward me, stopping short in front of me. He bent over, panting, shivering.

"Who are you?"

I said, "Walt Whitman."

He cocked his head to the side, grinning, laughing.

"It's fucking cold. My balls have shriveled up." He was trembling, and his teeth chattered.

I peeled off the quilt and tossed it at him. He quickly wrapped it around him.

"Thanks," he said and paused. "Look at this. We don't need the acid."

"No, I don't think so."

Jon turned in all directions, now looking up at the emblazoned stars, now at the ocean, now up and down the beach, now at me, smiling.

"Here," he said, and he opened up the quilt for me to join him within it. "Sit your ass down."

It felt strange and good and scary to be sitting next to this naked boy who I felt attracted to in ways I had never felt before, had never felt for any girl or boy I could remember. High tide. The sea was rushing in. Looking up, I saw a shooting star and a plane that seemed to join the stars it was so high moving in a straight line among them. Jon stopped shivering against me.

"Amazing show," he said.

I was feeling a part of something magnificent—the plunging water, the far horizon, the deepening night. And maybe Jon was, too, but then he said, "But it has no meaning, does it?"

"Does it have to?"

We sat for a time, and then Jon said, "If we swam straight ahead, where would we get to? England? The bulge of Africa?"

"Heaven or Hell, I expect. Most likely Hell. We would be pulled under by the undertow and drown, in the graveyard of the Atlantic."

"You are a realist, after all."

I didn't reply.

"I have a need to know where we are," he said.

"Ocracoke Island."

A laugh burst out of him, and he laid his head against mine. I started to move mine away.

"It's okay," he said.

In the distance, we heard a pure soprano. Her voice formed a song, and we could hear the words, but it was a song I did not recognize, or maybe she was making it up as she walked on the shore. She was wearing a peasant dress, white, sleeves and skirt fluttering in the wind.

"We can sit here under the stars," he said. "The wind can blow, nature can throw its magnificence at us, but in the end it means nothing, does it? I mean, it's just a place."

"I think I just let it happen and am grateful."

The girl approached, and her song, made up in the moment, I think, spoke of what she saw and felt. She was typical of girls we knew who wore the same sort of gossamer dresses and let their hair grow down over their shoulders. She didn't look at us, although she was very close and passed on down the beach toward the tables and the lights in that direction.

"Jesus Christ, I'm horny," Jon said.

"Me, too," I said.

We listened until we could no longer hear the girl, only the waves and wind.

"Maybe we should come here, say, annually, from wherever we are, meet up and eat canned stew and beans together," I said.

"I don't think so. Not that I wouldn't want to meet up with you again, but it wouldn't ever be the same, would it?" Jon asked.

"I suppose."

"I want to remember this just as it is this moment. I want to remember this night, this empty, magnificent scene, this wind passing over the water. And you. How we shared this together, you and I. And the girl."

"Maybe." I felt disappointed.

"Jesus, in three months I'll be in fucking Germany."

"Yes."

"Will you come see me?" he asked.

"If I can. Who knows where I'll be then. I have no plans except to go home."

"Will you?"

"I've been wanting to see Paris since I read *A Moveable Feast*," I said.

"It's not there anymore," Jon said. "Not *that* Paris."

"No, I suppose it's not."
"But we could make our own."
"Yes, I suppose we would have to."

◆

Caroline Maun

WHAT IF I TOLD YOU

It was all a misunderstanding.

You would never have been able to please
your parents sober

you could not reverse their folly
by being smarter, better,

more beautiful, or by anticipating
their needs more.

What if I told you that you couldn't
have made a difference.

Even with all the magic
in the universe

those sad, broken, selfish people
would still break your heart

over and over; they would still
just want to die slowly their way

even if you could drive the darkness out
with a feather-touch to their temples.

GET INSIDE

His hand on my shoulder
a paw to hook me back
in the house, away from the boy
I would make all those mistakes
with. Stupid, defiant stoop kiss,
as much pageant for a jealous
father as a *good night, sweetheart.*
No control at all over those soupy
organs at my seat, time bomb
breasts and string bikinis. I'm fourteen
and drunk on the cocktail my glands
concoct. I'm weeks away from
the standing sex in the Gulf
of Mexico, the hours slipping
on slick vinyl seats in a parked
hatchback, fogging and stuck
in golden sand. That one
shoulder swipe, my father's
only violence, what brought him to it,
what he must have seen ahead.

CAROLINE MAUN

LUCK

In the middle of it,
I realized what was oozing
out of his ears was cerebral
spinal fluid. He tried to escape
the bed but couldn't, pain
pinning him, a full-throated
scream, then restraints,
a fall risk. I saw not a different
man, but maybe a variant,
a strange cousin,
a glimpse of someone
related but angry
and estranged. Eyes said
there were more important things
than remaining oneself. Getting out
of this was more important than love,
more urgent than a plan.
His old friend visited, staying
a long time. I remember
telling him how quick
and then it was a fight
for your life. By tiny degrees
it was different. The self
reassembled itself. At the rehab unit,
stalwart and unexpected against
the wall, we found an electric

piano. I wheeled him
to the keyboard where he struck
first one note, then the others,
a melody he'd written
we had fallen in love to.
The luck of it,
those things still there.

CAROLINE MAUN

TELLING IT

What if depressed you'd fallen
asleep on a couch in your living room,
the geometry test you'd failed that day
in the wastebasket, the cigarette
pack on the ottoman. You'd wake up
and he would be there, surprised as you.
Sleep so deep you did not hear the lock
jimmy. Your parents still out at dinner
they'd invited you to, thirty miles away.
It takes a minute. How do you know
to keep talking? How do you know
you should go along with the charade
he's looking for yard work?
You write down the fake name and number
he gives, which becomes more evidence.
You don't know it, but in this before
time he is figuring out you
are really all alone in the house
on two acres of land backing
up to the shallow creek. Even if raised,
your voice would die at the windows,
absorbed by walls of concrete block
and a roof of Spanish tile.
The nearest neighbor is beyond
a stand of pepper trees and yucca.

Not knowing what else to say
but somehow knowing your life depends
on connecting to this person
you have never seen before
wearing a muscle shirt, blue jeans,
sneakers gray with grime

and hands seamed with oil like he'd been
working on an engine. I offer him one
of the cigarettes and pull the failing test
out of the trash.

♦

Kim Roberts

BOOK OF KNOWLEDGE

Etruscan priests wrote an encyclopedia
called the *Libri Fulgurales*, or Lightning Books.
Lightning, properly read, carried omens of the future.

Nine different gods hurled eleven kinds of bolts
and each strike needed categorizing:
whether it pierced, forked, or burned.

The priests noted its acrobatics,
entry and exit points, the exact places it struck.
Lightning melted the coins inside a bag

but left the bag intact. It destroyed
a sword and not its sheath. It killed
a fetus but not the mother.

The horizon was mapped into sixteen sections.
The priests recreated a sky map
on the liver of a sacrificed bull.

To read lightning was to learn a tongue
awesome and holy. The sky's tribunal
waited for its cue, then opened its dark maw.

◆

Marilyn Janus

FIREWALKING
Fiction

We had no clothes. That's what the empty trunk of our Albuquerque Sunport Budget rent-a-car was reminding us. Not that we didn't know where they were: fat, warm, and happy in their suitcase, 2,000 miles away, on a comfy sofa with access to cable, no doubt laughing their asses off. Only what we were wearing, plus the change of underwear in my carry-on bag, distinguished us from Adam and Eve before The Fall.

All the way up to Santa Fe on I-25, we reenacted the five stages of grief.

"Pull over and look again." (Denial)

"How could you be that f----- stupid?" (Anger)

"Buy me a new wardrobe and I won't tell the kids." (Bargaining)

"God, we're going to stink." (Depression)

"Screw it, we'll never see any of these people again." (Acceptance)

Not until the turn-off to Los Alamos did we notice the snow, three feet of it stacked like a white shadowbox frame on either side of the main drag. Not only were we without clothes, we were without the wrong kind of clothes.

"Freak storm." our motel keeper says. "Just missed it."

Tom was there for his first face-to-face with his email contact at the Los Alamos National Laboratory. Their agenda was peacetime uses for nuclear war technology. My agenda, clearly, was clothes shopping. Happily, in a government town where the phrase "one size fits all" applies only to IQ levels, The Company Store did not blink at 2XL Long requests.

"Wanna go look for elk?" our Science Guy host says at the end of Day One.

Los Alamos sits about 7,500 feet up an ancient volcanic cone, a mutant bump on an atomic log. Science Guy downshifts his 4-wheel drive, steering hand-over-hand, peering and pointing, all the way to the top. The snow glare penetrates my photo-gray lenses right into my eyeballs. Worse, the rising, curving altitude tells my gut it is seasick. At 10,000 feet, with my Western omelet threatening to revisit, we reach Valles Caldera, a rock-ringed twelve-mile wide lake of snow.

"Youngster," Science Guy says, referring to the fact that it is only 60,000 years old.

You couldn't prove it by me.

Agnes Sasagawa, a nineteen-year-old Buddhist, awoke paralyzed from a botched appendectomy. She remained immobile for the next sixteen years. During her recovery at a Catholic clinic, Agnes was converted by a nun. She joined a religious order, where she had a relapse and spent ten days in a coma. The Sisters sent her water from Lourdes; she recovered. By January 1973, she had joined the Lay Institute of the Handmaids of the Sacred Heart in the Eucharist in Akita, Japan, founded by Bishop John Ito. She was also losing her hearing.

Meeting day two: the rental Mazda and I set off on our pilgrimage to Abiquiu, Georgia O'Keefe's "black place." Los Alamos, known locally as The Hill, may be America's only hometown with a near-vertical driveway. In lieu of pollen, the air harbors conspiracy particles. After all, the top secret in top-secret Sandy Hook, New Jersey, where I grew up, turned out not to be buried gun emplacements or Nike missile silos, but the *Bali Hai*-like Officer's Beach with its stem-to-stern view of Manhattan island.

What if the top secret in top-secret Los Alamos was not The Atomic Bomb, but this four-lane divided drag strip with no speed limit, the only way in and out of town?

Once down The Hill, I follow the road that says "scenic overlook." It is flat, lined with back-to-back soccer fields. Ridiculing my naiveté over what the government would consider scenic, I follow it to its end. Beyond the last paved parking lot, the world drops off. Snaking along so far below it as to be indifferent not only to me, but to life itself, is the Chama River. It is that shade of green museum shop catalogs call celadon. Everything is so still, I actually look around for objects that make noise. There are none: no birds, no wind, no water over rocks. It reminds me of the summer I was ten, when the eye of the hurricane blew over South Cottage. Being warned how dangerous it was, I promptly went outside. For some immeasurable time, we shared the same silence: me, the Shrewsbury River, Grandpa Rowland's silver maple trees, and one lone seagull, circling and re-circling in its own time zone.

At around Espanola, I notice I am the only person on the road, man or woman, not driving a low rider. Somewhere along Okeyh Owingeh, formerly San Juan Reservation, I notice I am the only woman driving anything. The country, high and flat, is open, just this side of desolate.

Robert Oppenheimer, the Manhattan Project's "Coordinator of Rapid Rupture," was no stranger to black places. As early as the 1930s, he had written papers suggesting the existence of "black holes." Nor was he a stranger to depression. Or to the more pessimistic nuances of the Bhagavad Gita, which he read in the original Sanskrit. Or to self-destruction (a chain smoker, he had recovered from tuberculosis not far from Los Alamos).

Abiquiu comes and goes, no more than the map dot it deserves. The Chama River reassembles itself into Abiquiu Dam with back-to-back concrete boat ramps. (Duped again?) I drive onward to the end of the world. O'Keefe's hills—the ones in my twenty-five-year-old Santa Fe Chamber Music Festival poster—are finally there: pink, gray, white, black, parfait-striped. All they need is a cherry on top.

Agnes Sasagawa, now totally deaf and forced to resign her catechist job, went to live permanently at the old farmhouse on Yuzawadai Hill that housed her Lay Institute. On June 12, while praying in the convent chapel, she experienced the tabernacle engulfed in flames. On June 28, the eve of the feast of the Sacred Heart, she experienced intense pain in her left palm. She told Bishop Ito. No abstract theologian, the bishop told Agnes to ask God if this was a sign that his Institute should continue.

The exact location of O'Keefe's Ghost Ranch was proving as elusive as its name.

"Back in Abiquiu," the gas station attendant says. "Second building on the left after the traffic light. Up on the hill."

But the "*Ghost Ranch Visitor Center*" sign points ahead on the right. My idealized reclusive O'Keefe would no more emblazon her name across her driveway than she would, well, live next to a traffic light. After some dithering on the matter—considering the traffic on Route 84, I could have slept on it—I turn into the gravel entrance.

While in her coma, Agnes Sasagawa had reported a vision of a "gracious person" who taught her a prayer, unknown in Japan but familiar in Europe as the Fatima Prayer. Now, on June 29, this gracious person appeared to her. On July 5, Agnes received the stigmata, followed, on July 6, by Mary's First Message. (Agnes never actually named her, but specified that "the voice" came from the statue of Mary in the chapel that was carved with Japanese features. She also insisted that, while deaf, she "heard" the message.)

Ghost Ranch lobby smelled of patchouli. Next to the Holistic Cleansing Schedule brochures were scented candles for sale. Serenity was not among them. "We called down earlier," whined the female voice from a back door through which I could glimpse cabins, suitcases (!) and confusion. She was Sixties in both senses: rimless glasses, gray ponytail, turquoise earrings, turtleneck, L.L. Bean skirt not quite covering expensive boots. "We've been working with the kindling *and* the matches and we can*not* get a fire started."

This time, I had been duped. Nobody saw me leave.

On August 3, Agnes Sasagawa received Mary's Second Message. On August 4, the so-called "Malevolent Being" grabbed her as she was entering the Chapel for group prayer.

No one knew quite what to call Oppenheimer. To his students at Cal Berkeley, he was "Oppie," the Ph.D. at 22 whose theoretical physics was as good as his arithmetic was awful. To his lab mentor at Cambridge, on whose desk he left a poisoned apple, he was presumably Snow White gone bad. He cheerfully called himself a radical leftist but refused to be labeled a Communist. It all depended on the girl he was chasing, making him, in the scientific community's judgment, a womanizer, an adulterer, even, but not a traitor.

From August until September 29, Agnes Sasagawa's diary records nothing.

Leaving Ghost Ranch, like a compass on autopilot, I keep pointing north. *Did Kit Carson trek this high, flat county?* I wonder. Did he wonder, as I did, whether, when he reached the vanishing point, he would just vanish? Whatever disrupted his pioneering—rattlers? Apaches? bad water?—it would not have been this white woman's bladder, demanding immediate (and indoor) relief. At the Carson National Forest welcome sign, I turn into a parking lot. Bracing against the wind, focusing on the loo-containing lodge dappled among its evergreens, I quick-step past a line of empty-looking cages.

An eye catches mine.

Can't be, no time, gotta GO.

I back up.

It is, I think, a coyote. His name plate says "Bert." And where there's a Bert, there's an...yes, right next door.

Walking backward, kennel by kennel, I fill in the story line. Bert and Ernie were not trapped together. They were not trapped at all, but rescued from Route 84 where two separate cars had hit them. Their new neighbors are two abandoned fox kits, a wolf who has, by his well-chewed look, lost his "dominance issues," and a roadrunner, victim of mistaken identity, shot-gunned in place of a quail. This is not a mini-zoo, but an R & R shelter whose residents rotate with the season's fender benders. Having brought neither flowers nor candy, I nonetheless observe the protocol of the convalescent ward. In my most comforting tone, I speak a few cheery words to each patient. Absent guardrails, I wonder how many well-wishers are tempted, as I am, to extend a misguided forefinger and tickle their noses.

Apart from the main ward, in a very large cage, sits a smallish bird with burnt sienna feathers. "*California condor, blown off course*" offers me a silent bored profile. I lean in to check out why it needs so much space. In a single twitch, it makes full eye contact with me and extends both its wings in a dry, ratcheting spasm. Only an aspen tree stops my backpedaling. *Dear Lord, I thank Thee I am not a field mouse.*

For the third time that day, it occurs to me, I am alone in a time-free zone. One, five, fifty miles ahead of me—how would Kit Carson have measured it?—an arc of purple mountains' majesty, drawn by some celestial protractor, starts and ends at my left hand.

A female, Hispanic voice trills behind me. (Only in Northern New Mexico—and only the women—can sing small talk.)

"You're cold," she says.

Cold? You think? It's forty degrees, the wind is jackknifing through my spring windbreaker. Even as I turn around, she has removed her Forest Ranger jacket and is wrapping it around my shoulders.

"We've got a fire inside," she coaxes me, "and some nice beavers to look at."

The A-bomb test is scheduled for July 16, 1945. "Oppie" has decided to name it, from one of John Donne's Holy Sonnets, Trinity.

On October 13, 1973, the anniversary of Fatima's Miracle of the Sun, Agnes Sasagawa's Gracious Person issued threats of catastrophe: "Fire will fall from the sky...survivors will find themselves so desolate, that they will envy the dead."

When it goes off, at 5:30 a.m., the press reports that Oppenheimer, purveyor of the poisoned apple, quotes from his *Bhagavad Gita*: "If the radiance of a thousand suns were to burst at once into the sky, that would be like the splendor of the mighty one." But the *Gita* is only what he quotes for print. His actual words, according to bystanders, were: "Good. It works." Newspapers around the world covering the Potsdam Conference, which starts the same day as the Trinity test, quote President Truman, urging the Japanese to surrender: "They may expect a rain of ruin from the air, the like of which has never been seen on this earth."

"You can see The Whale," Science Guy says.

It is our last night in Los Alamos. Wine glasses in hand, we're inspecting his collection of aerial photographs. Sure enough, on a line dribbling down the side of the volcano is a lump we recognize as the Los Alamos Aquatic Center, having passed it this evening on the way to his house.

"Room for two kayaks side by side," he says.

The Hill, he tells us over dinner, was originally the Los Alamos Ranch School, a "fresh-air" camp for sickly boys. Modeled after the Boy Scouts of America, the residents slept on covered outdoor porches and washed in cold water. Among its alumni were future Beat writer William Burroughs and future Lincoln biographer Gore Vidal. In November 1942, the U.S. Army bought it for $440,000 to build the bomb.

Akita is a remote, mountainous area in the far north of Japan's main island. It is notable for the highest national consumption of sake, which is locally brewed, the most severe population declines and its "Akita beauties," women renowned for their round faces, white skin and high voices.

"Gotta card game for you," Science Guy says after the dinner dishes are cleared.

With the girls and their mother taking leave for home schooling, the "you" includes me. Tom picks it up in five minutes. Science Guy makes me a cheat sheet on his napkin, the way I learned to play bridge in college. In the heat of competition, he barely remembers not to keep score on the tablecloth.

"Occupational hazard," he says.

When we have played long enough that he can beat Tom fairly, he drives us back to our motel.

On January 4, 1975, the statue of Mary in the Institute Chapel began to weep. Over the next ten years and eight months, it wept 101 times. On August 6, 1946, the Catholic Feast of the Transfiguration, the atomic bomb was dropped on Hiroshima, Japan. As predicted by the Blessed Virgin nine years earlier, Agnes Sasagawa was permanently cured of her deafness. Three days later, another bomb followed on Nagasaki. In April 1984, Bishop John Ito declared the events at Akita to be "supernatural." On August 14, 1946, U.S. bomber pilots flew 3,800 miles to the port of Tsughizaki to destroy Japan's last operational refinery which produced 67% of their oil. It was in Akita. East had met West.

After the war, when he lost his security clearance, Robert Oppenheimer took Albert Einstein's old job at Princeton University's Institute for Advanced Study. He died of throat cancer. Agnes Sasagawa may or may not still be alive. The Catholic Church has not issued any further formal statement about her visions. Nor has the statue wept.

In May 2000, the slopes of Cerro Grande, a 10,000-foot summit on the Valles Caldera, were tinder-dry. Reluctant to remain at the mercy of heat lightning, National Park Service officials started a controlled burn at Bandelier National Monument. High winds and drought turned the perfect snow-filled lake into an inferno. Four hundred homes and 48,000 acres burned, causing $1 billion in damages, but no loss of life.

◆

Irene Fick

THE LONELINESS OF SUPPER

It was such a splintered time. We ate in shifts
at the Formica table. Mom, always worried
about her weight, settled in with her diet: steak
and iceberg lettuce drizzled with vinegar
and Wesson oil. Dad worked late. Ate elsewhere.
Kid brother's meal was mobile and quick
just before Little League or whatever he did. And I,
the *fussy eater,* nibbled on pizza pockets warmed
in the toaster or plain tuna on Wonder Bread
or some careless dish as I paged through *Modern Screen*
and *Motion Picture* and imagined the stars aligned
at supper, dining with cloth napkins and real plates,
awash in witty conversation where someone, anyone,
asked *how was your day?*

I DONATE MY AUNT'S CLOTHES TO THE UNFINISHED BUSINESS THRIFT SHOP

My maiden aunt lies in that uneasy truce
between living and dying, cradled in the calm
of hospice on the health care wing. Each day,

another small loss. We falter through shards
of conversation—*what about the good times? Tell me
about those family dinners, vacations in the Catskills...*

but she dwells on the loneliness of being left behind,
her four sisters dead, nieces and nephews who play dead
all year long. On the dresser, a black and white

photo of the tight Italian family. Better times. Each day,
my aunt grows smaller, yet she is a giant in the shadow
of her misery. Her apartment is now bare,

prepared for new tenants: rose-colored sofa and chairs,
mahogany hutch, old hope chest, all sent to auction.
Last week, I donated her clothes. She smiled

when I told her the shop ladies were thrilled
with her tailored black wool coat and the turquoise silk
dress and matching jacket. I told her the ladies admired

her impeccable taste. We are near the end. Each day,
another small loss, and truth becomes the intruder.
She will never know how I crammed her things

into jumbo plastic bags, then dropped them off
at the shop's back door. *Just some women's clothes,* I said.
I don't need a receipt.

◆

Chris Jansen

WHY DO WE NEED POETRY ANYWAY?

Because the roof is still held down with tenpenny nails.

Because that very long knife that sleeps in the kitchen block.

Because we take hands and say the prayer.

Because there are whole cemeteries with headstones just for pets.
(They have boxes for mice, rats, turtles, collies, even
a horse.)

Because she touches your arm when she talks to you.
Because you noticed.

Because televangelists can heal the deaf with a word of knowledge
from the Lord.

Because of you.
Wasn't it always you?
Of course it was.

Because holding blackberries always stains your fingers.

Because you slipped.
Because you fell.
Because it left a cool bruise.
Because it still hurts.

CHRIS JANSEN

Because after coming home from a great movie, my mom would say don't turn on the TV.

Because Goodwill has a toy aisle.

Because we're so fucked.

Because it's a long way home.

Because hell if I know, maybe

because the Sufis say a man or woman
needs a soul
and a soul needs wings to fly to God.

REQUIESCAT

My cat got run over.
I don't have a cat.
And yet it got run over.
I loved that cat.
I raised it on fresh albacore
and pretty cat toys.

My cat got run over.
I've never owned a cat.
Nothing against cats:
It's me who is allergic.

The poor thing, it was running
from the neighbor's madman
midnight-whiner of a pug.

My sweet cat!
Now it's just a bloody gray pelt,
lying in the public street.

O God, O Cat!

I don't even fancy the animal,
still I can't resist
petting every stray,
though I know I'll wind up sick
and wheezing.

CHRIS JANSEN

My cat got run over.
The cat I never had.

If dogs go to heaven,
where do cats go, mother?

I've never even cat-sat for a cat.
I find them cold and amoral.
My precious cat!
It never had a chance:

Nothing so flat
as a cat
of the imagination

run over by the
yellow school bus

you never saw coming.

CHRIS JANSEN

THE GOOD NEWS IS

I'm dead.
And I'm so happy!
I just regret all the time I wasted
worrying, procrastinating
with vitamins and sunscreen,
thinking it would be like going to
the dentist.

It doesn't hurt at all.
In fact, how can I explain?
It's like the first night
we were together-together;
it's like swimming in God.

The bad news is,
despite the many humiliations
on my curriculum vitae,
it turns out I never suffered properly.
So they're sending me back.

I'll be a woman named Miss Corinne
who takes the bus into the city
to work at a nursing home.

I'll be a poor farmer in the South,
a farmer whose crop has failed.

I'll be a boy with Down syndrome
who takes away the trays at Burger King.

I'll be a fat man who invests
way too much *eros* in football.
I'll be his wife who makes beautiful hand-crafted wreaths.

CHRIS JANSEN

I'll be a Marine with no legs
who is learning to work with computers.
I'll be his fiancé who slept at the hospital.

I'll be your neighbor's dog,
the one that whines all night
for fuck's sake why don't they just let him in?

I'll be that woman you see every day
on your way to work,
that beat-down woman
who stands
at the off-ramp
holding a sign
that says
Homeless and Hungry.
Anything Helps.
God Bless You.

CHRIS JANSEN

SPIN THE BOTTLE

'Round and 'round and 'round she goes,
where she stops, nobody knows.

This time maybe on depressed Cassie,
who came home from school
and found her mother
swinging from the rafters.

Maybe on Kyle, whose boots
have no laces; his father told him he was cancer.

Maybe on Jonah, who could always make you laugh;
relapsed after 6 months.

Maybe on Brittany, the linebacker with a purse
who was born in the wrong body.

Maybe on Junkiemind Jerry
who was sent home to die.

When it comes to my turn, I will pray:
Lord, let it land on pretty,

green-eyed Destiny
who always wears long sleeves.
(She liked my poem.)

In rehab we played games
to help us learn how to be human again.

Now, almost fully human,
I drive toward night,
convinced that I'm grateful for it all,

CHRIS JANSEN

though this evening's sky is bloody as a botched abortion,
and the bottle never stops spinning,

and the earth never stops turning,

and the moon revolves through the houses,
her face always illuminated,
her body always in darkness.

'Round and 'round and
'round she goes.
Where she stops
nobody knows.

♦

FEATURED WRITER
MEREDITH DAVIES HADAWAY

AN INTERVIEW AND SIX POEMS

The River is a Reason: Meredith Davies Hadaway
Interviewed by Poetry Editor Anne Colwell

Colwell: I know most people would begin this interview with a question about ecopoetry—and that's coming!—but I want to start out instead by talking about music. You are a poet, and you are also a musician, a harpist. Those two vocations overlap and support each other, and this is clear in your poems, both in the poems that directly refer to music like "Heron and Harp" and "Basso Profundo," and in the music of all of your poems, the strong feeling for the rhythm and sound of the language. Can you talk about the connections that you've found between music and writing in your life? How aware are you of being a musician as you write?

Hadaway: My father taught me to play the piano about the same time I was learning to read, so music and words have always flowed through me on parallel tracks of expression. I think they are so integral to my sense of self that I am unaware of being one or the other in a particular enterprise, whether I am playing the harp or writing a poem. Often a poem begins as a rhythm that plays out on the page. The impulse is sonic, and I try to "hear" its melody, tone, and timbre, rather than imposing demands of content or structure. So at least initially, poems—like tunes—play out in real time, and I try to be a good listener.

Colwell: According to James Engelhardt, ecopoetry tries to connect to and define the human responsibility to the environment. Ecopoetry, he says, is "surrounded by questions of ethics." One of the things that occurs to me about your stance toward nature and the natural world is that your poems present and illustrate the human connection and responsibility to the natural world without ever "preaching" about it, without becoming shrill or didactic. I'm thinking of the delicacy of images like this one from "To a Sycamore, Lately":

> *I cannot know the hundred*
> > *springs when tiny leaves uncurled*
> > > *to grasp the sky,*

Or, these beautiful lines from "Here on the Chester":

> *Rivers grow larger, rivers grow*
> *small. Here, where the dead like pebbles rise*
>
> *among the weeds, I'll build my house*
> *on water.*

Can you discuss how you balance the need to talk about taking responsibility for our impact on the natural world and the desire to celebrate that world and all of its beauty?

Hadaway: I think the experience of connection carries with it an awareness of responsibility. "Ethics" feels like something imposed rather than something that arises from within, though the result may be the same. I seek to describe rather than define. The aspects of ecopoetry that shape my work most profoundly are the evocation of connection, fragility, and sense of place. The Chester River has been both muse and mentor for me. I learn so much from watching the osprey build a nest of twigs and twine, saliva, and shit—so precarious on its pole but somehow able to withstand summer's storms. I hope my poems open up possibilities—maybe no answers but deeply felt questions.

Colwell: Delmarva Writer's Almanac recently aired a program in which Sue Ellen Thompson, Adam Tavel, and I had a fascinating conversation about the question of poetry and influence. We talked about the idea that the writers who influence us are not necessarily our favorite writers, but are the writers who give us certain gifts at exactly the right moment: like courage, permission, a particular world view. You've said in other interviews that Linda Pastan was a writer like that for you. I'm wondering if you could enlarge on that insight, and maybe suggest some other writers who have had an influence on your work.

Hadaway: I love this notion of gifts at the right moment. Linda Pastan was the first poet I heard read when she visited my undergraduate class back in the 1970s—a time when women poets were scarcely studied. Pastan's gift to me was the idea that poems could illuminate the extraordinary moment in "ordinary" days. She continues to inspire me with poems of elegant understatement. Others who have brought gifts: Elizabeth Bishop taught me to hear resonance in pure description; Lorine Niedecker showed me how water can flow seamlessly through lines of spare verse; Jane Hirshfield let me feel the energy of paradox; and my favorite genius—Mary Ruefle—made me laugh.

Colwell: Like me, you have been a teacher and editor as well as a writer. One of the things that I love about your poems is their celebration of a real life "with one day / scraped against another," with cats who knock over perfume bottles, deaths and sicknesses, joys and "Ice on the River." Would you mind talking about how editing and teaching have influenced the way that you see poetry and the way that you find your voice?

Hadaway: Teaching remains the most revelatory and rewarding aspect of my life as a poet. Whether in workshops with adult poets, environmental studies students, or high schoolers interested in eco-arts, articulating a response to an act of creative expression amplifies it with a participatory power. As a teacher and as an editor, I get to share space—be it virtual or physical—with folks who feel the same tingle. Every poem has this potential, enacting the circular connection between writer and reader—we become a buzzing hive. And being an editor gives you the chance to put together an entirely new poem in the larger work formed by your selections, creating a chorus of voices in what Wendell Berry would describe as a "convocation." In either case, you are involved in a communal exchange, and isn't it interesting how sometimes you find your own voice when you lose yourself in a larger enterprise?

Colwell: One last question, connected to the one above—many of our readers are writers themselves. Could you talk a little bit about your compositional process? How do you begin a poem? How do you work it, revise and restructure? Is there a way that you know when a poem is finished?

Hadaway: I am a packrat. I collect resonant phrases, images, sounds, from omnivorous daily reading and from long sessions staring out the window. I try to free-write for at least ten minutes every day, always in longhand. From that free-write, anything that seems to shimmer becomes my jumping-off place—I look for a spark I can fan into flame. On a good day, this will unfold into a rough draft. On a subsequent day, I will turn on a computer and try to see the shape, arranging line and stanza breaks to better support that shape. Later still, I begin to revise by seeing how an image, a line, the rhythm supports or undermines the whole. Then, for the ending, I often go back to the original impulse and look for an image. This helps me avoid the tendency to "conclude" at the end and ideally will allow the poem to open up rather than shut down. If I succeed, the final image will shimmer like that initial impulse but in an entirely different context, the poem having taken me somewhere I did not know I was going. I've resigned myself to the fact that no poem ever feels completely "finished," but I've learned to let them go when they seem ready to take flight—however imperfectly. There's always the next poem. And where to find it? I tell my students, "Go where you can feel the earth's heartbeat." For me, that is here on the Chester.

◆

Meredith Davies Hadaway

IN GREEN INK

*Neruda wrote in green ink, to his mind the colour of
life and hope.*

—*The Telegraph*

It's 9:20 a.m. and Rachel Carson Osprey is
feeding her chick. We call her Rachel because
these birds were rare before the ban on DDT.

Now they patrol the river every spring, reclaiming
nests on poles and pilings, on platforms we have
placed for them. Like this one beside my neighbor's dock.

Rachel hatched three chicks but two are
gone, snatched by owls or eagles or maybe starved
by the stronger sibling.

We read that more than half of osprey chicks do not
survive their first year—and that's with two parents.
Rachel's mate has disappeared—

lost, we think, defending the nest. There was commotion
and a strange gathering of buzzards. Then all was quiet,
only Rachel remaining, with her single chick.

She's still there, this morning, when I raise my
bedroom shade, though she's grown thinner.
She has to feed her chick and then herself.

Fishing's harder when there is no mate to
guard the nest. A month to go before the chick
can learn to fly and fish.

An early breeze has brought relief from yesterday's
humidity. Rachel perches on a pole beside
her nest and stretches wings behind her, turning

slowly, like a weather vane. She chirps to let
the chick know she's close by, though her back is turned.
The chick, a tiny silhouette atop the nest, has also

turned to face the wind, small wings spread behind,
chirping, too, in perfect imitation of the larger bird.
Here, says one. *Here,* says the other.

The nest, a tangle of debris cemented by saliva—sticks
and bark from several seasons, straw from nearby farms,
some packing string from stacks of cardboard waiting

for recycling—everything now flutters in the morning air.
From one side I see two lengths of ribbon waving wildly.
I pick up my binoculars to take a closer look.

It's green, the ribbon—brilliant green. In a private
celebration, it spirals through the sky.

STATE OF THE UNION

Two gulls locked beak to beak,
wings rowing the water and battering the air so

fiercely I thought they must be dying—trapped
in this unnatural embrace.

Starvation, drowning—no good could come of this.

And then they broke
    apart just long enough for me to see

that this was combat.

The larger gull dove again into
the other, this time hammering the back

of his head. No mercy. The other trying now
to break away.

Another half an hour, their beaks
entwined, a parody of swans' iconic nuzzling.

No fish in sight, no obvious source.
Just two huge birds—the size of eagles—stuck

together, thrashing as the river slides beyond them,
the ebbing tide exposing mud.

THANKSGIVING

Because I wake up here where a kingfisher flits
to a piling, where the heron strides his patient

watch, and a sparrow chips away at the feeder.

Birds go about their business, the winged
body of one soul, lodged briefly

in another, stitching clouds to the tide.

From somewhere a shotgun stutters. One goose
tumbles—skims the edge of soft

and familiar. No wind, no sound beyond
my own breathing. Just a thick, hovering

sky. The bare limbs hold it
between them.

"ON A BROAD REACH
THEY ARE MAGNIFICENT CRAFT"

for Alex Castro

Every poem begins as a blink
in the sky, a slight turn of the

earth. It stretches the length of the
sun to where a cardinal perches, chipping

away at the morning. It gathers the leaves,
arranging them in riddles of rust and

gold, rubs each stone in its path.

Now it is midday and centuries lie
behind us, a litter of bones and

promise beneath the slurry of sand as we
stroll to the river.

Every poem is a long walk, the resurrection
of all the meters that brought us here, past

windows ablaze with sun. Every hand that
twirled a brush or twisted a knot to tether

us to something that lives on wind, bellows
in the breath of the water.

"DEAD ARE DEADLY"

—Headline from news.nationalgeographic.com

In the bath, I see one black
ant trundling across

my rug and though I hesitate—
apologize—I grab a sandal

so the crush will be complete.
It's hard to kill the big ones

who can ball themselves between
the fibers of a carpet and survive.

But this one, dead now,
lies in the fringe, forgotten

till I look down later and see
another ant lift up the smeared

body and struggle it toward the edge
of the tub where I suppose an ant

funeral has now been planned.
I sigh, feel some regret, then take

this mourner out with another slap
of the sandal. Soon two more ants

appear, one to lift each curled
body. Why is there no warning

in this litter of corpses? If Darwin
figures in, they should deduce

my bathroom is a danger zone
and look for shelter in a place where

sandals never tread—but no, they come
in ever greater numbers to collect

their dead. *Enough!* I say, sweeping
the bodies into a dustpan to dump

outdoors. Let them call for the fallen
there, where the wind through

the sycamore drops limb after limb—
but I keep moving.

SPIDERWEB IN A SYCAMORE TREE

I only spot the long white wisps because they
   hold a carcass, twisting

in the morning breeze.
   Invisible against my roof's light

molding until a puff of air
   disturbs it and I see it holds

a constellation of small bodies—some
   dead, some still scrambling up

the scrim of silky thread—waving
   gently from a higher limb.

◆

Charlene Fischer-Jehle

THE LAST CONCERT
Nonfiction

"This is the last concert I'll ever play," he said as I rolled his wheelchair onto the stage. I placed his water bottle and music on the stand. He unpacked his case and meticulously assembled his horns. His tone was perfect as always as he started his warm-up. His once-nimble fingers labored ever so slightly on the keys. I noticed a little slower movement, the dexterity slipping as he ran through the scales.

———

Larger sailboats control the rudder and thus steer the boat with a ship's wheel; the smaller boats use a tiller. A wheel is turned to the right to make the boat head in that direction, whereas a tiller moves in opposition. If you want to steer the boat to the right, you push the tiller to the left.

———

The program for the Salisbury Orchestra listed him on clarinet as Phil Jehle, a departure from the many names he used when playing non-union gigs...Phil Harmonic, Phil Dirt, Bertha De Nation, Ben Dover... It didn't matter anymore. There would be no more paying jobs.

"This is the last concert I'll ever play," he repeated as he sat in his chair, wearing his tuxedo, leaning to the left side. It was getting difficult to balance even while seated.

———

The sheet is a rope used to pull the sail closer or to let it out. While adjusting the sheet is 90 percent of sail trim, there is so much more. Halyard tension, outhaul tension and traveler adjustment change the shape of the sail. Each maneuver requires experience to contribute to the efficiency of the sail and can take years to master.

———

"We Need a Little Christmas," "Sleigh Bells," "What Child is This?" and "Ave Maria" were performed before the intermission. Phil adjusted in his seat, took a drink of water and rearranged his sheet music for the remaining selections of the holiday concert.

———

Apparent wind is the wind experienced by a moving object. True wind can only be measured by a stationary object mounted on shore. True wind is affected by the forward motion of the boat; therefore, a pennant attached to the mast will show wind coming from a different direction than true wind.

———

Phil and I retired to the beach in 2010. We planned to finally travel, pursue some hobbies in earnest, and live the laid-back beach life. Instead, almost immediately, his health started to fail. He began to have trouble walking and balancing. One by one, his limbs shut down. He saw a series of specialists who provided little help. The diagnosis finally came from UPenn: multiple system atrophy, a degenerative neurological disease that leaves its victim with a fate similar to that of the famous baseball player, Lou Gehrig, and the physicist Stephen Hawking.

Not long after the diagnosis, his left arm and hand contracted. His elbow and wrist were bent, and his hand held a tight fist. The right arm followed a month or two later. He could no longer hold a book, iPad, or cell phone. The remote control lay idle on the bed.

In the final stages, he couldn't feed himself and eventually had difficulty speaking. I learned more about medicine, home care products, and disasters lurking around every corner than I ever dreamed possible. I learned that a simple bedsore could take a person out of the ballgame. I had to be vigilant and fastidious in caring for any signs of skin breakdown.

———

It takes skill to navigate a sailboat into a safe port during a storm. I felt like I was trying to steer with a broken rudder, a severed mast, and sails luffing in the wind. I was turning a meaningless wheel, never knowing in which direction I was headed, or the timeline in which we would expect to reach the final destination. Each day, I was at the mercy of the wind, drifting aimlessly with the tide, unable to anticipate when the next swell might cause a tidal wave to wash over us, capsizing the boat, separating us, setting us each adrift.

The hospice center had a beautiful sentiment printed on the back of its guide. It spoke of a group of sorrowful people assembled on the shore watching a ship disappear in the distance until the tiny speck is no more. At that point, someone says, "There, she is gone." What they don't see is that there is as big a group assembled on the far shore eagerly awaiting the ship's arrival. They rejoice when they see that speck on the horizon. They see it grow larger as it approaches and jump up and down in great joy, shouting, "Look, here she comes!"

The concerts continue. Only the stage has changed.

◆

Martin Shapiro

BREAKING AWAY

Sunlight he cycles through is feathery, cool,
but he's burnt-out, his legs and ass ache.
The Potomac, below a mesh of tree limbs,
crests chocolate milk-thick above flood stage.
Rollerbladers lunge into his lane: He yields.
Parents scold a crying kid who crashed
into no object, and blocks the trail: He yields.

Racers on attack, patched with brand names,
hunch mantis-like over handlebars,
lean a steep-angled line into the corner
he's slowing through, so he steers nearer
the shoulder, over dog poop and debris.
But they're still closing, greedy for those few
inches he keeps, and he's clipped, sent skidding. . .

Before my character careens downslope,
snapping twigs and flipping into the river,
I set up a wormhole he can slip through to
bounce down on the sofa beside me,
minus the bike: here's the pimply guy I was,
dumbstruck before my too-familiar face.
He checks, amid whiskers, for my birthmark.

MARTIN SHAPIRO

I welcome him: *I'm writing my life. Relax—*
only words can wallop you in this realm.
Shelves across the room hold works he's read,
Catcher and *Cuckoo's Nest,* but all the gadgets
and screens distract him: little blinking boxes,
the machine I'm typing these lines into,
that big, blank rectangle flat on the wall.

He can't see what's lit inside himself.
Luckily, he's grown up strange. I let him know
he won't be marched into a quagmire.
He'll always go home from discos alone—
being extra picky, he'll escape a plague.
He asks how far into the future
he's been thrown; also, if I still smoke pot.

He could quiz me on my past half-century,
but I haven't time. So I shut my eyes,
dropping him into a bed of dust and leaves,
next to his bike. He waits for his wits,
which arrive by way of a migraine.
He finds no bone- or spoke-breaks, and walks
the bike to the trail. From there, he can coast.

♦

Mark Jacobs

THE HARP IN THE CELLAR
Fiction

The crown of the harp was a woman's head. The woman had
flowing gilt hair and an open mouth. Were there teeth? *Don't be
impertinent, Eleanor.* Teeth or no teeth did not signify. The
woman on the instrument's crown was a singer, her voice rising
from the nether regions on strings of gut. Watching Randolph
come down the stairs with a box of her neatly folded
undergarments, Eleanor wondered what in the world possessed
her to remember the harp all these years on.

The man held up the box. "In the bedroom, I'm guessing.
That right, Miss Malkin?"

She looked away, mortified at this inadvertent intimacy. But
what choice did she have? She had decided to move onto the
ground floor and needed help to make that happen. The stairs
were an accident waiting for her to happen. Randolph–she
suspected that was not his name, but he fulfilled the mental
function of Randolph for her–worked cheap and followed orders.

Now that the harp was in her mind, she recalled that back
when it was properly strung, before it donned an overcoat of dust,
her mother used to play the thing. No, that was wrong. It wasn't
her mother, it was her grandmother, a woman known for her
flowing gilt hair. Of course, the harp did not live in the cellar in
those days. Eleanor would give her eye teeth to recall when it had
been transported thither, and by whose agency and hand. The
topic fascinated her, although she had the wherewithal to realize
nobody else would give a damn.

She sat to collect herself, but a moment later here came Like
Randolph clomping down the stairs with another box of her

clothing. It was a relief, really, no longer being so deeply moved by the sinews of a man's arm that she could not think, could only quiver in fruitless response. *Root cellar fruit cellar coal bin harp, who sewed shut my pussy in the dark?* Now where did that come from? Unbidden, the little ditty horrified her.

Taking a breather, Randolph screwed his face into a social smile to let her know, "It's on the chilly side in here, Miss Malkin. You want me to caulk them windows before the snows begin with a vengeance?"

She shook her head. "It's not cold, it's just my poor circulation."

"Arrowhead's an old house, isn't it? Among the ancientest in Bradford County, or so said my ma in her day, God give her rest. And Malkins have been living under this roof for many a generation."

"My grandmother's grandmother sang harmoniously. She was known for her octaves."

That was not exactly how she had wished her response to come out, but once it got loose there was no calling it back. Then, when the man said, "How 'bout I hot the pot for tea?" the question took her by surprise. What did this Like Randolph want? Perhaps, she thought, nothing more than a cup of tea. She nodded, and they sat in the kitchen at either end of the table, which may or may not have figured in her past life; she could not say with certainty. The slippery nature of her recollections—that was another feature of a trying day like the one in which she found herself aswim. Like trying to scoop up fish with your bare hand from a fast-moving creek.

She watched the man dump half the contents of the sugar bowl into his cup, saying in his reassuring offhand manner, "Mind if I ask you a question, Miss Malkin?"

"Suit yourself." That sounded curt, so she rephrased it. "You go right ahead and ask."

"It's two questions, I guess. How come you left Pennsylvania? And how come you came back?"

"I was in the information industry, in Southern California. I wanted a career, you see. And, of course, the weather."

That made her California life sound like more than it was, although she had never tired of living near the Pacific. Even when the sea was turbulent, its under-calm steadied her. She started out as secretary to a newspaper editor, scaling the company ladder through the years to positions of more administrative responsibility. She bought a bungalow. There was a young pindo palm in the tiny front yard. As her career advanced, the tree grew. Six months ago, long retired, she had gone out into the yard to pick up the newspaper one morning and was taken aback by how old her tree looked. She had felt its rough bark with the palm of her hand and decided to come home.

Like Randolph nodded, stirring the sugar with a spoon that had belonged to a high-spirited Malkin bluestocking several generations back, or so Eleanor thought had been the case. The man across from her was rail thin and had what people used to call a shock of black hair, lightly streaked with gray. The frank expression marking his broad face led a person to trust him, and his teeth were virtuous. How strange he should wear the same green workpants the real Randolph used to wear.

"I came back to set my affairs in order."

His smile was comforting. "You're not thinking about giving up the ghost any time soon, I hope."

"That's not what I meant. I am sorry for not saying more. These are weighty matters, or they are to me."

"No need to apologize. I don't mean to be nosy. It's unusual, is all, a woman of your years moving into a humongous old mansion by yourself. Maybe you'll have friends to stay with you, help you look after the place."

She asked him to repeat his name. The instant he did, she lost it again. That was simply a game her mind enjoyed playing on her. Never mind.

He was right about the snow. It fell that night for the first time since her return to Towanda. She sat in a Hepplewhite chair by the bow window, wrapped in an ancestral afghan, watching the white make steady, quiet progress covering the sloping lawn as the lights of the borough disappeared behind a curtain of the swirling stuff.

The lawn looked enormous, even as the snow reshaped its contours. There must be a full acre. Come April, it would need regular cutting. Perhaps Like Randolph could be persuaded to take on the job. Was there a mower in the barn out back? She had not thought to look.

She rested in her nest for a long little while, beset by a sense of anticipation. At a certain point, the snow stopped, a gap appeared in the clouds, and the moon appeared, fat and sassy, like a pampered princess. The story of a little girl came back to her. It involved a wagon hurtling down the drive that bisected the vast lawn of Arrowhead. It was the green season, and she smelled lilacs. Surely the child must go smash. But at the last moment Randolph stepped into the drive and lifted her from the careening wagon, bruising her underarms where his strong hands grasped her. *That was a mighty narrow miss, Missie.* The obvious pleasure in his laugh punctured the swelling bubble of her fear, and she laughed as hard as he did.

That was Randolph, to a T. Being so wrapped up in forgetting other men, she had neglected all these years to remember the one who deserved her gratitude. He worked for the Malkins back when jack of all-trades was a respectable calling. He treated her, from a distance, as a doting uncle treated a niece to whom he was particularly partial. Candy canes at Christmas, a song from the lawn as he worked on a hot day, a bunch of peonies presented with a courtly bow.

Rising from the chair, she went to the mahogany secretary where Malkins traditionally kept papers of a certain magnitude. There was a letter from Ferguson, who in addition to his legal duties acted as steward of what remained of the Malkin money. She disliked the arid, chiding tone with which he admonished her not to die intestate. Why not? Let him go ahead and tell her why not. She had no heirs. *No heirs, no hair, nothing left down there.* They were coming fast and furious today, the ditties. It was exasperating. In his letter, Ferguson recommended a mix of conservative charities but of course had the delicacy not to mention the fees accruing to him as executor. Let him stew in his beef. She would not respond until she felt like responding.

Since coming back, this was the first night she had slept in the guest room. The family had always referred to it as the Cornsilk Room, although why was beyond her since for as far back as she could recall the walls were papered in a plum pattern. The bed was a high four-poster requiring her to climb a cherry step stool that a seafaring predecessor had brought back from a famous archipelago whose name she never had mastered, an Oriental port city where the men went around half nude due to the extreme heat. They carried a type of dagger in their belt; it had a name, now gone. She settled onto the comfortable mattress but had to get up immediately to locate another blanket. Maybe she would let Randolph, Like Randolph, caulk those windows after all. She fell asleep secure in the knowledge that mornings she was better, stronger physically and her mind less fractious. In the morning, she promised herself, the situation would be clearer.

But in the morning, she woke jostled cheek by jowl in the guest room bed. Hoo boy, what a crowd. Her mother was there, and her grandmother with the little sack of horehound candies she used to carry like ammunition, sweet little bullets she spread in scattershot fashion in a feeble attempt to keep the peace. Eleanor's father was in the bed along with them, in his absent way. Prince Malkin was anecdotes, to his daughter, always and only anecdotes, capped by the story of his departure from Arrowhead in a chauffeured Packard. From the library his wife, Madelaine, had watched, through mullioned windows, the car disappearing down the drive, Prince slumped in the backseat with his tie askew, preemptive tears of regret glistening on his cheeks, a bottle of the finest rye on the seat next to him like proof positive that one thing led to another.

THE HARP IN THE CELLAR

Crowded though it was, the bed in the Cornsilk Room contained yet another occupant. Eleanor knew him by his profile but could not look him in the eye, not on an empty stomach. Then, by the time she sat in the kitchen before coffee and toast with marmalade, she was distracted by the enormity of the task she had foisted on herself, coming back to Arrowhead. All the upkeep, the echoing empty space, the sheer size of the place, she had no business taking it on. There was a standing offer for the property that Ferguson had so often urged her to accept she suspected he would get a commission if the sale went through. *The proprietor is a little old lady. A spinster, as it happens. Lives in Southern California. She severed ties with Towanda and her family decades ago. Leave it to me and I'll bring Miss Malkin around.*

It would be foolish to stay on just to thwart the designs of the family retainer. She was capable, she had learned the hard way, of extravagant foolishness. But now, with the winter wind rattling old windows in their panes, the furnace laboring, the drive unplowed and no arrangement made, getting through winter felt daunting, let alone spring and the relentlessness of grass.

The smart thing would be to junk the whole idea. Let Ferguson sell Arrowhead. Take the money and go to Tahiti. Learn to drink. Write a new definition of profligate. But there was no way she would be smart. She had come back to Towanda for a reason. With time and luck, memory would serve rather than betray her. It was not only criminals who returned to the scene of the crime.

She heard an engine and made her wobbling way to the front windows to see a blue pickup with an enormous red plow clearing the drive. Relief felt like the instant after a spasm of gas. She watched the driver expertly manipulate the plow until she was sure it was he of the green workpants. Then she went back to the kitchen and brewed a fresh pot of coffee. There was no time to bake, but she fished some powdered doughnuts from the bread box and arranged them on a plate.

She waited, doing her best not to fret over paying him. She hoped he would simply hand her a bill but feared he would leave the amount up to her. She had no idea what the job was worth and dreaded insulting him with too little, or too much. She waited.

Waited. Until she heard the truck going away. He was not coming in to see her. Why? As she poured the coffee down the sink, her vexation with the man knew no bounds. She held the empty carafe for a moment. The room spun, its individual objects refusing to stay put in their assigned place. She closed her eyes and gripped the sink edge with her free hand. Opening her eyes again, she threw the carafe at the refrigerator. It smashed brilliantly, like a rejected present. Now here, thank goodness, was a mess she knew how to clean up.

"I'm scatterbrained. You'll have to tell me your name again."

"Izaak, Miss Malkin. Izaak Walton Duncan, after the famous fisherman."

"Fisherman," she echoed.

That was a mistake. Izaak was the word she needed to net, not some fish. Izaak. She had it. Now to keep it.

She was relieved he had come back, though it took him two days to get around to it. Thoughtfully, he'd handed her a folded piece of paper with the bill for clearing the drive written in legible numbers. Handing him cash, she had no idea she was going to say to him what she did.

"You put me in mind of a man who used to work here. His name was Randolph."

His smile was large. "Randolph Boggs. I'm sorry to say, Mr. Boggs passed quite some time ago. But he lived to a ripe old age. There was a big turnout at the funeral. People respected Mr. Boggs."

"He was kind to me."

Izaak nodded again. He was a patient man, which helped. They were standing out of doors, under the portico. The weather had moderated, and the snow was gone. It felt deceptively like spring, the leaping time of year. Eleanor had a black woolen shawl over her shoulders, knitted by a grieving female hand after a relation fell in the trenches at Belleau Wood. The shawl had the weight of ages, not such a bad thing. The sun made the trees stand straight. Izaak wore dungarees, a leather belt around his waist bristling with the tools of his various trades.

"Would you like to go inside, Miss Malkin? You look a little peaked."

"No, I would not."

He gave her his arm, and they strolled on the drying pavement of the drive. She said, "I suppose you know all about my father." That was unfair. She should not have put him on the spot. She tacked leeward and began again. "My father, Prince Malkin, left the family when I was a girl of ten. Irreconcilable differences, I believe is what they call the category."

"I'm sorry."

"At that time, Randolph–Mr. Boggs–was working for us."

That might not seem germane, but it was. She took comfort from Izaak's patience, deep as seven wells, and inhaled before going on. "After the Packard, that is, after my father left, my mother wrote to her brother. Lambert Thierry was the name. They are French-Canadian, originally. She wanted a man around the house to see to things."

"Seems natural enough."

It was coming. No, it wasn't. There was a block keeping it back. The block was her. Izaak pointed to a red fox going into a hedge on the edge of the yellow grass, its stiff brush pointing as if to indicate a direction for her to take. The direction was backwards.

She said, "There was a problem."

"A problem?"

"An incident."

"I see."

The way he said it made it sound as if she had been perfectly clear. Why didn't more men have that faculty, or choose to exercise it?

"Down in the cellar," she said.

It was all she could manage, and he walked her to the front door.

She had a restless night and got up to drink a finger's worth of rum. As she sat with the afghan over her knees in the study, pictures of her life out west came into her mind. They were snapshots of things that seemed to stand for more than themselves. A view of the unruffled Pacific from a sandy bluff at Torrey Pines. The aggressive fin of an enormous blue Cadillac in which she once rode very fast. At a stoplight, one summer afternoon, she had looked over at the driver of the car in the lane next to her. It was Milton Berle. He lifted a hand and waved, like a gentleman. She had made a life in California, her own life. She had persevered. Maybe that was enough.

It was not. When Izaak–she had his name, finally – showed up to caulk the windows, she stood watching him at his task. She had always enjoyed that, seeing a man apply himself to a job, losing and finding himself in the work.

"My Uncle Lambert."

"Yes, Ma'am."

"I cannot recall why I was in the cellar."

He kept caulking, which was the right way to go about this conversation.

"He bothered me."

Izaak turned around, understanding perfectly. With a level voice he said, "Your uncle molested you."

She nodded. All these years on, and she could not stop trembling. The tears were hot as shame on her face. "Randolph happened to come down. It must have been winter. In those days, the house had a coal stove, and he meant to feed the fire."

Izaak nodded. "Why don't you sit down, Miss Malkin?"

She let him guide her to a chair.

"Randolph beat my uncle. Beat him badly. It was a terrible thing to watch. I felt myself to be at fault. What was I doing down cellar in the first place? It was not a place for little girls. The next day, my uncle was gone. No one ever referred to the matter, or mentioned Uncle Lambert again. Mother cried for weeks. She would hold me to her for hours on end. That's why I came back to Towanda, you see. Back to Arrowhead."

"To tell someone the story."

"Not just anyone."

Being in his work clothes, Izaak spread a tarp on a chair before sitting down in it. "I am sorry, Miss Malkin. Can I do something for you?"

"You already have."

He stuck around longer than he needed to when he finished the window job, which was kind of him. She baked ginger snaps, and he ate ten or a dozen of them with hot coffee. A thin man could get away with eating cookies like that. He told her jokes she seemed to remember having heard when she was a child. He showed her pictures of his several daughters, which he kept on his iPhone. And he had the decency not to say a single thing that ought not be said.

That night, she knew before her head hit the pillow what fell to her to do. She slept well. Her dreams were densely textured, like so many blankets being laid over her passive body. In the morning, she took her time. She made oatmeal and drank a second cup of coffee watching four crows work the lawn for insects in a crew, their feathers glinting in the sun like the sleek, unloving creatures they were.

At some point somebody had put in a new staircase down into the cellar. It was sturdier than what her feet remembered, going down the steps. But the old-fashioned round black light switch was in the proper place, the light it cast as weak and evocative as ever. *This bitch will sing, the skies will ring.* No. That was not what she meant. There would be no more ditties, unbidden or otherwise.

The cellar was large, the size and outline of the entire first floor of the house that sat on it. There were crazy crooked rooms, there were nooks and crannies and gloomy corners. She twisted a block of wood that held fast the door of the coal bin, half expecting the harp to be inside, but no luck. The walls were black with coal dust. She traced a straight line with a finger on one wall and closed the door again.

The place had a smell, powerfully familiar, that no basement on the West Coast ever had or could have. It was a vegetable taint, what vegetables had in common with people, what they left behind. There was grease in the smell, too, and used-up oil. There were secrets, and old understanding. A whiff of the Devil's sweat. She moved carefully, keeping an eye out for stray objects that could trip her up.

It gave her a start when she finally saw the harp. Up against the back wall of what used to be Randolph's workshop, leaning at an odd angle, the instrument had a presence she briefly mistook for human. She stood there looking at it for the longest time, not daring to approach. The weak light abetted her imagination, and she sensed the thing was in distress, alone and unplucked in the Arrowhead cellar for so many years. Such neglect was a savage thing and made her shiver. Yet somehow the harp had kept its identity as a machine designed to produce beauty.

When she was ready, she grasped it by the column and pulled it to her. There were strings. They must be older than Eleanor was. She was careful not to touch them.

She pulled the harp by the base with extreme care, one hand on the column guiding. It took a long time to get the instrument out of the workshop and onto the rough concrete floor. She was breathing hard and felt sweat blossom under her arms, cold and damp as it was in the cellar. Her throat felt scratchy. Once, the base bumped over something on the floor as she dragged it, and the instrument moaned.

"I am so sorry," she said, not feeling the slightest bit foolish apologizing to a thing.

She took a break, sat on an upturned apple crate breathing deliberately until her strength returned. What was likely a rat scuttled somewhere low in the dark. Damn the infernal creature. What was there to subsist upon in a cellar like this one? Overhead, outside, the world tore by in its customary frenzy. She felt, for a moment, safely distant from the viciousness of people bloodying one another, from the high, maniacal scream of them.

She was worn out by the time she dragged the harp to the foot of the stairs. If she had thought ahead, she might have brought something to eat. That way she would keep up her strength. But if she went up now, she would not come down again.

She sat on a stair, not minding in the least any dust on the seat of her skirt. She rocked back and forth a little. Then she did the one thing that remained to do. She reached out a hand and touched the strings.

The sound her touch produced was horrendous. It was tuneless and discordant. With growing pleasure, she raked the fingers of both hands across the old strings. The harp responded the only way it could. The anguished, angry sound moved her deeply. A matter, now, of taking her time. Pulling it up she would have to lean the thing, somehow or other bracing it, when she stopped to breathe. But by day's end–there was absolutely no doubt in her clarified mind–by day's end, the harp would rest above ground where it belonged.

◆

Sherry Chappelle

HANDEL AND HENDRIX WALK INTO A VENN DIAGRAM

One dyspeptic darling of royalty
king of cantatas and concerti
(please rise)   Great Bear
hooks up with Buster
blackboy born into welfare
hellraiser from the Bag O'Bones
risen to hobnob with the greats.

Every generation throws a hero or two
into the firmament
and this they share.
They have come straight
from Brook St, Mayfair, London
their joint museum
separated by a wall
and two hundred years.

They pull a pint.
From flame
these long-haired wizards
birthed enchanted webs
swinging long
past hazy days of smashed
guitars and harpsichords
capes and velvet breeches
muses of lacy low-cut
figures and fugues.

SHERRY CHAPPELLE

The bitch of fame sits at their table
red dress tight across her chest.
For one more toothsome riff
the right notes
in sounds bloody waves
they'd toss her out the door.

◆

David Xiang

A CREATURE LIVES IN EVERY POEM

The first man was of the dust of the earth,
and the second man from heaven.
                    —1 Corinthians 15:47

I know him by his writings I can
see the green meadow and shade
that stabs blind pierces into dark
forest outlines questions with the

care of a boy learning cursive It
takes shape slowly Quietly And
there are barely seconds before a
flood erases the riverbank Tints

this black ink beneath our bodies
recolors the blood coursing from
vein to holy waters reunites dust
with his eternally estranged child

But none of this exists Naturally
this is nonsense So he preserves
them as dreams Locked Cut up
Sometimes when he thinks there

is no one writing the dust weeps
sculpts caskets of different sizes
hoping one will fit But he prays
too long Loses vision Becomes

a monster to be pitied Someday
maybe these sentences will melt
and change themselves Baptize
eyes into mud Bring him home.

♦

Kristina Morgan

CROSSING THE LETHE
Fiction

The Bus

Motion gives me a sense of freedom. Freedom isn't something I
take for granted. I grapple with psychosis. I grapple with
schizophrenia. I am a plastic pan not meant for the oven. That's
the way I feel when I struggle with the voices I hear being pulled
from the air with my mind. That's what it feels like when I can't
participate in the oven of reality. The heat of life is too much.

I ride the bus every day I can. Some of the same people ride
with me. I suppose I could say it's a social event. And I can't
jump out of the bus while it's moving, unlike a car: *open the door.*
Jump. Roll. You won't get hurt. Another car may hit you but you
are Super Woman. The voices get my attention. I fight not to give
in to them. When I drove, they also told me to hit pedestrians.
They favor people walking dogs or old ladies.

The bus commands the road, attached to the black asphalt of
Washington. The sun shines through the windows. Light
punctuates each passenger. I am a comma, I think. People pause
at my six-foot frame and black clothes. They aren't used to seeing
such a tall woman. I wear tough boots. They look like motorcycle
boots, black with a silver circle on the band around the ankle. I
sit still, watch wind lift scraps of trash thrown on the road and
littering the sidewalk, paper the size of small dogs.

The bus stops. I watch the feet of people coming down the
aisle. A woman with scuffed shoes the color of custard. A man
with large, white feet in flip-flops. Small cowboy boots on a child
and a larger brown pair, probably the parent's.

The door swings shut. A contralto.

Every time we hit a bump, the motion of the bus pushes my body up. I recall my father hoisting me from the backseat of our car when I was five years old. I pretended sleep, silently asking that he do this, lift my body into the air, his strong arms wrapping around me. He carried me into the house, gently placing me on the couch. I knew I was safe. For this feeling alone, I would ride the bus for hours.

Unit 6: Repeat Visit

I appear again at the Behavioral Health Center, Unit 6, after a psychotic break during which I ran from the Circle K bathroom out to the street, naked. I thought bed bugs were in my clothes. The first couple of days, I feel nothing. I stand in the hallway, still as a hinge. Days four and five, I start coming to. The medicine the doctor prescribes is kicking in. I'm beginning to feel safe in my own skin. The hospital a cocoon of warmth and clean sheets. Days six and on, I'm agitated. I want out. The doors will not accommodate me. Their lock feels permanent. Only the doctor can release me. My stay is usually ten days.

On the unit, Jeremy, a patient of one week who attempted to converse with me with no luck, leaps. The square window of the nurses' station allows for his shoulders the width of my sister's. His scrawny ass follows. He thought I was tucked between boxes of Haldol, an old anti-psychotic, on the other side of the nurses' station. The river Lethe flows between the patient's area and the nurses' floor. I imagine him drinking from the Lethe, inviting the Underworld to plaster itself to the patients' area. The nurses' station remains an area of light. Of hope. At night, it's the only place that glows. I know this because I've woken at midnight and ambled down the hall in search of a handkerchief, my nose runny and cold.

Pharmaceutical representatives bring Haldol with them. I believe it has a side effect of my fear that telephones send electrical currents and mice into my inner ear.

Jeremy wants to propose to me before I forget him—Jack be nimble, Jack be quick—before the nimbus becomes too thick, clouding my vision. Jeremy is worth only the weight of his smile.

The Bus

The bus approaches Seventh Street. The bus driver's voice as he calls out the street sounds like someone with a penchant for chewing gravel. I pull the cord without lifting my head. I bow in penance for the sin I have yet to commit. A sin I don't even have the words for. It is three o'clock. Too late or too early for anything I want to do.

Stop. The bus commands the road like a woman strolling her baby across four lanes of traffic, its large presence keeping everyone on the sidewalk and cars stopped behind it.

I step out. Where is the curb? The curb is not immediate. It is one lane over due to construction. A car comes close to hitting me as I step into the lane. The world stops for an instant like the final push of birth. Was there a horn? No horn. I hurry across the lane. On the sidewalk, I stand on the chalk drawing of a Minute Maid container.

Unit 6: Jane Doe

Unit 6. I draw a picture of wine and cheese the color of cranberries, the color of nurse Helen's fingernails, the color of tongues on a friendly day. I place it under my bed. The paper can't hide, its edges sticking out. The wings of a dove from a nest too small.

Kristina, the television calls from the lounge. *Kill the television or become a media whore. Lather your hair. Lovely lather loosens lice, lice loosens lovely lather.* I drank my shampoo. The alcohol in it didn't get me drunk. The voices force this diatribe into being. The voices pester me. I wish I couldn't listen. They're as clear to me as an umpire shouting "out" as a player slides into home plate.

I enter the lounge. The woman in the commercial looks clean under the spray of the shower. Water sprays her shoulders in welcome. I imagine a feather butterflying its way down her skin.

Matilda is in the corner kissing Jasmine behind the back of a psych tech scribbling notes in longhand this side of Lethe. It is becoming dark. The moon promises to be a boulder. Nikki shoots a marble across the circle, knocking the cat's eye loose. My voices tell me to call them fags, to call them gay geeks. This I don't do. I tap the voices, asking them, *please.*

I return to my room. My drawing is balled up on my bed, killed by creases I can't smooth out. The young woman who sleeps in the bed one over laughs. The hands that cover her mouth are dirty with charcoal. She has refused to speak her name. The laughter is the first I hear from her. She remains a Jane Doe.

Her person fills the room. It is overwhelming. She is locked into her depression, as limp as a rag doll. I am alone with her in the vacuum of my rage. Her long, greasy hair provides the handles. I wrap it around my hands like boxers do white tape before sliding on their gloves. I yank her out of bed, the yank as powerful as an upper cut to the chin.

Was there a shriek? No shriek. The voices I hear tug at my ears. I hear *kill the fucker, pull out her hair, let your anger hang as a silver Christmas ball on a tree.*

Before I decide what to do next, a psych tech is on me. His hands around my waist only tighten the grip I have on her hair. The weight of me is pulled back into his chest. The weight of her is pulled into me. She smells like shit. I pray they have to cut me out of her like Richard, my friend with the red hair, did the sun from a coin he brought back from Brazil. When not here, I wear it around my neck. Here, they confiscate it, thinking I might hang myself with it. Its thread is thin.

Food

I eat the Traditional Sub outside Quizno's on Roosevelt and Seventh. Mayonnaise runs from my wrist to my elbow and then drips between my boots. White beads flatten, roll nowhere. Applause. Roar. The voices said to leave a mark. I have printed myself onto the sidewalk with mayonnaise that dripped from my elbow.

The walk to Safeway is interrupted by kids selling lemonade for ten cents a cup. I can't resist them in polyester and plaid, with hats like Minnie Pearl's. I learn their names; Toni and Jerry or Toni and Geri are genderless, which makes spelling their names correctly difficult.

Unit 6. Wound

Nurse Helen is asking me something. Her mouth is lovely.
Jane Doe isn't to come within twenty-five feet of me. The rooms are not wide enough. I still remember how it felt to wrap her greasy hair around my hands.

I scrape one of my hands against the corner of a broken counter. Hydrogen peroxide fizzles. My wound cools like rose petals in winter. There is a heightened awareness of skin in movement. A slight breeze comes from a fan. I breathe lightly; a whisper harnessed. Heaven is just so far.

Tea Time

Tiwi waits tea for me in her upstairs condo. The condos are higher than the billboard promoting suitcases and long sleeves, graffiti along the bottom. They border the homeless who beg the occupants to play stereophonic jazz at dawn before the noise of traffic becomes the aggressor and interrupts the few dreams the homeless may have.

Dew beads winter grass. The scent of green arrives with me. The moistness of the smell clinging to the black stubble on my head.

CROSSING THE LETHE

Unit 6: Time
There is little to claim my attention. Time moves like a clogged hourglass, allowing only a single strand of sand to power through its curves to the bottom of the glass.

Aunt Tiwi
Tiwi is an aged aunt to me. I met her at the grocery store. She couldn't reach the top shelf of jams. Cherry. Tiwi wanted cherry. I was fresh out of the hospital and still had my hospital wristband on. She asked me about it and then invited me for tea. A year later, she is still serving me Tazo Chai—reincarnated tea. Throughout India, chai wallahs serve cups of chai to souls seeking inner beauty. Tiwi is not a chai wallah. She is an aborigine from Australia.

The tea tastes like the length of corridor to a kindergartner the first day of class. Its taste lingers long. It is the first I have had in a while. I still long for coffee. Coffee is closer, more immediate. Its taste provocative. A punch of drum in silence.

Inner beauty catches up to me at Tiwi's, just as God does. My hands are free. Nickels fall through holes or out the frayed patches of my jeans. I catch some. The rest hit the hard surface. I hear pings.

Tiwi reads from the box of tea, "To ask questions, share observations or simply have a bit of human contact, write us at Tazo, P.O. Box 66, Portland, OR 97207. Allow two weeks for a written response." The tea bag comes signed. Two weeks of no human contact leaves a person lost like a single red leaf that falls from the trash bag.

Unit 6: Leaving
On Unit 6, my mind matches the weight of rain. Rain slaps on the front windows of cars as they speed. Speeding in here, I do not. Everything is slowed, as there is nothing to do. My mind is axed open. My mind is open to life on the side of the nurses' station. The Underworld no longer appealing like it is mid-stay when I'm

convinced I cannot live in reality. Reality rolls through me down to my toes, staggering my walk, confusing my speech like an adolescent talking about Hamlet. Is it really psychosis again?

I don't consider psychosis tagged onto the voices. The voices are a staple in my world. I am prey to them. Sometimes they drive me crazy, like when they mimic everything I do. I pour myself cereal. They say, *you pour yourself cereal.* I walk outside. They say, *you walk outside.* I open my mailbox. They say, *you open the mailbox.* And then they comment, saying *don't pay your bills. You will be dead before they come due.*

Where is the tea? Where is Tiwi? I want to see her hand locked with Dream, poured into the sugar of my cup. I want to float around blind curves, survive like thistle in the forest.

Experts attempt to reach me with their faith in pills. Pills. Manage me. Will they manage me well? Please take the T-shirt from me and fill my hands with blue sky. I want to lounge beneath the sun on the patio outside the Unit.

Is it still 2018?

Notes to Dr. P., my psychiatrist on Unit 6—

Without poetry, I lie in bed haunted, or pace the floors dazed at the fact my body just won't die. Please don't take my pens away. Without them, I cannot write poetry. I promise not to write on the walls or stab anyone. Does the point really matter, anyway?

Scabs are forming thick skin, covering my vulnerabilities. I recognize that fragility, like the lip of a porcelain teacup, is something I live with. But also recognize that the porcelain is strong, is protected, is well loved and has been passed on through generations without chips. Do not leave the teacup in the cupboard to stay safe.

Voices follow me—*die, cry, die, cry, do all of it and die.* The voices remind me of a rabid dog looking for purpose, slavering at the mouth. This is true, but the truth goes beyond dogs.

Doctor, please listen deeply. There is truth as heavy as the moon held up in the palm of the sky. I don't want to be the teacup in the cupboard.

Home

The Lethe and a breeze have followed me home. When will the water quench my mind? When will the wind still my thoughts? I no longer have dogs that could drown in the river. Both dogs died. Sasha last year and Brutus eight months ago. The loss left me feeling like an elephant who lost her calf to poachers, like a light bulb with no socket.

My raft holds me and a salamander. It is pre-dawn. Fire will not hit the sky for another couple of hours.

My home smells of candle. Patchouli. I imagine getting off the raft. The river has run dry. The light wood floor tinkles from the light coming through three windows into my family room. I hesitate to think family room. There is no family aside from friends. My rolltop desk is in this room along with my favorite chair—burnished metal with a flowered fabric seat.

The blue couch calls my name, invites me to lie down and bask in the freedom from Unit 6. I do this. The length of my body just fits. My head rests on one of the red down pillows. Then it happens. The voices dig into me. *Motherfucker. You'll never be free. You'll be in and out of the hospital mimicking the every-three-months rotation of this past year. You can't run from us. We contaminate your mind. We are you, and you are us.*

"Stop," I shout. I have never done this before. I have never talked back to them.

No. Our chain runs around your throat.

I feel for the chain. It's not there. My fingers touch skin. My. Fingers. Touch. Skin.

The voices whisper, *Die, Kristina. Die. Your life is worth a Bobble Head. Lethe will come back. You'll be forced to melt into the water, become a part of the Underworld.*

Whispers. I can barely hear them. "Stop," I shout again and sit up. The sunlight washes over my face. I am in control. The new anti-psychotic medication, Clozaril, must be working. It's helping me to hold this space steady.

Tiwi will be proud to know I will grab the sunrise and make a hat of it. I shudder in my shoes, the ecstatic moment not lost to bees in the wind. The sun does rise. The darkness fades. Someday, Unit 6 will be a decade away rather than two days. I believe this like I know water will run out the faucet when pulled on.

◆

Kristina Morgan

THE HOUSE AFTER HIM IN THIRTEEN PLACES

1. Laundry Room

His shirts are missing from the bundle of clothes smelling of damp. Without him,
I no longer care to walk around the house. The silence before the dryer soothes me
   like the air on a hot summer day.

2. Kitchen

He fucked my sister over and over. The year of their affair ended
when I walked in on them, her splayed over the table. I stand in his favorite room,
still as a magnet before it catches metal. I regret that I miss him. He is under my skin
   like a vein with a mean pulse.

3. Nightstand

My dream last night offered my demons bread. There is a glass of water
on the nightstand. I remember his lips as being dry. A pagan prayer group offered me
a silk bag smelling of sage, to rid me of his bad mojo. It settles next to the water.

4. Small Table

Grandma's picture in a wooden frame is missing from the table.
He took the photo, a reminder of better times.
He baked her pies and served her milk.

5. Coffee Pot

Coffee leaves me wide-eyed and calm like a Ritalin baby.
He leaves the pot, tells me I should be grateful for this small thing.
He has quit caffeine. Lies fall from his mouth like coins
from the grocery register. A nickel carries more weight than a penny,
but they are both still coins.

6. Study

It was a day of red cranes and green grass. Call it Christmas.
I won't write him into being unless I cast a spell. The voodoo doll
holds many pins. He has no place in my study. The extra chair
does not sag with his weight.

7. Bathroom

His mirror reflects pale heartache in the lines of my forehead.
I won't miss his driblets of urine on the floor. I won't miss picking up
after him, his sour washcloth left in the sink. Heartache stills follows me
like the sun does noon.

8. Family Room

The couch can hold three people. After that, its arms get in the way.

9. Hall

From the hall, I could hear him shaving, the light scratch of razor
moving over his bristled cheek. There was no light. I stood alert in the
gloom.

10. Portrait

Move the ghost out of the family photo. I feel grandmother's gaze over
my shoulder.
She begs me to let go, my arms around his belly.

11. Living Room

The day turns purple to match the weave of my drapes, the waists of
which are gathered
by a rope. My neighbor peers in through the window. The dogs watch
him.
He growls, that low throat sound my ex used to make when rough housing
with the dogs.

12. Closet Shelf

The stuffed animals with *I love you* hearts in their hands
suffocate, bagged in clear plastic. He won't be returning.
My friend's brother got drunk and wrapped his head
in a dry cleaner's bag. Fatal error. There is a chill in the closet.

13. Front Door

I collect breath before opening the door. The world is a thief in brown
pants.
It has been months without him. He no longer has a place in the ink of
my pen.
I am free to love myself. The world is a kite with a long tail
bobbing with the breath of wind. I clasp my hands and think new.

COIN TOSS

A quarter spins like a cigar
in the mouth of an excited new father.
Heads, I move to the desert
buy a bathing suit and search for water.
Tails, I align myself in trees,
contented to whisper *I love you*
because you are far away
and cannot hear me,
after thirteen years.
You are living with my antique dresser,
empty except for your bronzed
baby shoes.

A blanket covers my lap
where my niece sits
on Tuesday mornings
at the coffee shop.
This consoles me.
My family is kind.
She likes chocolate milk
and I a large brew of Sumatra.

KRISTINA MORGAN

My sister reads tarot and promises
I'll find another man, one who likes shoes,
who doesn't wear sneakers
with fitted suits. But see,
the thing is, I would walk barefoot
across hills, leave my pale face full of sun
to join you now, fingers laced
in your gloved hand,
gloved because we took jabs
with our mouths full
of cuss words.

I need to follow
the coin, break free of violent love,
remembering only that then I was lost in your pocket.
Now my tufts of hair blowing in the wind.

NOTES TO MY MIND ON A HEATED AFTERNOON WHILE EGGS FRY ON THE PAVEMENT AFTER HAVING ROLLED OUT OF THE NEST PRIOR TO HATCHING

1.
As a child, I did not complain about you.
You were a locomotive running on rails of inspirations
that housed little people who exited my ears at night
holding school at the end of my bed.
I would not kick my feet
for fear of interrupting geography lessons.
It was then that I realized there was place
outside of what my fourth grade teacher told me.

2.
You were a jewel that cut blue glass,
On the playground, it did not matter
that I was not picked for kickball
or that I was teased for having a mustache and unibrow.

3.
I looked into a mirror and winked, saying just wait,
I will grow to beauty. And I did.

4.
Age comes hard like a woman chiseling Hermes
out of ice on a broken day during a heat wave.
My mother dies before she can understand me.

5.
It is a wonder that I do not drown myself
in the imagery and pulse of words that move
through you, unfettered.

6
I think of the luminous wing of a moth
on a lampshade and smile,

break my steady gaze at nothing
but shaded surfaces.

7.
I have met people dulled by the ordinary.
I am not one of them.

I stand in my height of six feet and beam.

GRANDMOTHER

The shopkeeper tells me elephants symbolize infinity
as he bags the wooden calf. You dislike fresh flowers,
say they hold death in their stalks. I offer you this calf;
it holds the heat of my palm in its belly. You take it.
You set it on the end table next to your recliner
where you spend most of your time.

I am hoping to collect you from the afterlife.
You say to bury the calf with you.
Let it be your guide back to me,
to the place on my shoulder where the soft weight of you
will sit. *Do you know weight can whisper?* you ask.
If you say so, I answer.

You make certain I know where the hair clip is
that you gave me when I was three,
a gift from your mother.

We have agreed I will serve marshmallows at your memorial,
keeping the day light, allowing children to play jacks. I don't know
how I will keep flowers away, imagine calla lilies walking on toe.

We spend Thursday noon at the grocery store, pause in the cookie aisle
to look at all the Oreos. Red stuffed. Green stuffed. Double stuffed.
You think you keep me too long this time.
How can I assure you my time is never better spent?
You are an alarm. You wake me to what is important.

I see your shoulders now slope forward. They have borne the tugging
of people who depended on you. You kept shoes on feet
and offered houses that sheltered.

You show me the spots on your hands. I think of the beauty of bark.
I know you are tired of being an old woman. If I could pull age
from your hair, I would. I, like you, have grayed. I use color; you
leave things white.

You walk before me, turn to see why I have stopped. The light of the
low sun
envelops you. It is hard for me to see. Will I still be kind in your
absence?
You have shown me how to extend my hand and sense the spiritual
deep within others. I see the lily pads supporting frogs as they settle
on the pond. Life can be like this.

It will be hard not to miss you. Have you ever tried to move an arm
after it has fallen asleep? It takes another arm to wake it up.
I will remember the way the sun lit you from behind,
how your smile strengthened mine
that Thursday noon.

You have been nine months dead. I hear you in the evenings. The
sky
is not crowded. I say *moon*, you say *yes*. I say *galaxies,* you say
roam.
I say *star*, you say *plenty*. I say *I miss you*, and you say
I'm not gone.

◆

Ace Boggess

BREAKDOWNS

First the car. Then my voice. Back up. *First* first,
she spends months shaping despair into claws.

I'm not safe around all these shattered windows.

Things fall, apparently—what the dead say
with their malice (afterthought).

Breakdowns come faster. I'm tossed about by storms
that don't know they've trapped me in their vortices.

As for my motorized carriage,
I've never shown it the love it deserves.
It wants to leave, go anywhere.

I'm at an age when I'd rather make comfortable bargains.

ACE BOGGESS

THE PRESIDENT IS KEEPING EXTREMELY BUSY

his press secretary says, & doesn't say
one in power ties so many ties:
green, gray, red, & red.
The President stares at the mirror for days
to get himself worked up
for laughing at the Chinese leader's jokes.
Such a strain. He sometimes naps
during briefings on the war in X,
entirely missing the musical number.
His spokesman says the President
spends his coffee breaks feeding birds,
annoyed they won't eat chicken
from his hands. The President,
a busy man, dresses himself,
plots & plans, scowls at his underlings.
Sometimes, he reads the *Post*:
he loves it for its funny pages &
editorial cartoons, too busy to recognize
it's him depicted there
riding his busy horse into the abyss.

ACE BOGGESS

WE SPENT LAST NIGHT WITH ALICE COOPER

It's the spectacle; no, the songs—
how well I know them,
knew them thirty years ago when gruesome beauty

seemed to fit & stage blood was more real to me
than any man's. Lyrics return
like dead lovers in the showman's act,

as each did last night while we bowed our sore,
worn backs & tapped our tired feet—
the withering dance & danse macabre.

How old it felt to feel young again, alive,
our bodies trembling from piercing riffs
pulsing to the drumbeat of yesterday.

Fuzzy chords nested in our bones,
although we've reached an age
theatrics thrum more loudly than the notes.

◆

Sepideh Zamani

WE ARE WAITING FOR THE STORKS TO COME BACK

Nonfiction

The minarets, tall and thin, had reached the sky.

The bitter winter's cold had completely destroyed the brushwood on top of the minarets, and none of the nests had remained intact. There was no sign of any nest until the arrival of spring.

Every spring, we watched the storks flying: flock after flock appeared in the sky of our town and then left us. Sima and I would leave our schoolbags in the courtyard and run to a particular spot with a tree and watch them fly away.

Sima's grandmother, Haaj Naneh, would tell her stories about storks, and she would repeat them to me at school without omitting any detail. She said all of the storks we see are flying to Mecca for Haaj so they could stay in God's house for the winter, and after the pilgrimage they would return here once more. When she was young, Haaj Naneh had gone on a pilgrimage to Mecca, and she said that going to Mecca and coming back takes a few months, and because of the distance the storks would take a few months to come back and that is why we didn't see them during that time.

And God's house was very far away. This was what Haaj Naneh used to say.

And it was this house of God that caused a separation between Sima and me.

We were having lunch when I asked my mum where God's house was. Mum looked at me and continued dishing out the rice and didn't say anything.

Once again, I asked her, "Is it very far from our house?"

She stopped dishing out the rice and said, "We are not supposed to go there!" She then asked me why I was asking about God's house.

I said, "Haaj Naneh tells Sima lots of stories about the place. I think it's nice. I think it would be good if we went there once."

At night, when she was tucking me in bed and putting a blanket over me, she said, "My darling, we don't go there! Our religion is different from Sima's religion, and we don't believe in what they say and believe in, but we do respect them!"

The next day I told Sima what Mum had told me. She frowned and said, "Haaj Naneh says I mustn't go out with you. I mustn't accept food from you. and I mustn't be friends with you at all." I laughed and Sima too began to laugh with me.

This is all that I remember from those days.

Today at Düsseldorf Airport, I am waiting for a plane to land. One of its passengers is Sima!

Two or three years ago, I found Sima on Facebook and sent her a friend request. It didn't take long before she confirmed my request.

In a comment I sent her, I had written that religions did not separate hearts! And I had put a heart emoji next to it, and she had replied with a kiss and three hearts. As simple and easy as that, I had found my childhood friend.

There were five minarets. Mum said when we moved to this town they were already there, and surely they must be at least fifty years old.

We were in the third year of primary school, and one day our teacher gave us a composition task asking us to write all we knew about the minarets.

I didn't know anything. It was from that time that whenever Sima and I didn't have school we went to see two of them, tall and high into the sky, down the road where we lived and just before getting to the river. Sima told me things about the minarets that she had heard from Haaj Naneh; and what I heard from Sima made me become more and more interested in them. She said that when the older generations who lived in this town saw the flocks of storks coming here around the spring for breeding, they thought of building the tall minarets; the storks carried brushwood and other bits of vegetation to build their nests on top of them. It was possible to guess that these storks were the kind of birds that built their nests on very tall and inaccessible places in order to be far away from us. All the spring and summer, they were the guests of the town, and as soon as the cold weather arrived they would start their migration. Mum would pack some snacks for my breaktime to share with Sima, and until that incident everything was nice and beautiful.

At dusk, when we returned from watching the storks, Sima told me that her father had warned her to stop being friends with me, and hard as I insisted on knowing the reason why, she wouldn't tell me, leaving me to spend the nights with frequent nightmares.

In our online chats, Sima had apologized for what had happened in those days and said if it was her choice, she would have never done that. She had written that after her family had died they had held a wake in the local mosque and many people had gathered there. The local Mullah who traditionally led the prayers had talked about our family; he had called us unclean and said that not a single Muslim should have any dealings or relationship with people who belonged to another religion. She had written that she hadn't really understood her father's orders and instructions about breaking off her friendship with me and, if truth be told, from that time she had really disliked herself, her family, and her religion for depriving her of her friendship with her closest friend and separating us.

She wrote all of this after telling me some news. It was only two years since she had gotten married and her doctor had told her she was suffering from a very rare cancer for which here was no treatment in Iran!

In the morning, when our school head checked our nails and hands as we entered in order to make sure we were clean, when it was my turn, she told me to leave the queue. I was surprised! What had always distinguished me from the other children was my neatness and cleanliness, and now, because of that or something else that she hadn't mentioned, I was forced to leave the queue!

After the commotion caused by the children going to their classes had died down, the deputy head came and stood right in front of me and said, "When you come to school tomorrow bring your parents, too." She didn't say why, and in the classroom she put a special seat for me well away from the other children and ordered me to sit on that chair from then on; it could be just that day.

I asked Sima to send me all her medical records and tried to comfort her, assuring her that these days cancer was not an incurable disease. Of course, my specialization is in another branch of medicine, but I would do all I could to save my childhood friend and bring her back to life.

Every day as we left school, I looked at her with sorrow and regret and saw that she missed me, too, but people around her prevented us from being together. I used to run alone to the outskirts of our town and look at the storks that were sitting comfortably on their nests since the time for their journey to Mecca hadn't arrived. Sometimes they turned their necks right or left, as if there was nothing that was important to them until the time of their departure.

Two or three years ago as I was passing by a cinema, the title of a film caught my attention: *The Suspended Step of the Stork*, a film by a Greek director. After I saw the film, I understood that it was the story of a political refugee who was stranded in a border town in Greece.

What persuaded me to see the film more than anything else

was the word "stork." I had found a sign from my childhood in the city where I was living now.

Later, I discovered that the title was only referring to the way these birds walk; they take one step at the time on trembling and unsteady legs. In the film, the director focused on the walking of the refugees, who were caught in a harsh winter while the way ahead and their future looked uncertain and hopeless. In the film and afterwards, there was nothing to connect me with the film except the storks...

The day my mum took me out of school, looked me straight in the eyes, and said that they wouldn't let me continue going there, I just looked at her confused and stupefied.

What caused me to shed tears afterwards was not the lessons or the school. Only Sima, with whom every day at dusk, I would go to look at those quiet and sad-looking birds and watch some of them on the bank of the river as they walked. Our storks, too, walked gently and shakily: long, thin legs that seemed fragile. One could sense their fear, although they walked with such pride, as if there was nothing in the world that could make them doubtful and hesitant.

I told Sima not to worry. I would do all I could; I would talk to my medical friends and try to find a treatment for her illness. I said, I would do what it took to relieve my childhood friend of her anxiety.

The deputy head had told my mum that the Mullah responsible for Friday prayers in our town had ordered the education department to stop the children of families like us mixing with other children. My mum had asked for the reason, but the deputy head had only nodded her head and said she didn't understand any of it. "I only comply with the orders and am not looking for trouble." This was all the excuse there was for keeping me away from school for a few years.

At dusk, I would go alone to the minarets to look at the storks,

and it always reminded me of Sima. After I was expelled from
school, I was sick in bed for a few days. Mum said I had high
temperature and was delirious, calling the storks and sweating.

My father stopped letting me go out at dusk to see them. For
some time, people we didn't know had been throwing stones at
our windows. Father, afraid of something horrible happening to
me, would not let me go as far as the bank of the river.

At home, I was wandering around looking for something
that I had lost outside the house, and I was pointlessly searching
for it here.

Sima had become thin and gaunt. Every time she wrote to me,
she said she found herself closer and closer to death. I tried to
comfort her and carried on trying to find some kind of treatment
for her.

In the film, there weren't any storks. The story is about a reporter
who is reporting on the refugees in a border town in Greece and
encounters an important person he had heard had been lost
previously. The old man is trying to avoid the reporter and hide
himself among the refugees, but the young reporter finds out that
the old man had been a great poet who had deliberately gone
missing. In order to discover the truth, he won't let the old man
alone until the moment of the climax of the film...

I prepared everything for Sima's arrival, and my colleagues made
positive and encouraging promises for her treatment. I was very
excited about seeing Sima after twenty years.

The last time I had seen her, she was holding her mother's
hand and shopping in the little bazaar. We looked at each other,
feeling lost, and I thought how the grownups' world can be
complicated and incomprehensible to children who just want to
spend time together and don't understand their world.

I have been working in a hospital in Düsseldorf. When my
mum took my hand and we left the school with her carrying my

schoolbag she said, "Here is no longer a place for us! We must go somewhere where there are no more of these Mullahs stopping people having anything to do with us." I remembered a quote from a German philosopher who said, "They kill each other without knowing each other for the sake of those who know each other and don't kill each other."

Of course, here nobody killed anybody. But as they made life more difficult for each other, they killed each other's feelings without ever knowing anything about each other.

During the years when we left the town and went into exile, the storks had also stopped coming there in the spring. The minarets were devoid of nests, and their tops showed the empty places of the storks.

People said that the older generations thought that the journey the birds took and until they returned the following season was because they had gone to Mecca for pilgrimage, and that is why they are called Hajji Laklak.[1]

At the airport, I was at every moment expecting to see the happy and cheerful face of Sima emerging with her bag from the arrival lounge. A few seconds earlier, they had announced that the plane had landed.

Afterwards, I took painting lesson here. In time, I was able to paint my dreams, and this helped a lot in keeping my childhood memories alive.

When I was returning home with Mum, I saw that she was hiding her tears from me and sometimes she would let go of my hand in order to wipe her tears with the corner of her chador.

A thin and gaunt woman with familiar eyes is coming from the side opposite to where I am standing, and she smiles at me. It is Sima. Sima, with those large familiar eyes and a smile that hides the moisture on her face.

She embraces me and puts her arms around my neck, and I feel the same childish excitement I did in the days when we shared the snack Mum had prepared for me.

She asks, "Have you been waiting long?"

I say, "No, not long, but it felt long."

As I drive home, she just keeps looking at me, and I look at the road, smiling. I ask, "Did those storks ever return to the town?"

She says: "No, never again...They also destroyed those minarets!"

She falls silent. She then says, "It was as if spring never came there because my mum, God bless her soul, used to say they definitely used to come every year with the spring, but then they never came."

I look at her, and she turns her head. She wants to hide her tears from me. She whispers, "You are an angel, very kind. I hope, for God's sake, you forgive us. We did you so much harm." I turn on the radio so the music fills the atmosphere.

I say, "Never mind; one day they will return...Even if those minarets are no longer there, for they have memories of the place...Surely they will return."

♦

[1] Haji Laklak is the Farsi name for stork, and Haji means someone who has gone to Mecca for pilgrimage.

Max Roland Ekstrom

LAST MOTHER OF SODOM

Years ago, before the girls were born
and thugs began nocturnal patrols
Lot's wife took evening walks by herself
through the avenue's gentle grade
like the slope of a man's thigh
passing the low walls separating
the town from swaying plains of barley
that would one day all lick into flame—
she was the sort open to the chaos
of her beloved town of scholars,
priests, peddlers and thieves
each with his own language and song
with which beneath the slanting moon
she too could sing, becoming someone else,
slipping for a moment into a different life.
Returning to herself well before
arriving at the hard oak of her door,
she yearned for guests who tell of their own
far shores and strange oaths, she yearned
for the generous arms of her husband—
her trusting and unworldly husband—
so they could pray together in the manner
of man and woman, gasps released lip to ear.

YOUNG AUGUSTINE

After pulling out all the stops
for the lecture on your favorite Latin
poet, you glide through the fire
of Milanese cobblestone noon
that bronzes piazzas' fountains
against the kilned sky to arrive
at your office and apartment
famed for argument and orgy
where you catch your girlfriend
and son dozing on pillows beneath
slanted rays and stopping to watch
makes you want to possess her again—
but your whetted lust cracks
beneath slow churning dust
motes dancing into the broken light
at which you wince—your African pride
tumbles into long exhausted anger
at the snicker of your many rivals
while these two strange gifts lie staged
as if by the hand of a lesser god.

THE OTTER

Eskilstuna
On the outskirts of my father's hometown
carved into sloping rock of former shoreline
within an ancient rune we watch the dance
of the sagas: Loki slaughters Otr for his pelt
but his brothers demand compensation
and the gods load fair Otr's skin with gold.
The earth speaks to us. A dragon belts
its perimeter, head to tail, and though Christ
had come, some stories must not be forgotten.
In town we pay respects at the family plot
where Dad's teen sister lies mute,
silenced while she walked with friends
by a young motorcyclist—the reckless son
of the town priest ran her over and never
paid apology. After, we wade in
the cove as a storm scatters boats,
the water new and strange, the water washing us,
the water that was supposed to forgive.

◆

Alison Thompson

A ROSE BY ANY OTHER NAME
Fiction

What's in a name? That which we call a rose
By any other name would smell as sweet
   Romeo and Juliet, Act II Scene II, William Shakespeare

I guess you're wondering who I am. I've been wondering that myself. My birth certificate arrived in the post today. Annabel Shoshana Smith. Born: April 3, 1982. Mother: Rosemary Shoshana Smith. As expected, the box for my father's name is blank.

Rose—my grandmother—said my mother didn't want my father (whose first name was Ron, I found out later) to have any claim on me if he came back. Not that he ever did, not even after my mother died. "A no-hoper," Rose said. I've always called my grandmother Rose. She said it made her feel younger, that being reminded she was a grandmother depressed her.

Anyway, back to the task at hand. Now that my birth certificate has arrived, I can fill in the forms that have been sitting on my kitchen bench for a week. Change-of-name forms.

You see, I'm recently divorced. Currently, I'm Annabel Butterfield. A lovely name, Butterfield. In hindsight, I think perhaps it was the name I fell for, not the man. Pity. Now that he's remarried and has little twin Butterfields on the way, it seems rather lame to keep it.

The question is, though, which name to change back to? This is not my first divorce. Butterfield is my *second* husband's name. My first husband's surname was Pritchard—very English and proper. Like him. I certainly don't want to revisit *that*.

But I balk at going back to Smith. *So* ordinary. It reminds me of roll call and nicknames. Smithy, Smitho, Smelly-belly-smith. I don't want to be that braces-wearing, pigeon-toed girl again. I've left that all behind. The funny thing is, a year or two following my first divorce, after some careful cajoling on my part and a couple of shots of Irish whiskey, I found out my father's surname from my grandmother. She laughed as she told me.

"Ron bloody *Smyth*," she chortled. "Smyth with a *y*!"

How unfair is that?

My girlfriends were less than helpful. My attempts at a discussion on the matter at my impromptu divorce party two weeks ago largely failed, probably on account of the quantity of champagne being imbibed.

"Take a famous actress's name—from the past," Stacy said.

"No, make one up," said Ash. "Like Daylight, or Seagull."

They started giggling. Stacy slopped champagne down the front of her blouse.

"How about Butthead?" she said, spilling more champagne on the floor. "Or..."

Angela interrupted her. "Just go without a surname—like Madonna, or Pink." She reached for the champagne bottle and refilled Stacy's glass.

Only Lucy, my best friend, could see I was serious. She pulled me aside, out of earshot of the others.

"Have you considered taking an old family name? There must be one you like."

I'd been pondering that idea the morning after the party when Jane, my flatmate, made a comment that stopped me in my tracks. I'd said I was considering O'Reilly, my grandmother's maiden name, given that she'd raised me from the age of three.

"And," I added, "it was her mother's name, not her father's. I like the strong female vibe of taking a *female* ancestor's name."

Jane was leaning against the kitchen bench, eating yogurt from the tub.

"True, though..." She paused and licked the spoon. "There's an argument that *all* surnames are male. Your grandmother's name, O'Reilly, her *mother's* name—it's actually her father's name, isn't it? Your great-grandmother's *father's* name?"

Damn. She's right. All surnames *are* male. Passed on to women by fathers or husbands. There are no female surnames, at least not in this culture, unless you make one up. So, I put the forms away, and now I'm back at square one. I check the time. A quarter to twelve. Time to get to the hospital. I'm running late. I leave the forms on the bench and grab my keys. Perhaps Rose has some suggestions.

She is sleeping as I enter her room. I pause just inside the doorway, taking stock as I do each day. There is her spare bathrobe, slung over the chair. Her overnight bag, full of clothes for me to take home to wash, her toiletries bag, hairbrush and glasses on the table by her bed. Today, though, I see something different. A leather satchel, a little smaller than A4 size, lies on the floor by the bedside cabinet. It is old and looks homemade, the leather lacing cracking around the edges. It looks strangely familiar, but I cannot place it. Then I remember, I have seen it before, in the bottom drawer of the wardrobe in Rose's bedroom in her house, where she keeps her sewing kit and through which I'd occasionally rifle looking for old buttons or bits of ribbon. For a moment, I am disoriented. I shake the feeling off and slip back out to the tearoom, where I make a coffee from the automatic espresso machine. It's awful, and at first, I only drank it for something to do, but lately I seem to have become addicted to its curiously metallic taste.

As I walk back into the room, Rose opens her eyes. Her skin is parchment pale. I can see the blue veins underneath.

She smiles.

"Annabel," she says. "I have something to show you."

The exertion of speaking sparks a coughing fit. A nurse glides in. I can't watch. It's a problem I have, confronting unpleasant truths. Probably why I'm twice divorced. I want things to be OK; otherwise, I'd rather not know.

You live in the clouds, Rose would say when I was little. *You have to learn to face up to things, or they'll knock you down.*

"I'm all right now, Annabel—you can look."

She hasn't lost her sense of humor. That's good, but as I turn back to face her, it's clear she's more tired than yesterday. She pats the bed and I half-sit on the edge, not wanting my weight to impact her in any way.

"Have you come to any conclusions?" she says, not without effort. "About a name?"

I try not to let my anxiety at her frailty show on my face. She doesn't like to see that kind of concern; it offends her in some way. *Poor man's pride*, she once said to me after I'd done something she didn't like, something that made her feel small. That admission was her way of apologizing. I look away and fiddle with the corner of her bedsheet.

"I thought perhaps O'Reilly?"

She looks at me, an eyebrow raised.

"By all means, though—if you're going to the trouble of *choosing* a name, make sure it *means* something. Don't pick one by default—that's just being lazy."

"It's *your* name," I say.

"Yes—well," she says, leaning forward. "Speaking of which…"

She coughs again, a long, drawn-out spasm. This time I stay put, perched awkwardly on the bed. After she recovers, she looks at me for a moment and then says, "I've made a discovery, albeit one rather late in the day."

"My satchel," she says, pointing down to the floor beside the bed.

I reach down and pick it up. It smells of stale boot polish and old newspapers and dust. I stifle a sneeze. The latch is stiff, and I tear a thumbnail opening it. It is full of old documents and letters, tea-colored with age.

"The envelope with the airmail pattern," she says.

I place the satchel on my knees and take out the envelope. It is not sealed. Inside are three folded sheets. The first is a marriage certificate. November 1943. London. Bride: Mary O'Reilly. Groom: Jozsef Telmann.

"That's my father," she says.

The second is a birth certificate. Rose pushes herself up higher in the bed and leans closer.

"Look," she says. "Look at what it says." She waves her finger at the document. "Shoshana Telmann, born May 17, 1944. That's me. I never knew. My mother said Shoshana was an old family name, so I gave it to..."

Her eyes fill with tears.

"...your mother as her second name. Then Rosemary gave it to you, as yours. She liked the way it sounded."

She sits forward, her hands animated.

"I didn't know. Shoshana is me. I'm not Rose O'Reilly. I'm Shoshana Telmann."

She lies back down again, her breathing more pronounced. After a moment, she says, "So strange to find this out now, at the end, that the name you have—that the *who* you thought you were—is wrong. That it's a lie."

She points at the satchel still open on my lap.

"Letters. From Mary and Jozsef. I couldn't read them. You can, if you're interested. I find I'm not. The time to find out has passed for me. All those years wondering. Now it's too late."

She closes her eyes and rests her head against the pillow.

"I'm tired. Come back tomorrow and we'll talk."

She was too weak to talk the next day, and for some days after that.

"She's deteriorating," the doctors said. "It won't be much longer now."

Each time they'd said that before, she'd rally, but even I can't pretend now.

Sitting by her bed, I reexamine the papers. The third document is a divorce certificate. 1949. Rose would have been five. Pinned to it is a newspaper cutting. An obituary. Jozsef Telmann—1962. The year before my mother was born.

Among the papers are some letters tied up with twine. I open one and begin to read.

When I get home that night, I search online for Jozsef's grave. I find it listed in the Jewish cemetery at Rookwood. Mary O'Reilly is there, too, in the Catholic section. I'm not sure why, but I decide I have to see them for myself.

Rookwood Cemetery is huge, and I'm terrible with maps. I wander around for most of the morning, my energy fading, until I locate the Jewish section. There is a simple headstone: Jozsef Telmann, 1919–1962. Beneath this, a Star of David and an inscription in a language I can't read, then—"Beloved Husband of Rina, Father of Ruth and Isaac." So, he married again. There are plastic flowers in the vase. I'm relieved my grandmother cannot see it. That she has a half brother and sister won't matter to her now. She's right. It's too late.

It's a long walk to the Catholic section. Mary's grave is in the lawn cemetery. 1984. The year before my mother died. I feel a curious sense of déjà vu. A memory of being carried. With Rose and my mother. I must have been very small, less than three. I glance at the grave next to Mary's. It's my mother's. How come I didn't know it was here? I hear my grandmother's voice inside my head.

Because you avoid everything unpleasant, Annabel. I've warned you, it comes back to bite you.

I drive home in a daze. How is it I've never given any real thought to my mother's death? About where she was buried? Or, come to think of it, much about her life? Something like shame passes through me.

My phone rings. It's the ward sister.

"You should come in," she says.

At the hospital, I hover outside my grandmother's room while they attend to her. She's drifting in and out of consciousness.

"How long?" I say to the doctor.

She's noncommittal. She touches my arm, a light but firm touch. Her eyes are kind.

"If you *need* to say anything to her—anything particular— now is the time. She'll need sedation soon. Once we start that, she won't be able to respond."

It's early when Rose wakes. I'm not sure if she knows I'm here. Her voice is surprisingly clear.

"I saw him once; I remember now. My mother took me to see him. He was in a park. I must have been about ten. He was thin and tall, with a beard. My mother said he was an uncle, but it was him. Something about him was familiar."

I lean in close so she can hear me.

"They divorced," I say, 'but they loved each other. The letters..."

She's drifted off again. I sit down, the letters crumpled in my hand.

I've read them all, night after night, waiting for Rose to die. I've been practicing saying it: She will die. I've watched how the nurses answer the questions anxious relatives ask at the end. *Yes, he/she will die.* They've learned the art of not flinching when the time for platitudes is over.

I know Mary and Jozsef's story now, as much as anyone can from the bits and pieces left behind. She was an Irish girl, working as a nurse in London. He was a Hungarian refugee who escaped to England just before the war broke out. He joined the British Army and served in the Jewish Brigade. They met while he was recovering from a minor shrapnel wound to his leg. She became pregnant and they married. They immigrated to Sydney after the war—for some reason separately—Jozsef in 1947, then Mary and the baby a year later. From the tone of their letters, they had hope then. I can't tell what changed, but there are hints. Mary mentions deciding not to convert. Jozsef writes of his renewed faith in God. Then nothing, just the divorce papers, and a letter transferring their house into her name. The grounds for divorce are listed as drunkenness and desertion.

There is another letter. This one is still sealed and is more recent, dated 1984. It's addressed to Rose. On the envelope after the name Rose is the word *Shoshana* in brackets. I turn it over in my hands, then tear it open.

My dear Rose,

I hope you are reading this in a forgiving frame of mind. It's not in my nature to ask for it, but impending death has a way of changing one's habits. There are a few things you should know. I loved the man who was your father, but we were not compatible. For more reasons than mere religion. The divorce papers state he was a drunkard and left us, but it is not true. I left him. It was the only way to procure a divorce. He was very kind. I changed our names back to O'Reilly. An Irish name was easier than a Jewish one in Sydney then, though barely. I'm sorry you could not see him again. I know he loved you. He named you Shoshana, after his mother. It means Rose. And you are. A beautiful rose. I know I have not been a mother comfortable with endearments, but there it is. I love you, my darling, my Rose.
Your mother, Mary O'Reilly.

I wonder how it can be that Rose hasn't read this. That she hasn't even opened it.

In the morning, she stirs. I take her hand.

"I have something to tell you," I whisper. She murmurs something inaudible.

"I'll read it to you."

And I do. I don't know if she understands or can even hear me. When I finish reading, I kiss her cheek.

"I love you," I whisper. "I love you, *Shoshana* Rose."

I brush away tears. I never allow myself to cry, but today is different. She doesn't release my hand, and for a moment I'm convinced she has squeezed it. Then the sensation is gone. Her breathing becomes labored. A nurse appears. Her eyes are gentle, but steady.

"You don't have to stay," she says.

"I'll stay."

When it's over, I head home. Jane is out. There's no one to greet me, not even a cat. Perhaps I should get a cat.

Lucy has left a message on the answering machine.

"Have you decided? On your new name?"

The name-change forms are still on the bench. I've filled in everything except the desired name. I like that description. *Desired.* I pick up the pen and write in my name.

Rose. That's it. I now know who I am.

I am Annabel Shoshanna Rose.

◆

Alamgir Hashmi

SEASONAL

I
Asked in, it has turned away.
It must be spring at the door
calling in half sleeves.

How it then appears is pointless.
Winter's snow still covers
every bough in the garden

refracting the sun—
the deep-white glare
of things made invisible.

These clothes I wear
may be the only season
passing.

II
Not Yet in the waiting world;
the light turns every now and then,
darkness is less shaded,

being inside helps.
Still, however you are or I am,
where are you?

ALAMGIR HASHMI

BREAD

Warm bread from the oven,
your hands smell of dough,
baking, the science of hunger
or satisfaction. You only say
we are out of cinnamon
just as yesterday.
Another mile to go for spring water,
more herbs, and nuts for the buns.

Year-round
it's been
plowing or gathering,
prayers for good weather.
Is it this we live for?
One waiting, the other away.

ALAMGIR HASHMI

ADAM'S PEAK*

Going along a loopy trail,
hours like days of walking uphill.
Gravigrades do it better.

Try a quick step in the narrow pass,
and it says: DO NOT GO OVER THE EDGE.
Step back, *back, back,* echoes the valley.
A thrill barely missed.

The final climb makes a minute
of the years it has taken me to get here.
I must stop a while to catch my breath.
The gravel crunching under my boots
almost threw me.
Air's light, the body hot as a potter's kiln,
fired up, wisping away.

'And then?' is a question others too
have carried this far up the rise of earth.
For this figure out of all that's heard
on the way, a sure footprint,
a departure?
Between the heaven and earth,
only a certain shape of stone makes sense,
its fine-cut toenails tickling the flesh
of my hands.

No one has stayed here for long;
it's only the beginning of descent—
to an aroma of tea gardens,

all the way down to the villages
of elephant men, coconut women.
I should train to look again
on breathing undulations of the land
where the sun flashes its sequins
from a blouse of green.
Every summer break, in my sleep,
the same pulsars beckon in the dark.

** A place in Sri Lanka. The legend says Adam landed on the
earth here. A Buddha relic on the top of a mountain enshrines
another memory.*

♦

Catherine Stratton

BIRDSONG

Fiction

Do you hear the birdsong?

Elizabeth, when you come, you will help me match the birds with their songs, as I can't recall which is which. I do know the robin's song, and I do know that, when we hear him sing *cheerily-cheer up-cheer up-cheerily-cheer up* you will rest the fingertips of your right hand on your chest, outlining your heart, and say, with an exclamation point, "Miss Robin wants everybody to be happy!" And I will be happy. So happy—when you come.

The birds don't sing at night, so I listen to my roommate cry in her bed. I don't ask what's wrong. I can't fix it. She wails and whimpers and sniffles and moans until the nursing aide arrives. "Here, honey. Take this pill. It'll help you sleep," and the sad woman takes it and sobs herself silent.

She's old like me. We're all old in this place with its yawning yellow walls and echoing footsteps and low mutterings. We keep to our beds, mostly. There's not much else to do. At times they drop us into wheelchairs and park us in the hallway. Or, they push our sorry selves into the common room. "Time to socialize," they say and leave us there to sit and stare and wait until they wheel us back to our beds to wrestle with memories that won't let us be.

I don't leave my bed anymore. I don't have to. I don't want to. I lie here and listen to the birdsong.

I wait for you, Elizabeth.

Listen! *Peter-peter-peter-peter?* A melody searching for what is lost. Is it a cardinal calling? A nuthatch? And, what about the driving *krrDEE-krrDEE-krrDEE*? Or, the hopeful *tru-ly-tru-ly-tru-ly-tru-ly-tru-ly-tru-ly*?

You'll know who's singing, Elizabeth. You'll know the names of the birds dashing and darting and swooping and blaring out ballads and arias and trillings.

Clara—my dear, dear niece—she comes to see me. She's the only one. Each time she visits, I ask for you. "Where's Elizabeth? Why doesn't she come?"

Clara doesn't answer. She remains still—eyes round, mouth knit shut—as if she forgot her lines.

How I miss our road trips. Remember how appalled our family and friends were when we drove from Massachusetts to Mexico the summer of 1934?

"Two young women drive to Mexico? It's dangerous," they said. "What could they be thinking?"

That must be over fifty years ago now. I guess women were deemed a more fragile lot back then.

We went anyway. Best of friends and then we fell in love— the moment still sharp in my mind while so much else has blurred. It was on Route 66, driving through Missouri, 200 miles southwest of St. Louis. I'd just seen the sign for Springfield when you leaned over, placed the fleshy tip of your index finger on my bare shoulder and drew an unhurried line down my arm lingering—electric—on my elbow. You showed me all love needs is a nudge to bloom. And, weren't we cagey, keeping our love secret all those years? Rooming together as spinsters did at the time, living our truth inside a lie. They called us old maids, but the joke was on them, wasn't it?

"Why didn't you ever get married?" Clara asked me years ago. She was still a teenager and, of course, teenagers question everything. I longed to say, "I am married. Elizabeth is my wife." Instead, I said, "I guess no man wanted me," which I suppose is true, too.

Where are you now my love?

The sheets in my bed stay cool—I'm hot, but they stay cool —wrapping me up tight like a mummy. I lie, eyes closed, still as a sloth. As light and silent as a feather that has misplaced its wing.

"Miss Audette. Wake up, Miss Audette. You need to eat something."

If only I weren't breathing, the nursing aide would leave me alone.

Oak-a-lee. Hear that, Elizabeth? Is it a mockingbird? A goldfinch? Or, the incessant *chuck-chack-chuck-chack* keeping the beat? The lilting *chik-o-ree, chik-o-ree*? The sporadic *pik-pik*? The low *pup-pup-pup-pup-pup-pup*—like soft, steady taps on a bass drum.

"Each bird's song is unique," you used to say on those Sunday mornings we nested in bed after working long days all week. You woke me at dawn to listen to a choir of warblings and chirpings and tweetings, and we'd lie like that, almost prayerful, and filled with birdsong. You'd sermonize about the birds, intact in your reveries, while I nuzzled into your softer parts, basking in your sweet and sour scent and syncing my soul to your rapid breath. Though you must have known, Elizabeth, it was the birdsong, not the bird, that mattered to me most. You needed the whole picture to feel cohesive—the how and why and what and who. I was fine with the result. I didn't care to know the story behind the song. But you savored your role as teacher, and I let it abide as you lectured me as to, say, why the males of some bird species are more colorful than the females and that it was Darwin who figured out that females are attracted to color and, as females can be in short supply, busy as they are taking care of their babies, the males must compete for their attention, and did you know birds see a much wider range of color than people do? They have colors in their plumage invisible to the human eye. "Imagine that," you'd say.

I confess; I often tuned out as you prattled on. You didn't notice, so enthralled in your stories. You would ask me, "Isn't that interesting?" And I would nod my head up and down in response with no idea what I agreed to.

Now I wish I had been more attentive.

We were an odd couple, weren't we? Me, short and stocky with wild curls and a too-large nose. You, tall and narrow. No breasts to speak of. "Just two raisins on a breadboard," you joked. That's when I'd whisper in the downy slope of your neck, "I love raisins" and remain a beat, waiting until I sensed your cheeks rise into a smile.

You wore that long face, Elizabeth, and as you aged, your features dipped on a race to your chin. People considered you sullen, and you did have your dark days. Those were hard. The fun times were best, like taking Clara and her brother, my nephew Sam, to see *The Wizard of Oz*. Was it 1938 or '39? They were little then, and Clara sat close and squeezed my arm during the scary parts. On the way out of the theater, we overheard them whisper in cupped hands, "Elizabeth looks like the Wicked Witch of the West." Do you remember how we laughed afterwards? And how you agreed, in jest, to stand in the bathtub, "naked as a jaybird," you said, so I could dump a bucket of water on you to make sure you didn't melt? Always the drama queen, you wailed and writhed, "I'm melting, I'm melting," and sank into the tub, and I jumped in with you and we made great waves that rose out of the tub and broke into deep and satisfying puddles on the tile floor.

Cheepings and chirpings, a chorus of stanzas and verse. Heavy *seets*. Hoarse *skeeches*. Urgent whistlings of *chur-wi-chur-wis*. Oh, I think I know this one; *ooAAH cooo*. The hollow hymn of a mourning dove providing the bass notes to the soprano chatter.

You loved flowers, and I often wished we had enough money to move out of our apartment into a small house with a garden. You bought me pink tea roses each Valentine's Day. Every year people asked, "Who are the flowers for?" And, you said, each time, "I bought them for myself as I don't have a beau" and they were embarrassed and felt sorry for you. Little did they know.

But why did you have to chide me to lose weight? Don't think I didn't hear you tut-tut if I reached for a second piece of pie. I guess I did the same to you about your smoking and you not emptying your ashtrays. Seems like a lot of hemming and hawing for nothing now. Why did it take us so long to learn that love isn't forcing others to change to suit us? But, then one day you started to cough and cough and cough until you became the cough and the cough was you...

I'll have you know I'm skinny now. My bodacious breasts—your words—have deflated into flaps of skin, my hands are skeletal, and each day my body lightens and I wonder how tiny I have to be before I float away.

So many birds chortling, sending clear notes. Refrain and response. Haphazard harmonies that somehow sound right. Wheezy *yank-yanks*, high, lisping *tzeees,* and rapid, nasal *whi-whi, whi-whi, whi-whis*. All of a piece. Overflowing into the empty spaces spreading inside me, softening my bones, tightening my skin.

"If you could be a bird, which would you be?" I asked you once.

"A Mallard duck," you said.

"Why?"

"Because they remain together for a lifetime."

"But it's a boy and girl duck who pair up, and we are two girls?"

"I'll be the boy duck," you said, with a certainty I couldn't argue with.

"Why?" I said.

"Because you'll love my colors and pick me out from the others."

You knew me too well, Elizabeth.

I wanted to be a swallow. I said, "Swallows fly like daredevils, so assured they won't fall from the sky. They're free to be their true selves and do what they want and somersault and skydive and, clearly, that's more fun than paddling around a pond, or lollygagging on clumsy webbed feet. Don't you agree?"

You stuck to your Mallards.

Hushed murmurings mingle at the foot of my bed—a sonorous male voice punctuated by interruptions of higher tones with question marks.

"Aunt Madge? Aunt Madge?"

Clara's face hovers over me in a breathy haze of warm peppermint. Her wide eyes blue wells to fall into. There's grief inside them that has nothing to do with me. I wonder why I never noticed it before.

"How are you, Aunt Madge? Why aren't you eating? They say you're not eating."

"Where is Elizabeth? Did you bring her?"

Clara's sadness drifts like a dark cloud, out and above her eyes and over and across her face's planes and slopes and crevices, but this time she doesn't stay silent.

"Oh, Aunt Madge. I know I keep telling you I will bring her, but, oh, Aunt Madge, I can't lie to you anymore. I'm so sorry, but she died a long time ago. Remember?"

My body fights fatigue while my mind is wide awake, buzzing with birdsong. It crescendos and hits wrong notes, no longer harmonizing. Major and minor keys clash.

"A cacophony of birds," I whisper.

"What did you say, Aunt Madge?"

"So many birds. Each with a different song."

Clara's brow contracts into gentle furrows of worry.

"I don't hear any birds, Aunt Madge."

The sheets stay cool. I'm hot, and they stay cool. The birdsong is no longer discordant but muffled, as if blanketed over by a gentle calm. I can feel my body billowing upwards with the grace of a sheet swaying on a clothesline as the wind picks up. It's nice here. Air caresses my tired limbs, lengthening them, stroking them until they're feather light.

BIRDSONG

The robin holds her breath behind a cloud. I breathe for her and await her song: *Cheerily-cheer up-cheer up-cheerily-cheer up*.

♦

David Salner

NIGHT TRAIN

Also published in Poetry East

The fields disappear
into the darkness beyond the tracks
as you listen to the clack-clack-clack
from the weight of the wheels bearing down
over miles of cross-ties and wonder
for no reason whatsoever what if
you could step down when it slows
for a crossing and become someone else
the man in that truck waiting by the tracks
gripping the wheel feeling
the heavy vibration at the engine's heart
and the miss that makes it stumble almost stall
until you rev it and a plume of exhaust
turns pink in the crossing lights. Could smoke
because what else would you do while you
wait for this long train to pass. Could breathe
a song of smoke into the country night
as you watch for the arm of the gate to swing up
and the road ahead to clear. Could follow
the center line as it unwinds between fields
into a forest where the tar of the two-lane
changes to gravel and the truck stops in a clearing
filled with the smell of pine needles
fallen on loam and the call and call again
of tree frogs through the window
the vibrant swell the pulse of their longing. Could wait
at the heart of that circle of trees where the air

had been washed by a shower that day
clear of all memory. Could walk
the stone steps to the porch
and turn the knob and feel how easily
the door swings open into a hallway
where someone is standing so close in the darkness
you feel her sigh on your cheek. Could breathe
that one word *want* one syllable
that would guide you through the night
and into a new life. Could step down
at this crossing and wait by the tracks
for this long train to pass.

DAVID SALNER

BLACK PAINTING, WHITE DUST

Also published in Poetry East

Goya purchased a country house where his friends
could hold picnics, bring baskets and bottles,
have a sweeping view of the gray Manzanares
flowing through hills full of orchards and vineyards.

He fought off grave illness in that pleasant cottage
away from the heat of Madrid—refuse in streets,
the court of Fernando maddened by rumors
of the French army advancing—then succumbed

to an artistic fever we can't explain, smearing
the plaster with a black oil chaos from which
eyes glinted like knives, crowds pulsed and clotted . . .

His son had the paintings shaved from the plaster
by a skilled curator and an unknown crew
who coughed white dust into brown work blouses.

DAVID SALNER

WHERE SHELLS COME FROM

Periwinkle, clam, or whelk—
like stones, these sea-worn shells,
all colors buffed away. An ivory sheen is left,
perhaps a whisper of purple across the upturned belly, purple
like the inside of the sea—looking upward through the waves,
if you were drowning, what you would see.

*

Once, these shells protected sea-blood, flesh.
Not sure what kind of life that was, what kind of holding
shells could give. But now a constant surf has broken,
beaten and blended them
to seamless seasoned stone.

*

True stones are heavier, wash lower in the surf.
Not like these whitened flakes, helpless as gull's feathers,
fathoming a way to happen here, so far from Africa,
where shells come from.

*

Our true home was never here, this sandy strip,
but in the sea, a sea of risk, that pure smooth
tumult pushing and sucking us, where we learn
to clutch at water, cling to liquid, float,
then glimpse the sun through waves—
rays lapping and flowing overhead—
as the wonder of our lives floats off.

DAVID SALNER

THE VIEW FROM HEAVEN

where the floors are made of a glass so clear
when I stare through them I seem to float, and it's breathtaking
and dizzying to hover like this, as on the top floor of a skyscraper,

looking into the dark cleft between buildings, slipping into the shadows
where everything seems to be happening, where the walls pulse with music, throb
like the chambers of a child's heart, and the streets fill with drunks and flowers,

and the nights are alive with voices that brawl with anger or whisper
hurt phrases of longing, and throaty laughter beckons the lively
through a network of tracts and hidden arteries, and there

in the depths by a flight of stone steps where I left it,
my soulful artifact, which lends meaning
to everything I can never have back

DAVID SALNER

WYOMING AFTERNOON

A long wait in the wind
for something that might not happen.

Antelope browsing right to left
on an oasis of grass. Sheep

in a dry creek bed, tearing
tufts from the shale-studded earth.

Then a change in the weather,
in the damp air, as the top-heavy

cottonwoods snap and nod
on the horizon. And at the trailer park

in Kemmerer, a shift worker wakes
as the sheet metal skirting flaps

from wind through the crawlspace.
She tosses her covers and puts

a bare foot down—can you feel it,
the chill of the flooring?

♦

Merideth M. Taylor

MISS MARY AND MERIDETH
Nonfiction

Mary Coates Somerville

Miss Mary

When Mary Coates and James Somerville were married November 12, 1925, it was just a few friends and family there. Mary walked to the church for her wedding. She and her sisters-in-law, Rosetta and Mary, walked through the swamp to get to the church. She wore a blue satin dress, blue hat, and blue shoes. She almost slipped in the water, but Rosetta caught her before she got muddied up. Joe Winters was the best man. He was best man for their fiftieth, too, and he got so drunk her sister-in-law took his place. There were five or six hundred people at the Fiftieth Anniversary Wedding. Daughter Magdalene made Mary's dress and the crown. The first time around, Joe Winters behaved himself.

The bride and groom were underage and were supposed to get permission, but Mary didn't tell her people she was getting married. Her sister would have moved her back to Baltimore. They didn't go on a honeymoon: they went right on home and went to bed.

They were married for fifty-three years when James died. Mary raised fifteen children, counting her son Lynwood's oldest, her daughter Dorothy's girls, and her own twelve. She was proud of that. The hardest times in her life were the deaths of her children. James Leo, he died at eighteen months. James had to carry James Leo about a half-mile to the road to take him to the car for the trip to St. Mary's Hospital. He'd caught pneumonia. Francis Lynwood died in a car accident. He and some boys were playing "chicken" on the highway in their souped-up cars. James Alexander died when he was six years old. He was struck in the stomach and hung upside down by a big teenage boy at school. The doctor came out to the house, but he only lived for two or three days after he was struck. When people asked her to talk about her life, Mary liked to talk about the old days.

"When I was a child the times was good," according to Mary. She worked hard all the time. But that was just how it should be. She milked the four cows and drove them to the woods every morning before school, and went and brought them back to the barn every night. She had no end of chores. She liked feeling grown up and useful. Mary's mama taught her how to cook and put up food for the winter. After she married, she won prizes for her preserves at the county fair. Won a blue ribbon one year for her peaches. She taught her girls to cook and bake and tried to make them and her boys into good hard workers like she was, but it didn't necessarily "take" like it had with her. Times were different.

When Mary was little, before she started school, her papa taught her the alphabet from off the quick oatmeal box. He used to read to her from the Bible and, when her mom would be gone, he would sit down and read fairy tales to her. "He was good to me," she said. "When Mama get ready to whoop me, he'd get between the switch and me, and he caught some of the licks. He'd say, 'Don't hit her no more, Mama.' He used to call Mama 'Mama.' 'Don't hit her no more, Mama.' [chuckle] He was old. Old fella, had rheumatism. I used to put his shoes on, put his socks on in the mornin'. He couldn't bend over to put his shoes on. Tie 'em up, take 'em off at nighttime."

Mary started school at five years old. She loved her teachers, and she remembered every one. Her mom boarded teachers like Miss Agnes Walton who weren't from around there. Agnes Walton found a husband "right from Mechanicsville" and got married in their parlor. Then there was Janie Bowie, who "wasn't tall as me, with legs bowed like pothooks. But she was just as nice as she could be. I was the littlest one in school, and everybody seemed to like me."

Mary's parents got the *Afro* newspaper out of Baltimore every week. They didn't have a radio. But they had a Victrola. They got their news from the newspaper and word of mouth. They also got information from an "old lady" who would travel from house to house carrying news. In later years, Mary didn't seem to care much for staying on top of the news. "Too much about all this drugs, rape, and murders."

Her favorite times as a child were at school and church when they put on pageants and she got to perform. "See, Mama Coates and all the society ladies always give a Christmas play. Three plays a year in the church hall, and they had me in every one of them. That's how I come to like to be up on that stage. In one play—the last play that had me in at the Mechanicsville Hall— was this song. [singing] '*Can you show me the way the city?*' Now, my father and some other men made crosses, made a whole lot of crosses. So, we had to kneel down at these crosses. '*Can you show me the way the city? To the city where the angels dwell? And the prince that we see on the mountain steep, he strayed to a cross of God.'* And we all was kneelin' at these crosses. That was a beautiful play. The cross was white—some red and some white. We all had a cross to kneel at. That was a Christmas play. The last one I was at before Mama died. And, yes, [singing:] *'We show the way to the city. To the city where the angels dwell. And the prince with his feet on the'*—That was Jesus. [sings:] *'On a mountain steep, please stray to the house of God.'* Real pretty."

"We had to study these dialogues, speeches, you know. I had to get it right. Mama made me say those pieces over and over. She would walk down to school with me and I said my part all the way to school. She right behind me. Come back at night, same thing. I had to get it right. When rehearsal come, Mama sat up, right up at the front. Right on the front seat. She had real big, full eyes, and I mean she could throw 'em on me—'Speak up there, Sister!' I was on stage! [chuckle] I just cracked! [laughter] I got surprised. 'Speak up there, Sister.' I mean, she wasn't smilin'. That little short fat woman was strong! [chuckle] Yeah, it was fun. 'Deed it was."

When people from the college came and asked Mary to talk about what life was like growing up in St. Mary's County, she loved telling them stories like that. She liked to make people laugh. She made fun of herself, too. Like why she didn't drive. She said she got registered to vote but never voted because she had no transportation.

She had folks in stitches when she acted out trying to learn how to drive and almost killing herself and James, who was sitting beside her in the old truck trying to teach her. The basic problem was that she was too short to see over the hood and she'd go barreling forward 'till he'd yell "Stop!" When she got out of the truck, she saw that she was headed directly into a building. That scared her so bad, she never wanted to try again.

Mary liked to talk about the families whose homes she worked in and how they were pleased with her and showed their appreciation. Especially the family she worked for who took her along with them on a trip to the Holy Land. It was the first time she had traveled farther than Baltimore. She loved to bring out her souvenirs and tell visitors about her trip.

Her favorite stories, though, were about being on the stage. And, at the age of 85, Miss Mary had a chance to relive the joy of performing when she was cast in a play called *In My Time* at St. Mary's College of Maryland. She played a character who was a real person and was a lot like her. The character was a hard worker who worked in the homes of white people. Mary enjoyed getting to know the young people in the cast, and they and the audiences loved her. She was, once again, a star, and it was fun, 'deed it was.

Mary Somerville and Merideth Taylor
Story of a Relationship

I met Mary Agatha Coates Somerville in 1993. I was casting for *In My Time*, an original play I had written and was going to be directing at St. Mary's College of Maryland. The play was based on oral histories collected and published by the Southern Maryland Documentary Project, a project spearheaded by St.

Mary's College of Maryland professor Andrea Hammer. I had received a call informing me that there was an eighty-five-year-old African American woman who wanted to join the cast and was hoping there was a part for her. She lived quite a ways from campus, but the friend who called was willing to provide transportation. Naturally, I was intrigued. I drove to Oakville, MD about twenty-five minutes from campus, to meet her.

I knocked on the door of her small, neat cinderblock house. When the door opened, I had to adjust my gaze downward to take in the smiling face that topped her four feet, nine inches of kinetic energy. She welcomed me inside, and we conducted a most unusual audition, which included an impromptu recitation and stories, rather than the script reading I had planned. These were accompanied by various spontaneous dance moves Mary provided to show she was ready for anything. She became the eldest member of the large cast, which ranged from five years old to eighty-five. Thus began a friendship that lasted until her passing in 2008, at the age of ninety-nine.

Over the years, we never went long without speaking. She performed again in *The Bigger Picture*, another original play, at the College in 1995. Aside from that, our activities typically included me picking her up and taking her to community, social, or church events. We visited fairs and festivals and attended oral history workshops together. As her health declined and she became bedridden, I would come and visit with her at her home.

In many ways, my relationship with Mary fit common friendship patterns, pathways, and progressions and was unremarkable. However, there were crucial ways that this relationship, in which there was a genuine mutual fondness, was far from typical and was often challenging, frustrating, and enlightening for me. It was an attempt at true friendship across difference. As I look back on the relationship, I am still tussling with important questions.

The overarching question I ask myself is: What did the role of racial, class, and generational difference, real and imagined, play in our relationship? It is one thing to know how a relationship feels from the inside, and another to look back and try to gain an objective understanding. During our years together, I had opportunities to learn about Mary in formal as well as informal ways. As a member of the Unified Committee for Afro-American Contributions of St. Mary's County, I spent hours interviewing her as a participant in an oral history project. I took my role as listener very seriously and understood the importance of withholding comment and judgment. Even outside the interview situation, I was reluctant to challenge or question too deeply the attitudes that surprised or distressed me. Maybe I should have been more open about my own reactions. I might have learned more.

There are things I would like to ask her if I could reach back into the past. For example, why did she go on sitting quietly in the back of the church long after the practice of sending African Americans to sit in the back rows was no longer considered acceptable? And was that still common practice in Southern Maryland? Did other African Americans her age follow suit?

And why, even in relating the tragedies of her children's death, did she show little or no anger toward the system that had discriminated against her and let her down in so many ways? She was very happy to be the subject of an oral history interview and enjoyed sharing her stories. But would the stories have been different if I had been a black interviewer asking her about her life, and, if so, how? I had already gained her trust by the time we sat down to do the interviews, so that may have lessened any reluctance she may have had to be frank.

For much of her life, Mary provided domestic labor for white employers. The fact that she showed neither embarrassment nor resentment when relating stories of accepting charity in the way of clothes, foods, and household goods from the white folks she worked for surprised me. Some even took her on trips, including a trip to Israel, which was, understandably, a high point in her life. She clearly seemed to feel proud of, and not at all demeaned by, her relationships with her white employers and happy to be given valuable things. Like most of us, I'm sure, she enjoyed being in good favor and pleasing people. And, after all, she gained very beneficial experiences like travel, as well as useful material goods that she would not have been able to afford for herself or her family. It is hard for someone like me, who did not experience living in a segregated system, to understand the feelings involved in the exchanges between patrons and the patronized. These gifts or "handouts" were valued commodities as well as signs of her success in winning over her employers. It seems, to me, she had learned to "work the rigged system" to her advantage as best she could with hard work, intelligence, wit, and charm. I have no doubt that her employers were genuinely fond of her.

In our interactions, there were very few moments that felt awkward. It generally felt natural that I would take the lead in making decisions. I was her director after all. And it felt natural that I would be "treating" her. She was an elder and deserving of extra care and respect on that grounds as well. I think we politely refrained from acknowledging any sense of discomfort we may have had. When invited to a meal at my house, she offered to do the dishes and clean up as if, maybe, that was part of the "admission price." It was not like the casual offer of a friend. How did that make me feel? Uncomfortable for sure, like being cast in a role I didn't want to play.

I noticed that Mary showed no reluctance or discomfort in receiving unreciprocated gifts from me. I bought her many gifts on our outings and became aware over time of what seemed to me to be strategies meant to encourage my gift-giving. Was I forever the white benefactor rather than the white friend? Does one preclude the other? I started to see her skills at manipulating her family members and me to vie for her appreciation or to feel guilty. I worried that the family would come to resent me. And I believe they did, at least to some extent. Once she was bedridden, they sometimes made it difficult for me to see her, and that was frustrating.

I've thought about Mary a lot over the years since she passed away, puzzling over the complications and contradictions of our relationship. I've learned that, embedded in my sense of privilege, no matter how unconscious, there may have been the belief that *I* would have resisted, that *I* would not have accepted so quietly the discriminatory treatment that she endured. Since I've never been put to the test, of course, this is a fantasy. How do I know how I might have reacted to the kinds of everyday insults or micro-aggressions and the much larger injustices she experienced? Was I judging her for her "failure" to be outraged and to resist more demonstratively? Was I asking her to see herself as a victim?

To what extent did she speak and behave differently with me because I was white? After a relationship of almost twenty years, did she suppress expressions of resentment and hurt because I was white? Did our class differences have an even more dominant effect on our relationship? She had less wealth, fewer material goods, less education, and less standing in the community. It was easy for us both to assume that I would be the one footing any bills. We were friends, but we weren't. How could we be true friends in an uncomplicated way when our social capital and economic resources were so unequal? When our mutual heritage was one of racial, gender, and class hierarchy and segregation? It was a lot to navigate. But we did care for each other. We genuinely liked each other and enjoyed our time together. She was a live wire with great stories to tell and a good sense of humor. I was interested in learning about local cultures. We both liked to laugh. We clicked.

Mary Somerville seemed to me to be a happy woman. Was she wearing the "mask" of double consciousness so powerfully alluded to by writers from Paul Laurence Dunbar to W.E.B. DuBois to Ntozake Shange? Or was it because she was, above all, a *survivor* and a woman who wanted to be happy in the world as it was? Had she taken our friendship at face value and chosen not to question the gifts of material goods or friendship and been the happier for it?

One spring day, Mary and I attended a strawberry festival at a local historic plantation. Mary had dressed up in the way that a proper eighty-five-year-old lady of very limited means could. In other words, she had dressed as she would for church. I remember she had a white Peter Pan collar with lace trimming that contrasted with her dark skin. A tiny bit of face powder had spilled onto the collar. A hostess met us as we came into the mansion. She was not outwardly hostile as she greeted us—I think she may have smiled stiffly—yet I felt a sudden drop in the room's temperature. I don't know how else to describe it. It was different from the welcome that, as a friendly-looking, middle-class white woman, I normally expect and get. It seemed so clear that we did not belong there. We stayed and did our best to enjoy the occasion, saying nothing to each other about the chilly reception. Mary showed no sign of feeling hurt, and I was afraid to hurt her feelings by remarking on it.

Our long, close relationship helped me to learn uncomfortable truths and to better understand her, myself, and the wider society. Our relationship provided benefits for both of us. I enjoyed making Mary happy, and her appreciation of my efforts was gratifying. I greatly benefited from her participation in my theater productions and believe that the oral history she provided is of value to the community as well as inspiring to me as a writer. On several occasions, I attended church services with Mary. This was a real cross-cultural experience for me. I, a lapsed Unitarian, was new to the Southern Maryland African American church experience. Mary was open to any denomination and especially liked the "homecoming" services, where all were welcome. We attended AME, United Methodist, and Catholic churches, including her home church, St. Joseph's. I never pretended to believe, and she never held it against me. She probably hoped it was doing some good for my soul. It probably was.

The specious old canard of the "happy darkies" was a concept and expression devised and utilized to rationalize the inhuman practices of slavery and Jim Crow. I wonder if there exists a bitter irony in the unaccountable ability of some people who, subjected to lifelong unjust and often brutal treatment, manage through their own devices to survive, develop resilience, and even find joy. Mary Somerville, dark-skinned, economically disadvantaged, and hard-working woman that she was, made "a way out of no way," as they say. She chose to squeeze every drop of enjoyment and love out of the life that she saw as something that she was given and had little power to change.

♦

Brice Particelli

DANCING AT THE BAY OF SHARKS
Nonfiction

Most of the people I met in Kiribati got their first tattoo when they were thirteen or fourteen years old. The tattoos were small—often just a friend's name in bleeding blue, hand-written with a needle and ink.

Etiaroi's were cleaner, more complex. Her first was an armband of barbwire for her father when she was twelve, she told me, "because he is in jail." The second was an armband of Samoan symbols, "for my first love, a Samoan boy when I was very young."

Even without them, it would be easy to tell that Etiaroi wasn't from here. Her voice boomed louder than anyone around, and she walked like she was too big for a rural island of 2,500 people.

Etiaroi and I met on the basketball courts during my third week on Christmas Island. I was twenty-six, on a grant to visit several of the Republic of Kiribati's thirty-three islands by freighter and write about the impacts of climate change. I was also in the social hole that is graduate school, where debt and uncertain job prospects encourage adolescent relationships. I was more focused on intellectual pursuits.

In fact, it was a metaphor that drew me to Kiribati. With an average altitude of only two meters, most of Kiribati's islands will be uninhabitable or underwater within fifty years. Kiribati is also the world's easternmost nation, pressed against the international dateline in the middle of the Pacific, making them the first people to welcome the new day.

It's a stunning metaphor: the first people to see tomorrow will be the first to lose their entire country to climate change. I knew I needed to see it, so I hopped a plane to Christmas Island, ready to spend the summer soaking up as much as I could.

Etiaroi barely said a word the day we met. She was the only woman in a three-on-three basketball game, pushing and playing in a place where it was rare to see women older than sixteen unmarried, let alone playing sports.

I'd stopped to say hi to a friend when one of the players came over.

"Do you play?" he asked.

"Sure," I said.

I don't, but I rarely say no while traveling. Besides, at six feet tall, I had a good four inches on anyone out there. How hard could it be?

Etiaroi lined up against me. She was the tallest of her teammates and had short-cropped hair and long, athletic limbs. She stared me down with big brown eyes and was as beautiful as she was intimidating. She was all business, while my default is a quick smile. I knew I was in trouble.

I tried to flirt, hoping she'd ease up, but she ran circles around me and left me defeated without a word. The game wasn't even close.

"Come dance tonight," Alice said the next day. Alice worked at the Communications Office, the only place that offered internet or phones on the island. "There is someone I want you to meet."

I was wary. Alice was nineteen and unmarried. Her parents had arranged a marriage for her at fifteen and while she'd talked them out of it then, American missionaries from Georgia were trying to arrange one now between her and their twenty-one-year-old son. Alice's family seemed unlikely to let her say no again, but she was struggling with the decision. Kiribati offered women very few choices, she told me, and she desperately wanted to go to the U.S., "but I don't love him," she said. "I hoped it would be you, but maybe it is him."

I'd been trying to be friends with Alice, but after that conversation I realized it might not be possible. I determined to only see her in the office.

"No dancing for me," I said. "I'm not much of a dancer." But she wouldn't relent.

The dance was in the town *maneaba*, a large grass hut in the middle of the village. It was a family event—bright lights and no booze—not like the bars on the outskirts of town where proper young Kiribati women weren't supposed to go.

"Come with me. Let me introduce you," Alice said, walking me over to Etiaroi. "Maybe you like her instead of me."

Etiaroi and I talked on the outskirts of the party all night. She was twenty-one, from Tarawa Island, Kiribati's capital 2,000 miles to the west. She was bartending at The Bay of Sharks, one of those outskirt bars, saving money while waiting for a visa. She was staying with her cousin Tuutana, and they planned to visit family in Honolulu once the visas came in. They'd been waiting for a year, but this was a place where the mail only comes every few months.

"Maybe I can find work in Hawaii," Etiaroi said. "Maybe we can stay."

"You don't like Tarawa?" I asked. I'd assumed Kiribati's capital was more cosmopolitan, in part because of Etiaroi. "Why do you want to leave?"

She scrunched her nose like I'd asked a stupid question. "There is so much more in America. There is so much more I can do. Here, there is nothing."

"Christmas Island is quiet," I agreed.

"No. I like Christmas," she said. "It is nicer here, but very traditional. Tarawa is fine, but it is dirty. And small. There is so much more out there for me."

For the next two weeks, we spent almost every moment together—picnicking on secluded beaches, walking tropical lagoon flats, and dancing to Australian and Fijian pop at The Bay of Sharks. We talked music and dreams, and she told me she wanted to go to nursing school in the U.S. "I just want to help people," she said.

She was more secure in her desires, and I found her confidence intoxicating.

None of it felt romantic, not really. My flirtations were often ignored, and it became my day's goal to make her smile. Mostly we talked about our own plans, as if we were young friends dreaming of our own possibilities—her as a nurse in Hawaii, me as a professor in Colorado.

Occasionally she'd sneak into my room late at night. In bed she was timid, hesitant, and she'd sneak out before sunrise, looking both ways as she implored me to whisper like we were kids at summer camp. I made a joke of it one night, and she squeezed my arm hard. "You don't know what it would be like if people knew. You don't understand."

When the freight ship that would take me to the other islands arrived, I thought I saw tears in her eyes.

"I'll be back in a month," I said.

They couldn't be tears, I thought. I was the soft one.

The freighter bounced between islands for the next month unloading rice, flour, and sugar. Kiribati is one of the most cash-poor countries in the world, with only 20 percent of its 140,000 people participating in a cash economy. The rest live off whatever the land and ocean provide, so the freighter only visits four times a year, bringing basic items and picking up dried coconut meat and seaweed, their few exports.

With no hotels on the outer islands, I stayed with families along the way. I explored Tabuaeron Island by bicycle with an ex-Navy Seal who had married a Kiribati woman and become one of three foreigners living on an island of 1,500 people. On even more remote Teraina, I drove a Kiribati Minister of Parliament from village to village by scooter so he could tell people what had been going on in the world over the past three months. In almost every village, I was asked if I was single. In several, I was thanked for my country's role in World War II when the U.S. ended Japan's occupation of Kiribati.

I asked about the rising oceans as I traveled. Most people understood it was happening—they saw it, and they were building seawalls by hand to fight it, but the reasons were less understood or too overwhelming to focus on. Most cared more about food or schools or roads than where their kids would have to live in fifty years, or how their tiny nation could fight something so large.

I collected experiences I would later write about, and while I occasionally thought about Etiaroi, she was quickly becoming a memory to carry through later life.

When I returned to Christmas a month later, Etiaroi shrugged her hello. I was excited to see her, if only for a few days before my flight home, but I felt myself checking my excitement to match hers.

We danced that night at The Bay of Sharks and then drove to the beach, laying a blanket among the stars. As we kissed, her long dress flipped up and I saw a new tattoo—a dozen hearts, hand-done in bleeding blue, wrapped around her right ankle.

"When did you get that?" I asked.

She covered it with her other foot, curling toes around swollen skin.

"One month ago. Tuutana did it."

"What for?" I asked.

The question escaped before I could stop it. I closed my eyes, hoping they'd suck the words back in, wishing I could instead pull her close for our last few days together.

Etiaroi stared silently at the ocean, past our feet, then up at me.

The blood emptied from my face.

"Because," she said, looking away, "I—I have a lot of love."
She didn't say anything more. Neither did I.

I tried to cuddle as if nothing had happened, but the night was over. Her face went as quiet and distant as it was when we were among other people.

I left three days later, catching a plane back to Colorado.

I never saw her again.

It's been over ten years, and I've told many stories of Kiribati. The metaphor of this sinking land only becomes more real through time. A few years ago, Kiribati bought 6,000 acres of land in Fiji. While it was purchased for farming, their president warned that the land might become Kiribati's permanent home if the world didn't start addressing climate change.

"In a worst-case scenario, and if all else fails, you will not be refugees," the Fijian president told the Kiribati people. "The spirit of the people of Kiribati will not be extinguished."

I tell these stories, but I still don't know how to tell the story of Etiaroi.

I am now a college professor in Manhattan, happily engaged to a wonderful woman. Being engaged has caused me to pause on past failures to make sure I don't repeat them, but I still don't know what to make of Etiaroi.

A part of me wonders if I'd become the thing I was there to investigate, taking advantage of my power in the world without considering the consequences of my actions. I'd treated our time casually, as if it were a vacation—a word that implies the ability to step away from reality, a word that holds little meaning to most people in this world.

I was a deeply in debt graduate student, sure, but my options were wide open based entirely on where I was born. I could fumble through possibilities. I could treat relationships and experiences as collectible or discardable. I could walk away.

I was there to question the consequences of our disposable culture—to explore a nation sinking because of habits led by my own culture, and I couldn't help but fall into the trap myself. I didn't know how not to.

At the same time, I hesitate to turn Etiaroi into a metaphor. I hesitate to oversimplify. We'd been together without promises or pretense, after all, and relationships lead us in different ways. I don't know how she felt. I don't know when she felt it.

I write and tell stories about that beautiful and disappearing place, but I have avoided telling this story. I can never make sense of what happened. Not really.

I avoid it, but it's there, imprinted on me forever.

◆

Marvin Jonathan Flores

EL SALVADOR

What you recall is not your body

Intolerant of the heat, the thin shriek
Of mosquitoes homing for flesh, the roof tiles
Above you shifting with the gibberish of mice

Or the impossible darkness that drops

And freaks your comprehension like a blown retina;
It is not the endless stream of soldiers
Passing from boyhood
Into death, manhood into torn flesh,
Or the drinking water
That made your blood uneven with fever.

It is not even the clamoring for a father.

What brings you back are the rain-flecked rocks

That loom red and dominant along
The stony paths, the smell of burning wood
Wafting in the air like a pueblo's flag,
The frenetic cluck of chickens, the deep
And resonant low of distant cattle…

MARVIN JONATHAN FLORES

What brings you back
are the people,

The wild and giddy poetry of a *campesino*
Standing in the doorway, doffing
His straw hat. It is the way

The stars at night iridesce and sag
With dappled vastness, the chill of tropical dawns
And the sudden creak of rafters
As you stir in your hammock, caught
Between a dream and a dream. It is

The way Carmela looked at you
When, in her notable manner,
She said back in America you would forget her,
                              And her ways,
                                    And her laughter.

◆

Barbara Westwood Diehl

FOR THE GENTLEMAN
AND HIS FEDORA

The gentleman sitting next to me in Penn Station
has a fedora in his lap. Not a porkpie
or Panama hat. Nothing you'd call retro.
No, his hat reminds me of Humphrey Bogart
lighting a cigarette with his hands cupped
around a match. A hat my grandfather
would have worn reading *The News American*
on the number 8 streetcar. This gentleman
with the gray fedora, with its perfect crease
along the crown and a small brown feather
tucked inside a shiny black hatband,
tells me he is waiting for the train
to Philadelphia, where he will be met
by his grandson, Bill, who is quite the bigwig
in the computer biz. They will drink scotch,
while dinner cooks in something called a
crockpot. He chuckles at the word, crockpot.
The gentleman rubs his thumbs along
the fedora's felt brim and tells me
he will not need to go to assisted living,
after all. Then he blows his nose
into a white handkerchief with ironed creases
and an H embroidered in pale blue stitches.

BARBARA WESTWOOD DIEHL

My grandfather's initial. I like this H. I like
his small brown feather and perfect creases.
I like Bill and his crockpot, too. I would like
to drink a glass of scotch with Bill in Philadelphia
and the gentleman in the gray fedora.
I would like to go to a city where someone
will be glancing up from a newspaper
to check the time that I'll arrive.

◆

Christopher Linforth

YADDO OF THE SOUTH
Nonfiction

Across from the picturesque redbrick campus of Sweet Briar College, show horses share the lush green pasture with silky black Angus cows and twenty-five artists-in-residence. At Mount San Angelo sits the Virginia Center for the Creative Arts—a 450-acre site in the remote countryside of central Virginia. I find myself at the colony for the first time, newly graduated from my MFA program, desperately unemployed, and looking over the meager notes for my novel in my girlfriend's 2001 Toyota Camry.

Maria squeezes my hand. She tells me two weeks is plenty of time to write a book, that she believes in me, that I just need to believe in myself. I tuck the single piece of paper with my dashed sketch about 1950s Levittown into my pocket and thank her, kiss her on the lips.

"No kissing anyone else while you're here," she says.

She half-smiles to signal she's joking but also a little worried. This will be our first extended time apart since we started dating. Eighteen months—that's a record for both of us.

"I'll call you every night," I say.

I exit the car and wave goodbye. For a moment I listen to the Toyota, the thrum of the motor fading down the hill. I turn around, ready to get the next two weeks over with. I roll my suitcase into the Langhorne Residence, a dorm of sorts, with a spacious lounge and attached library. A little lost, I meander through the hallways until I find the mailboxes near the dining hall. A line of people waits outside; voices grumble it's already past the allotted start time for dinner. A trim man in beige slacks and a crystal-blue chambray shirt, introduces himself as Tom and asks if I am new. I nod, and he says don't worry about settling in. "It's time to eat and drink," he adds, brandishing a bottle of red wine.

The doors spring open and the cadre of writers, artists, and composers troop inside, scooping up white china plates and serving themselves pan-fried pork, hearty roast potatoes, and blanched green beans. I follow Tom to the sideboard brimming with steel chafing dishes but then realize I still have my suitcase. I park it against the wall before filling my own plate and sitting next to Tom. There are four other people at the table, but a bespectacled woman in her late forties holds court. Lean and pale, she immediately deduces from my plaid shirt and two-day beard that I am a writer, and she asks me the name of my agent. My lack of an affirmative answer leads to a long spiel about her memoir and her big advance, the opportunity she had to live in London and to visit the capital cities of Europe.

Later, over bowls of vanilla ice cream and more wine, the woman—Strawberry—divulges the covey of men she slept with in Europe. Something more than her hippie, free-love name signals dangerous territory. I sense a pattern of behavior and refuse her offer to refill my wineglass.

Up at six in the morning, a dull ache thudding in the back of my head, I leave the living quarters determined to write. Past the horses and cows, already feeding on the cud, I walk up the tarmac path shimmering with morning dew. The studios lie several hundred feet away, housed in a converted barn and stables. A trio of old grain silos looms over the complex of yellow-gray brick buildings and rectangular lawn courtyards. Inside my studio are a small bed, a grand-looking mahogany desk with chair, and a window with a view of the trail. I am momentarily confused by the bed and why anyone would sleep out here, alone, with the work, the unrelenting pressure of getting it done.

I pin the notes for my novel to the corkboard, turn on my laptop, and stare out of the window at the thorny bushes, the canvas of indigo sky blushing a yellowy-orange at the horizon like a time-lapse video. Sunrise should be inspiring, a call to action for the creative process to kick in, a reminder of our limited time. Instead, I shift my gaze between the blank screen and my novel notes. The memory of what I'd decided to write about and why exists as a fuzzy remnant of completing my graduate degree, a sudden realization that no one in publishing cares about short story collections. Novels, my thesis advisor counseled, are needed if you are to have a career.

For my first hour of work, I study the signatures on the wooden boards near the door—they seem like a rite of passage, a claiming of a time and place. I recognize a few of the names, wonder what novels were written in this room. At my desk, still curious, I Google the other writers currently at the colony. Several teach at fancy liberal art colleges and have multiple prize-winning books. Tom, I learn, lives in New Orleans, writes scripts for HBO, and has novels blurbed by Bob Dylan. Strawberry's memoir was published shortly after the turn of the millennium, the reviews chiding the book for its narcissism. A little more digging reveals she comes from a family of famous California writers.

My handful of literary journal publications means little around here. I know I should get to work—to hit my minimum of a thousand words a day—if I am ever to join these writers as a peer. I fight against my headache and my urge for coffee. But I cannot even write one sentence. I decide to read for a while, and I lie on the bed with a copy of the most recent *New Yorker*, yet I soon fall asleep.

When I wake a few hours later, I check my email and find an invitation for a job interview at a college in nearby Lexington. My research reveals that the institution describes itself as a military liberal arts college. I ponder for a while whether this is an oxymoron. Undecided, I call off the rest of my writing day and go for a walk on the grounds. Boxwood hedges line the paths that curve around beech trees and red oaks and large sculptures nestled in discreet pockets of landscaping. I skirt the swimming pool and an old cottage, and I see a handful of rabbits hop in and out of the briar. I track one of the braver rabbits around the side of the main living residence. There I spot, in a white picket gazebo, Tom playing his banjo to a gaggle of women. They seem rapt with his obvious talent. Pangs of jealousy hit me as a bluegrass tune floats out into the thick, humid air.

At a late-afternoon cocktail hour hosted by the administrative office, we drink gin and tonics with slices of cucumber and coins of ice. The colonial-style front porch bustles with the small talk and polite laughter of almost everyone in residence. The executive director mingles among us, talks eloquently about the colony's future. It has been around for decades, he says, at one site or another. VCCA wants to move, though, pressured by the exorbitant rent in the lease agreement with Sweet Briar College. The director suggests it may move closer to Charlottesville to rein in wealthy donors interested in patronizing the arts.

Somewhat tipsy, I lounge in a rocking chair and talk to an old married couple who spend their summers traveling from residency to residency. They tell me they get their best art made here. "Yaddo of the South," the husband says. "Only too hot," adds the wife, "and worse food."

I feel well fed with the healthy portion sizes of the meals and the constant supply of ice cream. The heat is stickier here, a lower elevation than my house a hundred miles south, tucked beneath the Blue Ridge Mountains. Even now, I feel a cold prickle of sweat on the small of my back.

"Are you being productive?" the man asks.

The wife slaps his knee, then looks my way. "You don't have to answer him."

"This place is a change from Blacksburg," I say.

Maria is back there working on her Ph.D. I miss her and the lack of pressure of completing a book. They both nod, and we continue to drink, talk more about the balmy weather before I make my excuses and stumble back to my studio. Inside, instead of writing, I tackle the stinkbug infestation. So far, I've been largely ignoring the rotund winged insects. They flutter and buzz across the room, disrupting any sense of concentration. I roll up my *New Yorker* and use it to flick the stinkbugs into a coffee cup. As I do so, I see poets walk past the window, enjoying an evening stroll on the trail. They seem happy, content with their day's work. I dispose of the stinkbugs in the courtyard and then return to the studio, desperate for inspiration. I scan the bookshelf, for one of the books must be of some help. I flip through Anne Lamott's *Bird by Bird* and a battered edition of *Moby-Dick*. But the alcohol has ruined my attention span, and I slump at the desk and rummage through the drawer. There is a thick stack of paper scraps, all written upon. Dozens of messages from former fellows speak of hope, of overcoming writer's block and stifled creativity. Stick with it, they say, and trust the work. I read through them all, then start typing and don't stop until late.

I fall into a schedule of rising at a reasonable hour and writing until lunch. Afterward, there is time for pleasure reading, some exercise in the outdoor pool or over at Sweet Briar's gym. I attend some of the impromptu poetry readings by the grand piano in the lounge, *umm* and *ahh* at appropriate moments. Many of the poets tell me their objective is three to four poems a week. To me, that seems underwhelming, but they say that number of poems is a lot, even mentally draining. Post-events, I write a couple of pages more and call Maria, talk about anything but the novel. She's concerned as much as I am about my impending job interview. I have a Skype session booked for midway through the residency.

When the morning of my job interview arrives, I've written fifty pages of so-so prose. The narrative is flat, lacking in energy, in anything happening plot-wise or to the narrator, a seventeen-year-old boy on Long Island. I am thankful to think about something else: a job that can pay the bills, make me feel less worthless about the previous three years of workshops and literature classes. My late-night research about the military college dredged up a recent scandal in the English department: seven professors fired or quit. The college is something of a Southern institution, a place of honor, famous for its spartan conditions and hard work ethic. For the Skype interview, I've tucked in my best plaid shirt and combed my short brown hair. I look halfway presentable.

I've set up my computer so a bookshelf is behind me. *Moby-Dick* sits over my right shoulder—the novel makes me seem scholarly and employable, or at least that's the plan. The Skype window opens, and two women in white military uniforms come into focus. Sitting behind an imposing black desk, they arch their heads forward, trying to inspect me. I am not military material, but it is an adjunct position, and I know they are desperate. They pepper me with questions about pedagogy and my experience in teaching composition, which I answer well enough that they nod and smile. Then the Wi-Fi cuts out and the internet connection is lost. After a panicked minute, we continue the interview on the telephone but just tie up a few loose ends concerning my skimpy résumé.

For the next couple of days, I try not to think about the interview or if I will leave the colony with a job. I double down on the novel and accelerate the pace of my writing. I begin to sleep in the studio and write for eight, ten hours a day. The air is cool at night, and I open the windows, let the breeze in, the brittle chirping of cicadas, the faint sound of voices in the other studios, or conversations out on the grounds. Then I hit page one hundred and feel stuck. I have no idea where the novel is going or what it is really about.

One evening, in the library, I confess my problems to Tom. He chortles at the premise of my novel. He is from that area of Long Island; his first novel covered similar thematic territory. My shoulders slump; I feel derivative and confess this to him. Yet he tells me not to worry about it. "There's room for another great Long Island novel," he says. Tom goes on to explain his process of sketching out scenes, filling in much of the connective tissue later on. "Just write the drama," he says. "The beats of the story."

The last week of my residency, I take his advice and map out the narrator's arc, how his story will unfold. All the sitting, though, leaves my body coiled with energy, my buttocks more like fleshy pillows than I remember. I write all the time I have. I make real progress. Then I get an email from the military college offering me the job. The news stalls me, derails my writing. The thought of teaching officer cadets, of being a faculty member at the same place Stonewall Jackson once taught, of joining the unorganized Virginia militia, hits me. I am neither a Southerner nor someone particularly invested in the military.

When I talk the situation through with Maria, she reassures me that it is not the actual military, that I will be fine. She is glad that I will be close in the fall, less than two hours away. I admit to her that my novel will be far from finished. She says she never expected me to really write a whole book in two weeks—that would be silly. With her blessing, I feel all right again to take in the evening readings, to show up to the visual art open houses, to drink red wine and listen to Strawberry's salacious tales of Europe and Tom's banjo playing. I walk the grounds again, watch the fireflies buzz luminous in the trees, in the air around me.

On my last night, I am invited by another young writer to a dance party in the library. I say I should pack, but perhaps I will stop by. For a couple of hours, I tidy my studio, then, as I leave, I sign the board. More than earning my place with these other writers, I made this time and place my own.

Around ten in the evening, I stroll through the residence, intrigued by the thrum of bass vibrating the rafters. In a small anteroom, I discover fifteen or so writers and artists drinking and dancing to bad nineties pop. Beer in hand, I sit through Bon Jovi, Britney Spears, NSYNC, then some other acts I don't recognize. Eventually, I am dragged onto the makeshift dancefloor and forced to strut my best moves. Around me, sci-fi and literary writers, classical composers, illustrators and oil painters alike flail and jump, as such introverted, desk-bound people are wont to do. Before I know it, the music is turned off. I want it to keep going—this party should not end. But it has, in its own civilized way. It is midnight, and some of the artists, upstairs in bed, are sleeping.

Early-morning sun beats down on me in the parking lot. As I wait for Maria to pick me up, I thumb through my manuscript, all one hundred and fifty pages of it. I have a good deal more than I thought possible. Something about the place brought it out of me. I turn to take a last look at the cows and horses, but I can see neither in the nearby field. Yet I can sense something: I can hear the familiar drum of the Toyota's engine. I believe it is her.

♦

Andrena Zawinski

ANCHORLESS IN THE LIGHT

...And in that veil of light/the city drifts /
anchorless / upon the ocean —Ferlinghetti

It starts this way each morning—house wrens
flirting potato vines, spray of sea on sand,
then the crows and their warnings, mornings
dewy under sun. Come step onto the porch with me,

> the view no longer blocked by the diseased pine.
> We have this, the gift of water beyond the marina,
> its rocky channel gateway to a smooth bay.
> Listen with me to buoys singing with wind in the fog,

old tug announcing its entry against the bark of a seal,
swoop of pelican wings. I cannot resist lingering here
in this veil of white light blinding with beauty, reminding
to hold on to this, hold it close and dear.

> I was once stuck inside glass and brick, sight set
> on neighboring city decks, their chatter, drunken songs
> and brawls, all of it weedy with ivy, bats circling chimneys,
> unlike these distant hills yet to be peopled. But last night

> I dreamed their mounds became an unlit stretch of halls,
> splintered doors on every wall, dust motes flecking air
> over a muddy cliff where nothing stirred, except a ghastly
> parade of dead who nodded, waved, winked, then dissipated,

sending my heart pounding. Here in this new day I can moor,
watch with steadied breath the rise of light. Come here.
I want you at my side, want you to look and listen with me
to the mourning dove's coo, anchorless in the light.

ANDRENA ZAWINSKI

I DIDN'T WANT HIM TO SEE ME

"He's a priest. I trusted him," one of the
1,000 Pennsylvania clergy abuse victims said.

The young priest slid up the lattice confessional screen
in a soft familiar hum. I could not see his face blurred
by gauze and mesh from where I knelt on a step
on my side, could not see him Romanesque
in white clerical collar and penitential purple stole
embroidered with crosses, could not see him sit stolid
dimmed behind his shield, didn't know he had seen me
fidgeting in the pew waiting for the door's green light.

I didn't know he had seen me mornings at Sunday masses
until he called me by name, called me one of his gigglers.
I nervously interrupted with "Bless me Father for I have sinned."
And sinned I had, confessing a carnal act that took me to him,
giving up my virginity the night before at fifteen. He wanted
to see me, later in the rectory after housekeeping went home.
Recoiling and rolling my eyes, I didn't know he could see me
there in the confessional, parish pastor in pressed black cassock.

I did not want to see him, proffered a false promise I would,
one he warned if broken to a Man of God would be mortal sin.
Dismissed without penance of ten Hail Marys, three Our Fathers
or good Act of Contrition, without "Go child and sin no more,"
with neither atonement nor absolution, I faced damnation
for a covenant to be willfully broken to avoid becoming prey,
Polish girl from a tough neighborhood in the Ohio River flatland
with its trinity of smokestacks, sooty sky, sulfur-spoiled air.

ANDRENA ZAWINSKI

Striking my chest three times, as if I could loosen some scarlet
letter of transgression, I headed for the door, signing the cross
across my breast with Mother of Sorrows holy water in a farewell
to the Father, to the Son, to the Holy Ghost. Saints Agnes
and Magdalene flanked at my sides. Parishioner in defection,
I pushed open the weighty church doors on their raspy groan,
wide sleeves of dust-speckled sun raining down over me,
where I would never return, and where he could not see me.

ANDRENA ZAWINSKI

SELF PORTRAIT, OUT-OF-FOCUS

(at Hotel Le Saint-Yves, Le Tréport, Normandie)

> *I was far outside the frame, beyond*
> *the pale, lost in the margins, smudged...*
> —Maggie Anderson

Legs spread beneath a garden party of a dress,
at the armoire's mirror I tap the shudder button
for a self-portrait as you doze off tucked inside
wide wings of sleep. Our Bordeaux, baguette, gruyere
on the bowed windowsill, sky freckled with late light.

Here other women once flagged white kerchiefs
at soldiers leaving alabaster shores of Normandie
for places far from here where we have dug in
to listen to the roll of surf, terns all whoop and wail.

In this snapshot, this is how I like to construct myself,
my image the image of any woman in a hotel room
watching wind skip the emptied beach, listening
for the last milk train coming in on a whistle and grind.

Self-portrait caught where craggy cliffs of the Atlantic
hunch over the channel and coast, the flash of camera
reflecting me back in a blur, I wrap myself inside
the fluff and frill of hotel bedding, drift off with you,
undisturbed, embraced by the long arms of dream.

ANDRENA ZAWINSKI

CIRCLING THE TABLES

We have circled so many tables, topped
by Formica or wood, marble or glass
with our mugs of tea and fortune cookies,
our espresso and chocolate, wine and biscotti,
baguettes and cheese—spreading, crunching,
filling up on tireless conversations,
our grand opinions on the state of things
spilling freely across their surfaces.

There, too, was just the backyard fence talk
about the woman who cries every Saturday night,
that wayward girl who ran off with the local
bad boy and his guitar on a Harley, a man
with Alzheimer's who turned fire starter,
whatever wasn't as we'd like it—
too much war, not enough money, all of us
growing wider and grayer than expected.

How often we squeezed in around those tables
in small kitchens or long stretches of dining rooms,
as if our heart-to-hearts would solve it all,
come to transform our worlds. Today
I find myself quiet and alone, hungry for a feast
of table talk, dreaming us back again, chewing over
breaking news and fearlessly writing recipes
for all our protests, actions, revolutions,
living it up like it really mattered.

◆

R. H. Emmers

CROWS ALWAYS TELL THE TRUTH
Fiction

Having left my lover—an excellent cook, diligent housekeeper and graceful dancer but totally indifferent to those issues that startled me awake in the deepest hours of the night—I decided to return to my childhood home for a period of reflection.

What were these issues that thrust me shuddering out of sleep? No, they had nothing to do with the current Regime, but rather were symptomatic of our modern age in general. For instance, I would suddenly jerk upright in the pitch dark with the overwhelming sense I needed to go to the window, throw back the drapes, and reassure myself that the searing moon still hung whole and uneaten in the relentless void of the sky. My lover, awakened by my leap from bed, would sit up, regard me with glaring eyes I could feel boring into my back, and grumble: So what if the moon disappears? Why do you persist in worrying about what you can't change? Didn't Einstein say that was the definition of insanity?

Well, no, but we'll let that pass. (Idiot.)

Oh, you dear and lovely moon, how much longer will you be with us? Will we be granted advance warning of your going, like all the other things we've lost? But about my childhood home. A small white cottage with green shutters, it stood just below the crest of a grassy hill in the middle of a forest clearing. All around was a gathering of heroic trees. Forest creatures great and small gamboled beneath those sheltering branches. How as a youngster I had loved to play in that forest where I knew those stately trees would protect me! Grumbling lovers weren't on even the most distant horizon, and heavenly bodies were assumed to be with us forever.

So, homeward bound it must be.

Since my childhood home lay in the most distant part of our dilapidated country, the journey there would be long and fraught, but such journeys should be. As the Bible tells us: *"The path of the righteous is beset on all sides by the inequities of the selfish and the tyranny of evil men."*

The train trundled along the ill-kept rails, rattling and bucking. Passengers swayed back and forth like storm-tossed sailors. Some bore the worried expressions of travelers being propelled into a future they now weren't sure they'd clearly thought out. Others tried to hide smiles; they were the absconders, relieved to be gone. Some passengers were thinking, *Oh woe! What is to become of me!* Others did all they could to suppress a shout of *Yippee-ki-yay, motherfucker!*

As for myself, I concentrated on rejecting unwholesome thoughts. My new regimen! I was leaving behind those bad times when my thoughts would grow dire, sprouting like dark weeds I couldn't kill no matter how much mental pesticide I'd spray. Those bad times when, realizing with absolute clarity how the disappearing moon would take with it all the light of the world, I would turn to thoughts of the knife. I would imagine the silver mystery of its edge, honed to such an infinite sharpness that it disappeared into itself.

(Sometimes the poetry of the blade would arouse my blood to the point where I'd point at my lover and order, Stay there! Then I'd scurry to the computer and fire up Google to search out images of that exquisite moment when the edge first kisses flesh and draws forth into life that tiny wondrous red bud. Such images were difficult to find, but when I did, my blood would blast through my veins like an IV of cocaine, and I would hasten back to my lover, who had stayed in bed as I'd ordered, and we would engage in…. Well, I will leave the rest to your imagination. But to ease your mind, no, I never cut a lover, even in fun, except once.)

So, I knew what I was leaving behind and what lay ahead, and I was happy about it. I ate my ham-salad sandwiches with contented chomps and filled my mind with the lush and lusty forest of my youth while the brown, wasted scenery of today passed slowly by in the train's filthy windows.

Oh, that forest! My dog, Sean, and I would wake up long before my parents and set off for a day of adventure. Above us, a great tide of brilliant stars would wash across the night sky while the moon gleamed unabashedly. (I assure you, it was like that in those days!) We would hasten out of the clearing where the cottage slumbered and make for our breakfast spot, sheltered in the ample bosom of towering firs, to eat corncakes I'd baked the night before. Then, satisfied and eager, we'd spend our day roaming among the rabbits and the deer and the squirrels and all the other forest creatures who were our friends. Birds we knew would flutter around, telling stories about what they'd been up to. (Stories that were probably made up; you know how birds are. Except crows, who always tell the truth, no matter how uncomfortable. Oh, how much we need the return of crows these days!) When night came again, we'd head home. My parents would already be locked up tight in their room; they might as well have been dead.

That's the way I remember growing up—until I met my first lover, and Sean was found dead, and I was alone.

So, the train carrying me home clattered on. Slowly, of course, the tracks being one more bit of crumbling infrastructure. I often dreamed about infrastructure. After checking to make sure the moon still clung to its precarious perch, I would return to bed and fall asleep, only to be pursued by a dream of everything crashing down, highways, bridges, aqueducts, buildings, you name it, all crashing into fiery ruin while I ran frantically about calling out for past lovers—possibly to save them, but I doubt it; more than likely I was seeking one final opportunity for orgasmic release among the bloody ruins. (I will relate more of my dreams later if I have the time, but not the really creepy ones.) I would write adamant letters to every politician I could think of, from the Leader on down, demanding action or else there'd be dire consequences. (What these consequences might be, I never spelled out; nevertheless, two Regime agents, one male, one female, paid me a visit. Needless to say, they entered my dreams: as Sean watched, waiting his turn, we frolicked, sometimes the three of us together, other times one on one; how earnest were the howls!)

At any rate, as I said, we were making our slow way west across the vast prairie. During the day, dark storms of high blue wind occasionally raced past, tossing the prairie grass into black teeming waves before the sun blazed again. You'd look out expecting to see a wagon train or a band of wild Indians, but the landscape would be vacant except for the shadows dragged across it by soaring carrion birds. That's the way the boring days went. But the nights! The nights thundered down with a blackness so profound it was like dying and being sealed inside a coffin interred in the blackest depths of the earth. I would sit rigid and guarded, lest I slumber and, awakening, look out at the night sky and find all my worst fears confirmed.

You're probably wondering about the other passengers. They were a varied lot, but typical of what you see these days on a public conveyance. Workmen searching for jobs. Brides going to meet new husbands. The usual orphans hoping for new families. Footloose middle-aged women. Dour salesmen with their unsellable wares. A couple sociologists. A prostitute or two. Several expensively clothed middle-aged men with neat haircuts, glittering nails, and big bellies, either Mafia dons seeking new territory or hedge fund managers looking for more victims, all of them accompanied by husky young men in bad suits, their bodyguards. I was wearing a disguise, of course, given the possibility that former associates from my time in the drug business might still bear a grudge. From behind the dark glasses that were part of the disguise, I was able to study these husky young men relentlessly, imagining them naked and hot-breathed, bending toward me, wearing their pistols belted around their slim waists. (Of course, I did the same thing with the young female passengers, especially those wearing *hijab* and *abaya*, imagining them naked and sweaty under all those dark, mysterious layers.)

There were many other people in my car, of course, but I won't bother to enumerate them because I'm sure you're familiar with the various types you see traveling these days, always traveling, as if traveling were a substitute for hope. (You'd be familiar with them, that is, unless you're one of those who has decided to stay hidden for the duration.) Anyway, from behind my dark glasses, I examined the young men and the young women and ate my ham salad sandwiches and gazed out at the infinite prairie and listened to music on my eight-track. I had many tapes of old-time murder ballads, especially those in which the defiled woman seeks revenge. Revenge is a fundamental human right, in my opinion.

And so, the end of our journey was approaching.

Little tickles of arousal jittered through the passengers, either anxiety or eagerness, depending upon the reason for the journey: Deathly sick uncle vs. deathly sick *rich* uncle, etc., etc. Several people discoursed into their phones, as people do when approaching their destination or calling loved ones in the midst of an air hijacking. Outside, the once barren plain had begun to hump into little pimply hills. In the distance, sharper hills rose like cardboard cutouts against the gray sky. Somewhere over there was my childhood home! Somewhere over there was my forest! Somewhere over there was the body of dead dog Sean!

Across the aisle from me sat a young woman. Wispy hair beneath a blue polka-dot kerchief, plain dress, flinty face, large breasts. She sat upright, looking straight ahead. She was speaking softly, apparently rehearsing a speech. Was it congratulations for some accomplishment? A justification to a parent for outrageous behavior? An apology to a loved one left behind? A suicide note?

No, none of these.

"Dear Theunis," I heard her say, "here is your loving bride, Joanna, dispatched to you by the agency after you selected me from the website and sent...No, no, no, wait. How stupid. Okay. Dear Theunis, here before you at last is your eager bride, Joanna! How I have longed for this moment through all my long journey..."

I turned away, unable to listen to any more of this drivel. Just shut up and take your medicine, you believer in love! Look, the train will arrive soon at the station, and there will be your stout Theunis with his thick ploughman's hands and dim, doughboy face, waiting for the fourteen-year-old bride he'd ordered, and the two of you will stare at each other as you try to reconcile what you see before you with the image you saw on the internet, and then you will move together into an awkward embrace, subsequent to which you will follow Theunis to his wagon, already filled with supplies, and begin the journey that will take you fifty miles north into the tall-grass wilderness where the lunatic wind always blows and to the sod house where the centipede- and spider-laden dirt drifts down constantly from the sod ceiling into hair and bedding and cook pot and where there is no Wi-Fi, and where you, Joanna, will wait until eventually you...

But should I tell Joanna what is coming?

Should I give her the benefit of my experience?

Nah.

The anticipatory commotion grew stronger. There were discussions about the best local restaurants and prostitutes. Joanna, across from me, continued her nervous rehearsal. The Mafia dons and hedge fund managers smoothed down their suit jackets and moustaches; their bodyguards checked weapons. The train slowed, lurched. The concrete-block station came into view, its parking lot crowded with cars, trucks, and horse-drawn wagons; taxis and rickshaws lined the pick-up lane. Atop the station's slate roof stood a statue of the Leader in one of his patented no-nonsense poses.

As I gazed out the window at this welcome scene before me—my childhood home was just over that ridge to the west! my guardian forest awaited!—my reflection in the glass surged into focus. My face looked haggard from the exhaustion of travel, of course, but seemed still imbued with the good humor I've always been noted for. But wait: another face appeared, then a third, a fourth, a fifth, my face, yes, but all with marked differences. Smiling, leering, eyes rolling, grimacing, laughing, sneering, baring teeth, recoiling in terror!

Was this the way death arrives? In a clown car? Or was I having one more brush with insanity?

Once, back before I set up on my own in the drug business, I worked as chief of staff to the mayor of a medium-size city, privy to all the deepest secrets of his administration, chief among them the fact that he was in thrall to the local crime family, the Gillespie Sisters, who'd ensured his victory with their army of social media trolls and bots. (It also helped that the mayor's opponent met an untimely death—it was *ruled* a suicide.) After the election, favors were demanded, and I, as chief of staff, was in charge of their fulfillment.

It wasn't a bad job, as jobs involving organized crime go, but I'd entered that phase of life when the nights were a torment. I would close my eyes. Sleep would make its hovering approach but then quickly become untethered, spinning away to some remote nook of the universe I knew I could never reach. You might think this was at least in part due to paranoia occasioned by my work with the Gillespie Sisters, but you would be wrong. Yes, I knew many dangerous secrets, any one of which might prompt the Sisters to ensure permanent confidentiality. But the truth is, I got along fine with them—we were all three of us oenophiles and Jean-Pierre Melville freaks. There was never a hint of suspicion of me on their part, and we might have continued our relationship for many happy years had they not been assassinated by Regime agents.

No, the paranoia that stabbed my nights like a large, terrifying needle had to do with the fact that I'd come to the sudden realization I no longer knew who I was. I mean, I felt as if I were unmoored, floating free, capable of being tossed by even the merest whisper of a breeze, all sense of personal reality brushed away like lint. Was I here on *this* Earth or a different one? Had our universe collided with some parallel universe, in the process sluffing me off into new territory like some errant quantum particle? Had all the accustomed equations been juggled, the cosmological horizon tilted?

Nothing looked different. Everything felt different. I thought I might be going mad.

Of course, one can learn to live with anything, including madness conjured by the Great Physicist in the Sky, as long as one has the loving support of an empathetic partner. Needless to say, I did not, my lover at the time being thoroughly consumed with protesting recent fertility regulations, but I endured, secure in the knowledge that whatever madness this was, another would be sure to take its place eventually and make the current bout nothing but an unpleasant memory.

And sure enough, my worries about the moon soon arrived.

I stood on the station platform with my backpack, breathing air that only moments before had wafted through my beloved forest. How sweet it was in my city-scarred lungs! Passengers milled about, seeking luggage, greeting family and friends, buying fruit from the pushcarts, haggling over taxis or rickshaws. I looked around for the young girl from the train, Joanna, finally spotting her at the end of the platform past the Stuckey's. She was standing in front of a bulky young man with blond hair and a face broad as a shovel, on it a grin: Theunis, of course. He was holding out a sausage-shaped object that, after a moment, I identified as a pecan roll from Stuckey's. A wedding gift for his beloved he was seeing for the first time! (Jesus!) It was clear what was going on with honest yeoman Theunis—that look of pleased befuddlement at his good luck in scoring a mail-order bride who didn't look or smell like a rhinoceros—but what intrigued me was the string of thought pulses coursing through Joanna's mind. I took out my notebook and wrote down the thoughts I witnessed:

Kiss or handshake?

Why is he grinning like a big Swedish idiot?

Why were Mother and Father killed at the mill?

Could they have saved me if they'd lived?

My life forever, I guess. Unless death. Mine ...

Or his.

What is that odor? Oh Lord, is it...?

Is this Love?

Or Fear?

What's the difference? (This was my thought, not Joanna's.)

In the Stuckey's I bought an egg salad sandwich and a pecan roll of my own and stowed them in my backpack, which also contained, among other things, change of underwear, Bible, small revolver, bearer bonds, my childhood stiletto, diary, and tin box of opium. While I browsed among the Stuckey's trinkets and striped blankets, I found myself pondering Joanna's situation. It is my observation that the only way two people can come together as partners in this buzzing hive of humanity in which we're all trapped is through the intervention of the Great Physicist in the Sky. It is He who disposes. And how does He do that? According to His own whimsical quantum principles. SNAP! and He has set two lives on course toward each other. The problem is that when they come together, there's a likelihood that, like stars colliding, all that will be left is a black hole destroying all light and time.

When I went back outside with my purchases, I saw stout yeoman Theunis, striding purposefully toward his wagon, Joanna trudging behind as if drawn by a tether.

To the west of the train station, a low ridge wiggled across the grassy plain. Although it seemed more raggedly eroded and careworn than I remembered—I suppose the same could apply to me—the sight of it warmed me, for beyond that ridge lay my forest and my childhood home. Oh, my friendly forest, waiting to welcome me with your embracing branches and titillatingly barky trunks and smiling, scampering forest creatures. I made my way through the station parking lot, hoping to catch a ride, but I could find no one heading west into the forest. Why should they? What allure did a forest of smiling trees and gaily chattering creatures hold for modern folk immune to magic and governed by the principles of rampant capitalism and quantum mechanics?

This attitude was brought home to me during a conversation with an elderly pigtailed gentleman sitting in a rocking chair on the porch of the station hotel, smoking his pipe and reading the Special Prosecutor's Report on his iPad. I asked him if he knew of anyone heading west with whom I might hitch a ride.

You aim to go to the Forest? he said.

I told him I did.

He scrutinized me. Then he said, No, no one goes there. And I would advise you against such a course.

Why?

That place where you want to go?

Yes?

Death is there.

Oh, you crazy old man!

As I set off walking, westward toward my forest, toward my childhood home, I found myself thinking about Joanna. An image kept appearing—so real I might have been wearing VR goggles. There she is before me in the tall grass beside a sod house, standing straight, hands at her sides, serious expression: she's making a speech. Dear husband, here you see before you your bride, Joanna, having traveled to you from the East. She clears her throat. She runs a finger slowly over her lips as if to mold them into an apparatus that can produce the words she believes are required. Dear Theunis, husband, all I ever wanted was for you to adore me, for you to place me above all others, for you to tell me how valuable I am! That's all! And then, we'd stride forward through life side by side, always and forever...

Husband, damnit, do you hear me?

Well, this is a new Joanna, isn't it?

Then the vision drifts, blurs, dissolves. A new video takes its place:

A low, solitary hill in the middle of the endless prairie, atop it a cemetery. A procession making its way across the grassy plain toward the hill. Men and women in their Sunday clothes, a scattering of children led by the hand or carried at the bosom. In the middle of the procession, a coffin borne by a horse-drawn hearse, its driver in a black suit and top hat. Mournful wind. Mournful fiddle music, drum beating a slow, sad march.

The video camera embedded in my brain pans across the scene, then focuses in on the cemetery. Stone markers tilted this way and that, silhouetted against a sky of swirling gray and black clouds. The hearse halts beside a freshly dug grave; a headstone rests against the shoveled dirt. The camera moves along the solemn faces of the mourners—good, solid American faces—then focuses on the headstone. A name is engraved on it.

Theunis Wessels.

A few of the things that *might* have killed Theunis:

Disease. Snakebite. Centipede or spider. Accident with a scythe. Kicked in the head by his mule while trying to shoe it. Struck by lightning. Bitten by rabid fox. Drowned in flash flood. Hypothermia after being caught in a blizzard. Shooting accident. Crushed by a wagon that collapsed atop him while he was trying to fix a wheel. Unlucky fall from the roof of his sod house. Prairie fire.

Or..?

The gray clouds swirl and the drizzle falls and ladies weep and a hatchet-faced minister preaches: *Listen to me, brothers and sisters! As the eternity of sleep overtakes us, we will be changed! Hallelujah! Brothers and sisters, I tell you it is the greatest mystery! In a flash, in the twinkling of an eye, at the last trumpet! All changed!*

Joanna wipes her nose with the back of her hand. She leans against an older woman, the preacher's wife, who supports her with an arm around her waist.

Are we not all sinners? Will not the final trumpet sound for all of us? So seek your Father's mercy before it's too late!

Oh, Joanna, I applaud your performance. As good as anything I ever accomplished.

Night after night in her tiny room in the home of her birth, lying on the thin mattress. The white light of a kerosene lamp. The blackness of the sky outside her window. The skeletal hands of an elm wavering across the moon's blotched face. (At least she had a moon!) Night after night in her tiny room, reading the magazines, roaming the websites that proclaim love and marriage to be the answers. (But what were the questions?!) Night after night dreaming, feeling the disappointment of the stern-faced old women in the parlor below seeping up around her like a noxious gas. Night after night. And finally coming across the website for Frontier Brides. Scanning the faces of all the young, handsome, hopeful, solid farmers. Sending in her pitiful savings, waiting anxiously for the response, not daring even to whisper her hopes to the old women in the parlor below sipping sherry and expelling noxious gas.

But did Joanna ever let herself gaze up into that night sky? (As I used to do before fear of the moon's disappearance, taking with it all the light, entered my blood like a deadly bacillus.) Did she ever let herself take in the immensity of that heaven soaring beyond the ragged rectangle of sky trapped within her room's lone window?

(As I used to do…Sean and I sitting on a soft carpet of moss beside a stream winding through the forest, and we are gazing up at the billions upon billions of cubic miles of overarching universe, at the billions upon billions of planets and stars and galaxies all spinning onward and outward in their infinite tracks, and we are realizing how tiny a speck we truly are in that gigantic tapestry, and we are understanding finally and irrevocably that whatever we would do with our lives, whatever action we would contemplate, whatever decision we might think needs to be made, all of it would be totally without meaning in that gigantic context. Save a child from drowning, murder a child with a knife, it wouldn't matter because either course would have exactly the same impact on the cosmos.)

Joanna watches as the casket is lowered into the muddy grave and the shovelfuls of earth splatter against it. She thinks of those many long months in that sod home while the dirt drifted down and the centipedes and spiders fell into her hair and the winds flamed down across the prairie as if they might eventually shear away all her flesh, all her soul. All that time in the sod house waiting for God to apologize, or at least exhibit some knowledge of her.

So, she took to going out at night while Theunis snored, she would go out and stare up into that infinite sky and wait for an answer, but the only answer was His silence, and His silence stretched on and on as the uncaring galaxies swirled away on their uncaring paths, and at last understanding came to her:

No, it didn't matter what she chose to do.

So, she did it.

And there it was before me at last, my forest. I stood at the crest of the ridge amid a clutch of blueberry bushes and took it all in. I felt all the jiggling tribulations and cancerous thoughts of the long train journey from the city to the prairie sluffing off me like dead skin from a snake. Joanna and Theunis? Just some unimportant people who flitted across my peripheral vision as they traveled from one life into another. The hedge fund managers and mafia dons with their bellies and $3000 suits and whiskey coughs and bodyguards? I don't know what those words mean. Girls in *hijabs* and *abayas* covering their sweaty nakedness? Be gone from my ken!

A breeze wafting through the trees of my forest pranced out to greet me, carrying the pine-oil scent of firs, the honey musk of poplars, the citrus of walnuts. I tore off my disguise. Disgruntled drug customers, do your worst!

I longed to plunge into my forest, but I made myself wait so I could enjoy the anticipation. Those heroic guardian trees of my youth, how I remembered them in their stately ranks! Through them we would romp, my dog Sean and I, chasing the little spirited forest creatures who thought it was just a game and we'd never *really* catch them and eat them.

But speaking of poor Sean.

Well, never mind. Sometimes the knife just grows impatient and decides to take matters into its own hand.

I have entered my forest.

There's something amiss.

That clamorous, ugly sound! The trees are shouting at each other. Snarling. Hurling insults and invective. Raising barky fists.

My dear forest creatures, what's wrong? There is brawling: maddened bears against maddened bears, elk locking horns, deer tearing each other with razor hooves. The smaller creatures, the rabbits and foxes and squirrels and raccoons, they peer from the shelter of dark thickets with frightened yellow eyes.

Birds are tossed about on angry winds!

Crows black as night sit on branches casting murderous stares.

I make my way deeper into the forest, still hoping to reclaim the comfort of my dreams.

But the brambles are thicker and thornier than I remember. It's human flesh they want to feast on! Branches grasp and rake like the skeleton fingers of unrequited old women.

Now there is a sound ahead of me. A thrashing of branches! Angry turmoil!

A great dark creature shows itself. It glides like a ghost among the fronds of the giant ferns.

Wolf? Dog? Mythic creature?

I cup my hands around my mouth and howl a question. The creature cocks its head toward me. It examines me with fierce, shining eyes. Its nose twitches with my scent. Is it remembering?

I howl again. My cry echoes from one tree to another, growing more and more plaintive as it skims the currents, as it dissolves into the mist.

My hands drop to my sides. Suddenly, it's as if I can feel the coolness of a nose nudging my palm. There is actually a moment when I think I feel familiar weight leaning against my thigh. My hand at my side strokes the black fur of a head, a neck.

I look down.

Nothing. Just the emptiness of fouled and departed memory. The emptiness of a ghost creature now gliding away from me through the fronds of the giant ferns.

Sometimes I dream I am Sean, that I am still alive, that I am searching through the forest. Then I awake, and as I lie there, I find myself wondering if I was a person dreaming I was Sean or if I am now Sean dreaming I am a person clutching a knife.

It is night. I have made my way through the forest to the clearing and the bungalow that was my childhood home.

I lie in the bed that was once mine in the small room upstairs that was once my refuge, my cell. The darkness is absolute, but I am comforted by the knowledge that I must be surrounded by all my things, my toys, my childhood clothes, my posters…

I hear a sound. What it is and whence it comes are impossible to determine. I leave the warmth of my bed and glide out to the hallway, careful to make no noise of my own in case it is an intruder bent on mayhem. In the hallway I stand still as death, listening, holding my breath so that I can better taste the currents of the air. But there is nothing further. I strain. Nothing.

Well, I decide, it must have been my parents in their bedroom down the hall. Dead thirty years and still going at it.

Back in my bed, I settle into the warmth of my blankets. On the opposite wall above my desk is the window looking out across the forest. Above the tree line hangs the moon and beyond the moon the stars, all uneaten, all whole, all undefiled.

Of course, I understand that they are nothing more than camouflage hiding the relentless black hole that will someday swallow us all. Maybe even in the next five minutes. Expect an apology from above? Dream on.

I go to sleep with that thought, and Sean stalks through my otherwise worthless dreams.

Then the crows awaken me with their deadly summons.

◆

James Norcliffe*

THE MAN WHO TURNED HIMSELF INTO A GUN

At first he thought bullets;
then he expressed them.

He became gun-metal gray,
cold to the touch.

He wanted to press himself
into evil's shoulder, be cradled there.

He wanted to be trained in evil's grip,
evil's telescopic sight in his sight.

Above all he longed for evil's finger feeling for,
feathering, depressing his progressive trigger.

He was sleek, he was balanced:
no longer flesh, no longer sentiment,

weighted,
then weightless

mechanically perfect,
perfectly mechanical.

◆

*Note: The author writes from Christchurch, New Zealand, where fifty
people were killed in a mass shooting at two mosques on March 15,
2019.*

Ron Riekki

ON REFUSING TO BELIEVE THE NEWS OF MY THIRD, YES, THIRD NEXT-DOOR NEIGHBOR BEING KILLED BY A GUN

Not in the same city. The guns follow all of my miles.
Except it's not the same gun. But it's the same America
with its copping for blood, how it loves its Walmarts

and walls but hates its wall art, its warts of oxygen
pooling on the ground, on playgrounds, into pools.
I boulevard it every other day as an EMT, so I know

that Alabama is a goddamn, and Georgia is a god-
less state too, and Texas, and every state really when
you see the little red stars speckled on a wall's cosmos,

the rainbows of angel-of-darkness purples, how more
gun owners need to do a shift with a medic, how their
opinions would shift, except one medic tells me he's

a gun owner, that seeing blood makes some thirsty
for blood, blood-thirsty, mixing up Molotov cocktails and
Mother's Day, turning hearts inside-out, fuses of living here.

RON RIEKKI

AMBULANCE, 2 A.M., I'M DRIVING

The red warning lights inside the heart
are bullied shut, this Packer fan/pack-a-
day smoker in back who doesn't understand
the stems of his body, or appreciate his
architecture, how we're set up to survive.

During the war—one of them at least—
I remember a man with no hand, how
intense the vasoconstriction was, as if
we have internal tourniquets, the quest
for shivering into tomorrow, smog-eyed,
but alive.

             And we drifted toward those
whose entire lives have been a ring of
dedication to curing the dead, or attempting.

RON RIEKKI

BUT WE CAN'T

There was a stop sign near my home,
or somewhat near, on the walk back
from work, high school work, which
means minimum everything, and my
cousin and I'd pass its octagon, a shape
that—to us—meant MMA, meant that
we didn't care about excommunication
in our flammable hometown, outsiders
where one kid said, "Seriously you're
the only person I know who has a goddamn gramma in prison. Who even
does that?" As if it was our choice,
as if we had the time or caring to explain that a psych ward is a different
sort of incarceration, one with rent
so expensive that my father hinted at
erasing her from our ancestry, and for
my cousin it was his own mix of how
marijuana and beer can drown family,
are not as much of a blessing as all
the addicts insist, his sister third-
trimester mid-semester and still
drinking in biblical proportions
and so we killed the stop sign every
time we walked by, the nights hiding
our pentagram fists, days, weeks,
years of us punching its hellhole O
& its sides until it bent, until its one
word begged loudly for us to leave.

RON RIEKKI

(THE NUMBER OF THE HEAT)
WHEN THE FIRES

behind our house insisted
they be allowed in our house,
my father took buckets of water
and asked the flames if they would
accept the water but the fire said
it wanted our house and our bodies

and everything it saw in front of its
absent eyes and my father said
he wanted the fires' death, the both
of them battling with my father
running to the house's hose, holding
it up at the sky that refused to take

sides, refused to rain, but accepted
all the smoke of our childhood
photos, the smoke of our money,
the smoke of our fingers and phones
and lamps and shoes and trees
and memories and air and hope.

RON RIEKKI

THE THREE WORDS

I stood outside of a pow wow once, the jingle
dresses dancing like the opposite of capitalism,

how each inch took time, gave time, kissed time,
and I felt so blessed to lean against a tree, yet

so outside, knowing the tribe of my ancestry
wasn't this tribe, that I was Euro-indigenous,

Saami, and not "Native American" when
an Anishinaabe poet I loved, her words

like the elimination of rush-hour traffic,
snuck next to me and whispered the three

words I didn't know that I longed so badly
to hear: *Indigenous is indigenous.*

♦

Gail Braune Comorat

THE WORLD'S A SHITTY PLACE

That's what my friend says every time I talk to her,
and some days I want to argue while other days I agree.
She wants to leave her husband, says she's young

enough to find happiness still, and I've tried
to point out all the negatives of living on one's own,

but today I'm doing my own leaving, driving toward
a weekend with friends, my husband left behind.
I understand that need, to be away from the daily dramas

of married life. I drive through farm country, past
brown rows of corn. I ride and try not to think about

all the shitty things: news of pipe bombs and rising debt,
families losing children. I crest a small hill
and from the roadside macadam, a vulture lifts

dragging with him the bloody carcass of a snake.
Sometimes when I'm walking through Target, enjoying

the music and bargains, I forget about the shitty ways
of the world. I feel light, happy the way the sun
is shining outside and that my old car still runs

well enough to take me places. Like today, on my way
to Chestertown, I saw a crowd of Amish men, all hatted

GAIL BRAUNE COMORAT

and bearded, dressed in dark overalls, working ropes to heave
the frame of a barn into place. I wanted to stop my car,
get out to cheer them on, but I kept driving. But such a rush

of sudden happiness, to know that there are still good people
in this sometimes shitty world, ones who don't stand left

or right, who believe in helping neighbors. Barns burn.
These men show up, save what they can, wait with faith and
grace,
with hammers and nails, ready to rebuild what the fire takes.

♦

Cameron Blais

WAS

Flash Fiction

Sadie and I are talking about being now. I say the problem with being is that anytime you say what being is, you presuppose being. The trouble is the *is*. Sadie barks. She has been dying any number of days, and she looks at me in her usual way. She hasn't read Heidegger. She doesn't know these ideas are Nazi ideas, and plagiarized. Except in her eyes, I see she knows her being, whatever it is, is coming to an end.

The highway is full of the kind of trucks that terrify me. They have additional vehicles stacked on top of them. Mass graves moving at high speeds. I think of them falling all over me, burying us both.

The sky is clear and blue and radiant with refracting light, and the snow on the ground reflects it too. Up at the sun I'm looking backward into time, about eight minutes. Every second that passes was an earlier second far away. In the water droplets of the sky and the snow on the ground, time bends around us. Do you see, Sadie? If you look far enough in any direction, you can see your whole life.

Sadie is curled in a ball, and her lumps fall against each other under the skin on her neck where I picked her up to adopt her. She peed then; she was so scared. Four or so feet in the air, her pee dribbled onto the carpet.

She peed again just now, before I told her about being. I don't think she was scared, I think she just knew I won't waste time being angry with her. Sadie has always understood me. She pierces the heart of my meaning. The smell of her urine is what takes me back to holding her by the neck as a puppy. I think of her always-twitching nose. The many memories it conjures for her, second by second, in the part of our brains we share.

The exit for the veterinarian's office is only a mile away. My iPhone alerts me again and again, and each time a bell chimes, I think, *already*?

This vet uses gas. Sadie will drift off to sleep forever. It will be painless, painless. Like a hole at the bottom of her leaky brain, and her light dripping out until she's gone. Weeks ago, I shared a Facebook post about how a little girl told her mother dogs only live fourteen years because they don't worry so much, and they don't need so long as people to figure out how to be. Well, isn't that nice, my mother commented. Must make you feel better.

She's heavy in my arms. I carry her through the glass doors held open by a girl in white.

◆

Sam VanNest

BROKEN ENGLISH, BODY LANGUAGE: A FRIEDRICH'S ATAXIA MEMOIR
Nonfiction

Author's note: Friedreich's Ataxia is a rare genetic disease that gradually causes difficulty walking, a loss of sensation in the arms and legs, and impaired speech. The disease causes damage to parts of the brain and spinal cord and can also affect the heart. The word "ataxia" comes from the Greek word "ataxis," meaning "without order."

At a café in Nice, France, in the summer of 2007 a Senegalese man asked me for a cigarette, motioning with his hand the universal gesture for smoking. So, we smoked and talked about whatever we stumbled upon the words for, as neither of us spoke the other's native tongue very well. I knew airport vocabulary from taking a French class back at college in the USA, so I talked about my flight. He knew a bit about music in English. He told me that he played the drums and liked System of a Down, an Armenian-American metal band. He'd tap his foot as if he were playing a bass drum pedal, occasionally bumping my crutch I had stashed out of sight under the table.

I finished my cigarette and espresso, got a baguette from a bakery, and walked back to the upstairs apartment where my girlfriend, Rebecca, was staying while she studied at the school in the city. I hadn't originally planned on visiting her at all. We had studied in England together the semester before, and I was broke. I took out a loan to buy the plane ticket to France, hoping for an internship in the summer to pay it off quickly. It was a spontaneous thing. I was depressed, and my friends had told me that it would pick me up to travel. I wasn't even sure she wanted me to come to Nice. I didn't walk well (I was walking with a crutch at the time but, in hindsight, I should have been using a wheelchair), and France isn't very accessible for the disabled. But we did it all—went to Paris for a weekend and rode the Metro, climbed Montmartre, saw the sights, drank espresso all day, and when we got back to our hostel at night, we drank cheap wine much better than anything we could afford in the States.

While in Paris, we went to a bread and cheese festival in the courtyard of Notre-Dame Cathedral, and there was a court set up and a wheelchair basketball game going on, all in the evening shadow of the façade. It was a very strange spectacle. Bec brought a plate of cheeses and a warm baguette to where I was sitting, sketching the cathedral as best I could. She wondered aloud how the disabled players got there, how they got around at all in this city, unforgiving as it is for anyone with a mobility issue. Along with my undergraduate alma mater, St. Mary's College of Maryland, I had applied to the College of Charleston in South Carolina, and they said their campus couldn't accommodate me very well, citing historical reasons to limit modernizing. Similarly, Paris has a history to preserve, of which people with disabilities have no part. When the game ended, the players, one and all, stood from their chairs to applause. The game had been a farce, a show where the players used the wheelchairs to tell a fictional story, a performance. I felt duped. In this place where I couldn't speak the mother tongue, where my body spoke loudest, I was a caricature.

I've read that Berlin, Germany, is a great tourist city for people with disabilities. After being bombed in the Second World War, the city had to rebuild with disabled veterans in mind. The physically disabled are part of the city's history, of its cultural DNA. The same is true in the USA, especially so since the passing of the Americans with Disabilities Act in 1990: freedom of access applies to all. In his book *Discipline and Punish* the French sociologist Michel Foucault accuses America of having no sense of its historical self; we build, tear down, and rebuild in an endless cycle of modernization. But I'm glad that I can get to the top floor of most places in my home country by pushing a button. The USA has, and I hope will always have, the freedom of contemporary construction. America, for me, is convenient, if less glamorous than France. Foucault says nothing in the USA is sacred, but I could only see Paris from the ground floor of the Panopticon, his metaphor for absolute power. The tower didn't have an elevator.

The whole trip was exhausting, but well worth it. I felt good about myself for the first time in a long while. I felt like I was doing something worthwhile, something that I wouldn't be able to do in the future. I wasn't sleeping, though. My knees and back ached from walking everywhere every day. I had gotten used to drinking myself to sleep at school during that semester before visiting Bec in France, something I wasn't proud of or eager to expose to her. Three beers usually did the trick, or a glass or two of wine. I needed a knockout plus a painkiller in France, so I'd drink a bottle of wine, slugging it covertly when Bec left the room. I slept like a baby but hated God in the morning. I spent ten days in France, four in Paris and the rest in Nice during Bec's school week. She'd leave for class in the morning, kiss my throbbing head, and I'd get up a few hours later, shower (like a responsible American), and hit the town on my own, looking for a café with cheap espresso where I could read and smoke and nurse my hangover.

I don't speak much French. I speak more Arabic than I do French, and more Spanish than either. Bec didn't like me wandering around on my own during the day, not because I don't speak the language but because Nice is even less accessible than Paris and I, being a stubborn man, brushed this off and did it anyway. I'd wander the town after I was cured by espresso and some variety of tomato and cheese on a baguette, find fresh strawberries at an outdoor market, get a sweet white wine to complement, and bring back something for dinner besides. I only fell once when I walked by myself during the day, down some stairs to an alleyway market. A big Frenchman hoisted me up and sat me on the bottom step, brushed the pigeon shit out of my hair, shoved a cigarette in my mouth, lit it, and began talking. Of course I didn't understand a word, and said so with the most useful French phrase for a non-speaker. He did his best in English. We parted ways when I stood up again, and then I bought Bec a purse.

One night during my sophomore year of college, back in the USA, my roommate and I threw a party in our suite. It was raining, and the people coming in made the floor slick. The foot of my crutch didn't do well on wet linoleum, so before long I slipped and fell in the middle of the party. It was at least a chorus of "Fight for Your Right" on the stereo before Bec swept to the rescue, like she always did, and hoisted me to my feet. I made a joke and everyone laughed, and Bec just squeezed my arm and said nothing. Having neutralized the situation with humor (like a responsible cripple), I left the party to stay the night in her apartment. It took three shots of rum to knock me out when we got in, but I slept like the dead.

I have dreams after being abroad that people I know here in the USA have foreign accents. I have one recurring that my father has an Irish accent while we're out sailing. In my dream, I yell at him, tell him to stop faking the accent, but he says it's fine and hands me the tiller. My dad was the high school quarterback and always pushed me to be physical before I was diagnosed at 16. Now he spends his weekends exercising his freedom of contemporary construction on the house, installing railings and ramps. I never asked him to put a railing on the dock to the cove in the backyard. It was just there when I came home from school, and I could see the blue herons again.

When Bec went to France, I realized the only person who knew the story of my body was gone. I hadn't told anyone but her. She was the railing on my dock. So, I went to her, braved airports with layovers with an ego that always declined a wheelchair from the wary airport staff. On the nine-hour flight home from France to DC, I discovered it only took two tiny bottles of airplane wine to knock me out. I think it has something to do with the air pressure.

On my mornings out wandering Nice alone, I was never uncomfortable not being able to speak French. It was actually refreshing, and I felt independent. I had these interactions with strangers in cafés, using what words I knew in French and some in Spanish, and they'd answer me in what English they knew, our conversations limited by our vocabulary. I talked for a while with the Senegalese man on several occasions, bumping into him at the same café every day. We'd swap buying the espresso, share cigarettes, and have these non-conversations that were much more based on effort than topic—our language broken, our bodies telling stories our vocabulary could not. We'd both get up to leave, and he'd hand me my crutch from under the table.

♦

Katherine Gekker

I AM THE LAST RADIUM GIRL

My daughter burned sulfur, released
        rotten-egg odors with her Build-a-
Chemistry-Lab-in-Your-Own-Home
        Kit, next turned solids into gases,
            liquids into air.

        I gave my daughter books –
Madame Curie: A Life. Then,
        Our Friend the Atom.

Now she props my thinned bones
        against the chestnut headboard.
She feeds me clear broth,
        tells me –
            This headboard only appears
      solid. It contains constant motion –
        excitations of atoms.

Just last week she said –
        Mother, your mouth glows at night.

        I wish I had understood even one thing.

◆

Kerry Leddy

BESIDE MYSELF
Nonfiction

So much about those first days following Sarah's death have
vanished, like a drawing on an Etch A Sketch that has been
shaken. All that remains are a few blurred images of the steady
stream of friends and family arriving at our door with
Tupperware containers filled with stews, casseroles, and salads.
Our refrigerator was overflowing; my stomach was empty.

But the visit of one condolence caller, a neighbor, has stuck
in my mind with an awful clarity. Almost as soon as he finished
hugging me, he asked, "So, did Sarah ever try this before?" His
tone was chipper.

"Suicide?" I asked, befuddled, certain I had misunderstood.

"Yes. Did she?"

Did he really want me to tell him the details that she had
been hospitalized once before? I hoped my terse response
signaled that I did not want to discuss this further.

"Oh, so this time she was successful," he said, his voice
rising at the end, injecting a bizarre tone of enthusiasm, as if
Sarah had finally broken a new swimming record.

Shaken, I responded, "Why, yes! We always wanted her to
persevere. She did it!"

Immediately, I wanted to take it back, imagining that in his
anxiety and discomfort, he wasn't thinking clearly, that he would
soon regain his reason and feel terrible. But, no, he seemed not to
notice my sarcasm. He just pursed his lips and nodded, as if we
were in complete agreement that kids today need to work harder
and stick to it.

With the death of my eighteen-year-old child, I had been plunged into a world I barely recognized.

I longed to disappear into sleep, but I couldn't. My mind was afraid of what I might see and feel in that vulnerable space. Instead, I walked and walked, through the rooms of our house, up and down the street, back and forth. I was like a caged lion trying to pace my way back to life as it should be.

When sleep finally came, it was more like taking the batteries out than gradually powering down. Usually a vivid dreamer, now I found only white space. My thoughts were saying "No, this I refuse to envision."

One morning, I was standing in my driveway retrieving the newspaper when my neighbor Janet walked over "for a visit." She took a deep breath, took my hand, and said, "Kerry, how *are* you? I don't know how you survive. I know I couldn't." Her words were meant as a kind of compliment, but they sounded strangely accusatory, as if she were saying, "How can you be standing here, surviving at all?" Were my grief truly devastating, I would not be standing upright. I would be forever prostrate, inconsolable. At one time, I too would have imagined I couldn't go on, wouldn't survive if I lost one of my children. But you do go on breathing in spite of yourself. In spite of the knee-buckling despondency that continues to overtake you.

Now I had a new way of understanding the word "visit." I lived in a world others did not want to stay in. A place where a child, once vital and full of hope, could become ill with bipolar disorder and wish to die. Friends might come and sit for a while, chat, drink tea, have dinner, but no one would want to feel at home here, to imagine this kind of tragedy could happen to them. Parents need to think they can keep their children safe. I was every parent's nightmare.

Before Sarah, I would have been right there with them—just visiting.

How could I be with others when every part of my body hurt,

even my eyelashes? Every encounter, every street corner, every moment brought deep pain, as if shards of glass were flying at me from all angles. Each outing was perilous and left me close to weeping. Seeing people do ordinary things—going to lunch, shopping, walking dogs—acting as if life were exactly the same. Didn't they know nothing was the same? For me, the very sunlight was an intrusion. I wore sunglasses at all times, even indoors.

Every word, every action, had a new context, a new meaning. One afternoon, I went to pick up my younger daughter, Anna, from school. I was searching the halls when the dean of students popped out of her office and inquired in a friendly voice, "Have you lost a child?" As soon as the words left her mouth, she looked stricken.

Another time during that first month, I received a call from a woman who ran a support group for parents who had lost children. I imagined there must be some database of grieving mothers, since I had received several calls offering help. After inviting me to their next meeting, the kind woman told me about the other parents in the group and the comfort they found in sharing their stories. "No one other than another parent who lost a child can understand what we've gone through," she said.

Her words struck me. What are we to call ourselves, we parents who have lost a child? If a husband dies, you are a widow; with the death of a wife, you are a widower; when your parents die, you are an orphan. We have ways of understanding these losses. But when your child dies, there is no word for what you become. It defies our language, defies our comprehension. Too dreadful to have a name.

Thinking about the group, I found myself hesitating, questioning whether I could sit with others, listen to their pain. On the one hand, it could be comforting to be with people who would understand what I was going through. On the other, I wondered if I was up to it.

As she went on, pointing out the many ways parents in the

group found solace in each other, my mind went back and forth between yes and no. It felt as though I had flipped a coin when I said, "Yes, I'll come." Grabbing a pad and paper, I jotted down the time and location.

When I was about to hang up, she asked, "How did Sarah die?"

My head whirled. "She was sick. Depression. Bipolar. Suicide."

Clearly sensing my hesitancy, she added, "I'm so, so sorry. You know we have another mother who comes regularly who lost a daughter to suicide ten years ago."

After a brief pause, she added, "And, even more tragically, three years later her other daughter took her life."

I felt like my brain was going to explode. "Oh, my God," I gasped, almost dropping the receiver, as though a shock wave had passed through the phone line and burned my hand. I wanted to cover my ears, tell her to please, please, stop. I couldn't get off the phone fast enough. In that moment, no matter how much sympathy I felt for this mother, or how much support I needed, I didn't want to get anywhere near her. I didn't want to be in a world where losing my other daughter was even a possibility.

A few days later, I received a call from a friend-of-a-friend-of-a-friend whose son had died a year earlier, asking me if I might want to get together. I decided lunch with just one mother, who had lost just one child, might be manageable.

We sat in a booth, across from each other, at a local restaurant that I have no memory of—but what I do remember was her very first question: "How many were at your service?"

I could barely absorb her words. I kept thinking I must be misunderstanding. I knew my brain was still not functioning properly—maybe that was the problem.

"I'm sorry…how many…What?" Gradually, understanding seeped in. "Oh, at the memorial?"

She nodded.

"Um…" I tried to envision the service, to calculate the

numbers, to give her an answer. I could barely remember the room. I started to feel lightheaded.

"I'm sorry. I don't know. I can't picture the place or who was there."

She continued, "We couldn't even fit everyone at ours. There were over a thousand people. They needed an extra room to hold our overflow. They had to watch the service by video."

I just stared as I pushed the food around on my plate.

For a second, I felt transported back to the early days of mothering: Whose kid read youngest, whose was the most gifted, the best athlete, whose kid had the most friends? Was I meant to feel that my daughter's funeral might not have been good enough, big enough, well-enough attended?

You win.

It took everything in me to get through that meal. I had already left the restaurant and was just waiting for my body to join me.

Time was passing. Bit by bit, I was being called to pick up the pieces of my old life, before Sarah's death, but that only made me more painfully aware that she was really gone. As was my former self.

When the email reminder arrived for my next book club, I didn't respond. I was changing my mind hourly. While several members were my closest friends, women I'd known for over twenty years, I still wasn't on safe ground. A part of me wanted to see them—they had been with me throughout this ordeal, we had raised our kids together—but I didn't feel ready to face the entire group.

Mostly it was my conscientious side that felt compelled to push through. But when I pictured myself sitting there, carrying on small talk, it seemed impossible. How could I go back to my old life when my old life was gone?

I said to my husband, Alan, Sarah's stepfather, "I don't think I can go." Then, moments later, "Maybe I should try." To each round of my obsessing, he would join whichever side I was leaning toward: "You shouldn't go if you're not ready," or "It might be good for you to get out. You can always leave if it feels bad. But only go if you feel up to it."

Book club began at 7:30, and at 7:30 I was still in my kitchen—not going. Then, at 7:35, I was going, but late. I'm never late.

Pacing the kitchen, Alan tried settling me down with a hug. "Please, don't!" I said. I was jumping out of my skin.

Finally, hating this indecision, I grabbed my keys and headed out to my car.

My hands gripped the steering wheel as I drove through strangely empty streets. My stomach clenched. Come on, I said to myself—it's only book club, not a root canal. Halfway to my friend's house, I pulled off on the side of the road. I would turn back.

My cell phone beeped with a text. "Where are you? We miss you."

I urged myself on, suddenly fearing that if I didn't go tonight I might never return, that I would let my former life slip through my fingers.

Pulling up to the house, I turned off my car lights and sat in the dark, staring up at the silhouettes of my friends milling about the kitchen. It was easy to imagine the conversations inside, conversations that I had been a part of for years, about jobs, husbands, perfect children, imperfect children—perfectly *alive* children.

Taking deep, long breaths, I climbed out of my car and approached the house. My legs felt heavy. I crept along the side path, out of the kitchen windows' line of vision, in preparation for flight.

As I reached the front door, I started to cry. "I can't do this," I said aloud and began my retreat.

But another car had just then pulled up. Without cover, I turned the doorknob and went in.

Instantly the room fell silent, but then quickly my friends all began talking at once, greeting me with long, deep hugs.

No one mentioned Sarah, perhaps fearing I would dissolve. Still, she permeated the air and every molecule of my body. She was the absent presence.

Through a haze, I watched as the ladies returned to drinking wine and nibbling on hummus and chips, as we always did before we got started talking about the book. I had no appetite, but to keep busy I picked up a cracker and with shaky hands spread some cheese. I took one small bite but quickly realized that I couldn't chew or swallow. I grabbed a napkin and tried to spit it out.

I could barely hear the words floating around me as the small talk resumed. I watched lips move, but no sound came through the loud humming in my head, the kind I do during scary movies, to block out the scene.

Yet somehow the clinks of the wine glasses broke through, and I heard a voice say, "Kerry...Kerry."

Oh, that's my name. Respond. Respond, I directed my brain. "Mmm...?"

"We made your favorite—brownies."

"Oh...thanks," I said through a half-dead smile.

Then the first land mine detonated. One of the book-clubbers announced, "Oh, we are so thrilled! Molly got this incredible scholarship to Brown."

There were some half-hearted congratulations as my closest friends cast sympathetic looks my way; one took my hand and gave it a tight squeeze. Another tried to change the subject, but I needed to get out. I headed for the bathroom. I stared in the mirror, repeating my now familiar mantra—breathe in, breathe out—willing myself to stop crying.

There was a knock on the door.

"Ker, you okay in there?"

"Yeah, sure. I'll be right out," I said as I wiped away the smudges of mascara.

"I know this must be horrible," a voice said through the door. Afraid to speak, fearing I would fall to pieces, all I could say was, "Yes."

Returning to the group, I stood off to the side, my arms wrapped around my chest. Nearby, Laura was telling several of the women about a historical novel she was reading. Suddenly, she stopped mid-sentence, touched my arm and gently asked, "You okay, baby? You're swaying."

"Yeah, sure," I said, adding, "I didn't realize I was moving," as I tried to quiet my body.

In my head, I repeated, *"Please, no one look at me, no one speak to me."* But within minutes I was moving again, shifting my weight from one foot to the other.

I thought of Sarah, how like most infants she loved motion—constant motion. Sometimes, as I swayed and bobbed with her in my arms, she would throw her head back or twist around to take in the world, especially faces, from another perspective. I think I found this rhythm as comforting as she did, like soothing music playing in my head.

During the first year of her life, whenever Sarah wasn't in my arms, I'd still find myself swaying. How naturally all that swaying came to me—maybe something wired in me from my own mother, maybe from all mothers to their babies. I remember disembarking from a weeklong cruise, returning to steady ground, and how my brain continued rocking and rolling for days—my sea brain, unable to recognize the solidity of land.

With Sarah, my brain never stopped registering her as part of me, her body as familiar as my own. Here I was, rocking myself to soothe my distress, as I had once soothed hers. Maybe my swaying brought her back, comforting me in a place where once I had felt so alive and essential, but where I now felt so completely adrift and alone.

Tears started.

"I'm sorry, I have to go," I said and headed for the door.

A week or so later, Alan and I ventured downtown for tapas. My old dance teacher, Lin, whom I hadn't seen in years, was leaving the restaurant just as we arrived. I was trapped. Knowing she had likely heard about Sarah, I steeled myself for her approach, the uncomfortable outbreak of "I'm sorry."

But Lin neither avoided me nor made light conversation. Instead, she walked right up, looked me in the eyes, held my gaze, and gave me a long, tight hug. Then she walked on. Not a word uttered. Nothing was required of me. I slowly exhaled. I couldn't have told Lin what I needed, but somehow, she had gotten it exactly right.

It was late October, three months after Sarah died, when Anna's first semester parent-teacher conferences were scheduled. It felt crushing having only one student, one child to consider. When I arrived for my first allotted ten-minute meeting, I sat numbly across from Anna's math teacher. I tried my best to look interested, but I'm sure I appeared to be in a trance. I was doing my own math, counting the tiles on the floor, then the ceiling.

My second conference was with Anna's Spanish teacher. As soon as I sat in the chair across from him, my mind flashed to Sarah's memorial service, where he had sat to my right, with the headmaster and the many teachers who had come to support Anna. My composure dissolved. With no place to hide, I wept. Not a few tears—this was a downpour. No matter how hard I willed myself to stop, no matter the embarrassment, there was no off valve.

My tears blotted Anna's test papers, which Señor Murga had laid before me. He continued on, telling me how amazing she was, about her latest grades and her homework assignments as I wept. The nicer his words, the harder I cried. When my time was up, I shook his hand and left the room.

I hadn't spoken one word.

No longer able to see or touch Sarah, I was in a constant state of dislocation. A few days later, as I was driving home on the Beltway, I heard Christina Aguilera's *Beautiful* on the radio—the song that had played as mourners walked out through the sanctuary at Sarah's memorial. Within seconds, my sobs made it too difficult to drive. I pulled off at the next exit to calm myself. I would take the local roads home. I started up the car to resume my ride, but I couldn't remember the route. I felt brain damaged, unable to make connections; it was as if I were looking through a kaleidoscope. In my mind, I could only see two spots— my home and where I was now—nothing in between.

Strangely, in that moment, my mind touched on a simple game from childhood that I used to play on long car rides. A little blue car sits atop a piece of cardboard with a picture of a road curving in all directions, like a maze. The car was held in place by a plastic cover. With a magnetic wand held under the board, my goal was to move the car from the starting point to the finish line.

As I sat, frozen, enclosed in my car, on the side of the road, my hands stuck on the wheel, staring straight ahead, I thought how I needed a magnetic wand to lead me home.

I called my husband.

"I'm so scared. I can't figure out how to get home."

As I drove, listening to his directions, I kept repeating to him how *beside myself* I was and how frightened I felt.

Only once before had I experienced anything close to this. It was the morning I took four-year-old Sarah and her friend Connor to the playground. The park had ten slides, a train ride, and, most importantly for Sarah, a plastic pig trash can that "ate" your trash. After watching the two of them line up for the longest slide, I waited at the bottom to catch them. Connor swooped into my arms first. I expected Sarah right after, but another child appeared. I felt a pang of worry, but I assumed she'd be out next. When she wasn't, I grabbed Connor's hand and quickly climbed up to the start of the slide. No Sarah. I started calling her name. Other parents jumped in to help. I don't know how long it took before we found her; she had wandered over to feed the pig some trash she'd found. Then, realizing she had drifted too far, she had set off looking for me, but in the wrong direction.

Right before a mother yelled, "I found her!" I saw myself from above the park, floating, as if in a dream—beside myself. As if everything was being recorded in slow motion, the image and feelings disconnected.

Now Sarah *was* gone, and I was once again pulling myself out of the scene at my most fragile moment.

For the rest of the day, those two words, *beside myself*, kept echoing in my head. I Googled the phrase and saw that it comes from the fifteenth century and meant "maddened or out of one's senses."

I thought back to Señor Murga, how I had been dissolved in grief, yet at the same time I was noticing his perfect composure. From this place, I was able to watch myself. The observing part of my brain was carrying on a conversation between my feeling self and the thinking one. Now, I pictured myself asking him, "Señor Murga, have you been speaking to weeping mothers all morning long?"

Yet even now, as I write these words, I notice it is the clinical part of my mind writing. The emotional part has gotten up and left the room.

Keeping busy became my fallback. When the weight of grief pinned me to my bed in the mornings, I would think of Anna. She needed me not to crumble, to be the mother she knew, not some ghost of myself. Yet I feared that if I turned my mind away from Sarah, I would lose her completely, shattering my past. I already felt I was losing a part of my future—seeing her as a college student, a young woman, an artist, a mother. All of that had been painted over with one brushstroke.

I needed to find a way to hold on to both my daughters and still move forward. After my mother died, I remember hearing my father say to friends: "I just have to keep putting one foot in front of the other." It wasn't until years later that I heard him add,

"I was so distraught. I was afraid if I stopped I would never move again."

I decided to get moving, clean out a cabinet, a closet, empty the dishwasher. I wrote thank-you notes to friends for all the meals and support over the weeks and months. I started to deal with the bills and insurance forms that had arrived in our mailbox. I spent hours on the phone with "insurance consultants" who rejected all our claims. Mental illness was not as "real" an illness as cancer or diabetes.

I became fixated on getting one bill paid—the ambulance that the residential hospital called when Sarah died. She had been there less than a week. That, I figured, was an expense that should be covered.

"I'm sorry," said the woman on the other end of the line "but that wasn't pre-certified."

"Pre-certified?" There must be some confusion. The bill was for an ambulance.

The woman kept repeating that it wasn't pre-certified, and I kept repeating that one could not pre-certify an ambulance.

I asked for a manager.

"I am a manager." We went on in the same endless loop.

"But you're not hearing me. It was an AM-BU-LANCE! You don't know you need one until it happens," I argued. "It was an EM-ER-GEN-CY."

"You don't need to raise your voice with me," she said.

I took a deep breath. "I'm sorry. I don't mean to take it out on you."

Pleading, I went on, "Just think about it a second—how can someone know they need an ambulance beforehand? Right? Even if you won't pay me, can you at least please see my point? Just agree that it doesn't make sense and I will go away. I promise. I won't even tell them you agreed with me."

No, she could not.

In the end, I gave up, saying, "Well, I'd like you to pre-certify us for five ambulances for the future, so that if someone else in my family ever needs one we will be covered. I want you to write that down and email me a copy."

"I can't do that," she answered.

"Exactly!"

I paid the bill.

A couple of months later, we applied for new insurance. Filling out the application, we had to list previous health issues. Fortunately, physically healthy, the only recent doctor appointments I had listed were the eight sessions of what I termed "grief therapy." As if that were even possible.

A rejection letter arrived explaining that they were not insuring us because of the therapy. Assuming it was an error, I called the insurance company. The woman on the phone, after briefly listening, said, "That's correct; that's why we didn't approve you."

"For *eight* sessions?" I asked.

"Well, one can never know where therapy can lead to, *can* one?" she replied.

Actually, I had a pretty good idea where it could all lead.

"What, as compared to bills for things like cancer, lupus? It was only eight sessions…after my daughter died…She was only eighteen." I started to cry.

Her curt response, "*Well*, my mother died last year, and I didn't *need* therapy."

"I am hanging up now," I said.

Unable to let go of this rejection and this woman's cruelty, I wrote a letter to the State Insurance Commission. Within a week, I received a call from one of the department heads.

After Donald identified himself, he began, "I wanted to call you personally. I was outraged when I read your letter—at what happened to you. Both for the rejection of your policy, but mostly for the way that woman spoke to you about your daughter."

Now he was choking up. "I lost my son five years ago, and not a day goes by that I don't feel grief. For that woman to so callously dismiss you and equate her mother dying to your daughter is outrageous." We spent the rest of our conversation talking about our children.

I no longer cared about the insurance.

The days grew shorter and the leaves on the nearby C&O canal turned gold and red and then disappeared—even without Sarah. How could anything happen without her there to see it?

One cool, sunny afternoon, I headed out to walk along the canal path. As I rounded a bend, I noticed Bridget walking toward me. Her pace was spry and brisk, despite her seventy-plus years. I braced myself. I hadn't seen Bridget since Sarah died. She slowed and smiled softly, her face flushed pink from the cold. Walking up to me, she caressed my arm and said, "Ah, Kerry. I'm so sorry, my dear Kerry." Her melodic Irish accent was as comforting and sing-songy as if her words flowed over a cobbled streambed. "But remember, she is with God. A good, safe place."

Earlier encounters with friends and neighbors had felt like blows that I couldn't recover from, but on the canal with Bridget I felt as if she were giving me a gift. While I have no belief that Sarah is with God, she most certainly would be if there were one. But I do think she is resting in heaven—a place that exists in the minds of those left behind, where a person is remembered with love.

Slowly, I returned to the routines of life, once again cooking, once again going to cycling class, once again shaving my legs. Some color was creeping back into a world that had been only black and white.

Yet the earth could still shake and the ground open beneath my feet—maybe for a moment or two, or maybe an hour—plummeting me back, with everything turning gray. I hadn't erased Sarah's number from my cell phone. How I wished her old phone messages remained so I could hear her voice. I kept time by how long it had been since she died. First it was days, then weeks, then months, and now years.

In some ways, I don't want the time to lengthen, or to have the immediacy of her loss lessen. And if I am honest with myself, there are times I am loath to give up the pain, because it binds me to her. Like a pebble I carry in my pocket that I turn over and over, its edges worn down by constant rubbing and caressing.

One afternoon, around the second anniversary of Sarah's death, I took a painting of hers to be framed and the man helping me said, "Oh, wait, now I know why I recognize you. Your daughter was with mine in school. Um, it's Sarah, right?" He seemed so pleased to remember. "Yes," I said, as that crushing feeling returned to my chest. I glided over to another wall, averting my eyes. Following closely behind, he asked, "So what has she been doing?" My face crumbled as I began to weep, momentarily, once again, beside myself. Almost as quickly, anguish spread across his face. "Oh, my God. I'm so sorry. I had heard about Sarah. How could I forget? I'm so sorry. How could I be so stupid?" Ruefully, in that moment, I wasn't sure which one of us I felt sorrier for.

When Sarah was a sophomore, she was a member of a fencing team. With her long limbs and quick eye-hand coordination, she was built for the sport. To fence epee style, one needs an arsenal of lunges. Grief had become my opponent, and I had learned some tactics of my own—when to expect the slash and how to shield myself from the flick of the blade.

I grabbed the painting and headed for home.

◆

Allen Stein

PAT-DOWN AT DALLAS-FORT WORTH

My seventy-year-old bones still carried a five-in-the morning chill
after twenty minutes of slow shuffling toward Security.
Surely, airports hadn't always been this cold.
The plane would be frigid,
and a blanket and airline coffee
would provide thin relief on the flight home,
where no one was waiting.
I took some tepid comfort in knowing
that my weekend with a distant son
and his family had been no less amiable
than obligation required, that nothing
had stirred the embers of old grievances.
At last, I reached screening—
shoes, belt, wallet and watch in a tray—
a man apparently divested of all he carried;
but a crumpled handkerchief and some loose change
in my back pocket sounded the alarm.
Released after my hands were held,
swabbed, and spectrometered, and my body patted over,
I sat tying my shoes, feeling, in the heat of the moment,
the irritation of being singled out and handled,
the remembered warmth of being noticed, touched.

EVENSONG

While they prepared the fatal hemlock brew,
Socrates learned a new tune on his flute.
Asked, "To what purpose?" He smiled and said,
"To master the melody before dying."
Those who loved him passed the flute on, hand to hand,
through time's slow carnage, until nothing
but the tale and the echo of a tune remained.

In July 1942, the inmate orchestra
at Mauthausen played on command
"All the birds are back again," a child's song
of springtime, as in striped pajamas
they shuffled before the cart that carried
Hans Bonarewitz, captured escapee,
to his hanging. The photo, blurry online,
shows Hans upright, his hands tied behind him.
As the noose was looped about his neck,
he was heard whistling the song, working
variations on its simple measures.
When his body was tossed to the flames,
some friends sought to hold the melodies
he'd achieved at the last, but the barking
guards and dogs shattered all possibility.

A ROOM WITH NO VIEW

(A Visit to Edward Hopper's "Room in New York")

They sit there as if waiting for something to happen.
But it already has, and they know it.
Have they just come in, or are they about to leave?
No matter—this plainly isn't working.
The three paintings on their walls,
others' notions perhaps of better times, better places,
are blurred, insubstantial, but the closed door
that rises and rears, slightly off-kilter, between them,
reaching up and out of sight, is solid,
its horizontal slats suggesting not ladder rungs
but bars. It even lacks a knob.
The window's vantage is one-way,
framing them in all that is inescapable,
unyielding as the stone column, the stone sill.
He leans into his paper, as if to evade
the enclosing arms of his chair
(only the merest shade lighter than his wife's dress).
She bends her head toward her piano
and watches her own finger listlessly
as it is about to sound a random note of lassitude.
On the interposing table, a doily holds nothing at all.
What is it that has happened,
what do they sit hunched from?
We can only guess—it's their marriage,
not ours, after all—but as we peer in,
our own shoulders slightly bowed
in the blanched moonlight,
and face the unfathomable white of his sleeves,
the pallor of her arms, of her downward curving neck,
we perceive that the window is cropped on the right,

not to offer them a way out, but to draw us inside,
where we begin to acknowledge, as they must have,
the vacancy that can encompass two in a room.

HERMAN MELVILLE, CUSTOMS INSPECTOR NUMBER 188

(From 1866 to 1886, Melville, unable to earn a living through his writing, worked as a customs inspector for the City of New York)

A salt spray dampens his cheek,
as the deck sways beneath him.
He walks the oaken boards
no less steadily than he did decades before,
and the chill breeze warms him with memories.
But the furled sails and the slack hawsers
looped firmly 'round the pier's bollards
remind him that ahead of the bow
are not open seas, scudding clouds,
and the Marquesas of his youth,
but Manhattan and its scrum of streets, spires, and dead walls.

He holds no whaleboat oar nor cutting spade now,
merely ledger and pen,
and instead of sturdy, weathered gray tarpaulin,
wears a blue uniform, faded with innumerable brushings,
and badge 188, tarnished with twenty years
of reading lading lists and taking inventory.
(He suspects he looks like a doorman
at a hotel no longer fashionable.)
A lingering glance at the sky, and he goes below,
walks among barrels of coffee beans,
crates of bananas, kegs of rum,
and inks entries in his ledger's tight lines
as with each breath he catches the scent
of the tropics he'll see no more.

Back on deck, he has a mad impulse
to scramble up the mainmast

and rest in the rigging, hammock-like,
drawing deeply on his pipe
and watching his smoke drift about lightly rocking spars,
and he almost expects Jack Chase will be there
waiting for him in the maintop with an easy smile
as in the old days.

But he knows that his tired limbs could not make the climb,
that Jack waits no more in this world,
and that the view would go no farther than Staten Island,
where his brother sits and broods
and stares from the windows of the Sailors' Snug Harbor.

His own journeys now are solely on ferry and cobblestone,
and his only harbor his small hearth,
where each night he gazes into the dwindling flames
and in truth sails far as ever he did,
pushing steadily toward a distant page
on which a handsome sailor, wide-eyed,
hangs by the neck.

◆

Roberto Christiano

AND THE STARS WERE SHINING
Nonfiction

E lucevan le stelle. And the stars were shining. My grandmother, Anna D'oria, wept when she heard Caruso sing this aria, which was usually during a live radio broadcast of La Tosca by Puccini. *O dolce baci. O languide carezze.* O sweet kisses. O languid caresses. Anna sat with rapt attention beside the radio. The tenor quavered with such longing tenderness. She, too, longed for tenderness. She had yet to take that long difficult voyage to Staten Island with her sisters. Marriage, a child, a better life but not easier—all that lay before her.

What lay behind her was the love of her life. And although she was only eighteen, she knew enough to know that love would not come again. It was too rare—a jewel that rivaled the sun for only a summer.

Turn, if you will, back to the aria *E lucevan le stelle,* to the phrase where Caruso soars effortlessly to a high note, to the grapes ripening on the hills of Martina Franca, a small country town in the Province of Taranto, to the hills on the ankle of the boot called Italy. Hear the crescendo in the heat of the sun, the cool nights scented by the sugar of white grapes that are waiting to be trampled and pressed for wine. Turn till you can smell the heaviness of olives grown from gnarled ancient limbs, and the richness of soil darkened from compost.

The year is 1919. Anna, along with her mother and father, three sisters and brother, work the land tirelessly. They live in a trulli—that iconic home of white limestone with a conical roof pointed like a steeple, the dense walls ideal for keeping the house cooler in the summer, warmer in the winter. Trullis are sprinkled through the whole region of Apulia along with the wild brown tulips.

This is the day Anna will ride on horseback with Lorenzo Costanzo, a mounted policeman, a *carabiniere*. He rides a horse named Bella, a mare the color of golden chestnut. Lorenzo is a tall man, an elegant man, young and mannered and proper. He has come from the Festival of Saint Anthony where he rode with his company in the parade. He wears his dress uniform, the pants his mother pressed, the crease still neat along the length of the leg, the blue serge coat smartly accessorized with gold braid and silver buttons, his head topped by a triangular hat with a white plume.

Anna wants to attend the parade, but there is too much work to do on the farm. Last year, the harvest was mediocre due to an early frost. The family has to work harder this year. She does not complain—she sees there is more food on the table.

Lorenzo always comes home this way, over the hill where the wild roses grow, and because he is a gentleman, he stops and tips his hat. And because she is also polite and good-natured, she responds with a gentle nod of her head. And because he is decent, he responds with a greeting.

On this particular day, she is tired and wants to get home. She can see, she cannot help but see, how remarkably handsome he is in his uniform and perfectly waxed moustache, his black curly hair spilling out from under his hat and onto his forehead.

Would she like a ride home? he asks. He knows where she lives.

He is a gentleman, a carabiniere—it is perfectly respectable to say yes.

He dismounts the beautiful horse and lifts her up. How easily he lifts her and secures her on the saddle. And then, in a single swift leap, he mounts the mare, seating himself in front of her. She has to put her arm around his waist to stabilize herself— the terrain is rocky, and the horse too nervous an animal. His posture is perfect, upright, his head perfectly centered, his waist firm and trim, all muscle and tone. She can smell the sweet smell of soap and sweat on the back of his neck, the vanilla note of pomade through the black curls.

It is then she knows, even though it hasn't happened yet. This is the man, these are the dark eyes, this is the back taught with balance, the lungs that breathe, expand and contract, the forearms, the hands holding the reins.

And indeed, the next night, he comes over for a visit, and the night after that, and after that. The summer quickly turns into a courtship of nights and flowers. And in the morning, sometimes, a trio of musicians play under her window to waken her.

Her family loves him. His family loves her.

Many evenings they walk into the higher hills where you can see the whole of Martina Franca. The wind picks up and causes her skirt to swell and billow. They weave among the tall grasses under the olive trees. The honeysuckle that has bloomed in the morning perfumes the evening. Sometimes even the nightingale sings.

The summer is long, and Lorenzo does not fail to disappoint in all matters of honor. They are allowed to be out until dark and are always accompanied by Anna's little sister, Maria Teresa. Lorenzo proves to be just as winsome with the ten-year-old girl. She never lacks a cone of shaved ice with cherry syrup or a strawberry gelato before the evening is over.

When Lorenzo says his last goodbye, the stars are just coming out against the indigo of the sky. He bends the long elegance of his neck down to kiss Anna.

Is there talk of marriage? Yes, there is. Both parents give their consent but advise a year's wait before announcing the engagement. So much passion in youth can easily burn out. A year will prove its constancy. The young people agree to their counsel because they are happy and happiness is a dream they can hold fast to.

Turn back to the aria and turn away from the indigo nights. Hear the ache in the wind and the roll of the hills, hear the gradual fading of stars at day. Turn to the rituals of the little town, the rhythms the Catholic Church provides, the customs and the feast days, the back and the bend of farming, the labor and struggle, the hardness and sweetness of days.

It is a Sunday morning. A six o'clock mass at Our Lady of Sorrows. Anna and her mother and sisters are here. In Martina Franca, everyone goes to church. The women and girls go several times a week and visit the confessional every other week. The mass is early because farmers are used to getting up early. The wealthier class goes to the high mass at noon with the big choir and incense, and the bells ringing out from the carillon. The six o'clock is shorter—especially the homily.

Afterwards, Anna's sisters go home to prepare lunch. Anna and Mother buy red and white carnations from the flower seller outside the church. On feast days, it is red and white roses. They go into the small cemetery, where granite saints and angels lend a charm to the sadness. Together, they lay the carnations on the graves and pull out the weeds encroaching on the tombstones. Everything is left ordered and beautiful.

And at the end of the cemetery is the mortuary.

The custom of the town is to keep open a presentation room where anyone can go in and see who has died. And even though the news of death travels fast, you don't always know. Anna and Mother are in the habit of paying their respects. It is a simple charity—to find out who has died, to know what family needs visiting or a meal made and brought over.

When they enter the room, there are three bodies on view. The first person they do not know, a youngish man with a rugged face, a field hand most likely from the calluses on his hands. The second, Mother knows, an old lady from church. Anna leaves Mother's side and walks over to the end of the room.

There she finds Lorenzo asleep on a slab of alabaster, the beauty of youth still present in the flush and rose of his cheeks and lips. He is wearing the dress uniform he wore on that day she first rode with him. The shirt starched, crisp, white. On his forehead a bright red gash in the shape of a star.

At first her mind cannot comprehend the vision. There is a long denial. And then the slow recognition and shock. And with the shock, the terribleness of it all. She screams out for Mother, who hurries over. Anna faints, and Mother barely catches her. Mother calls out for help. The mortician rushes out from the back room, his white shirt sleeves rolled up from work. He takes Anna from Mother and carries her outside to a bench. He waves a vial of smelling salts under her nose.

Anna wakes to grief, to pain, to tears. It is not a vision. Death has entered her life. No loss could be greater. No reality harder.

The mortician fans her, and Mother undoes the top button of her dress. She can scarcely breathe. She questions how it is that she is breathing. She feels she may faint again but the urge passes.

A young man is coming up the walk. He is Lorenzo's brother, Mario—he has been looking for Anna since dawn.

What happened? Anna asks, her voice slowly returning. What happened to Lorenzo?

He was thrown from his horse on the way home from his evening with Anna. It was very dark as he was riding along his customary trail. The heat was unbearable all day, and the night was alive with flashes of lightning. Bella, a tense creature to start with, was frightened by the lightning. A single bolt lit up the entire night sky when she bolted, throwing Lorenzo against a stone boulder. A shepherd witnessed the accident. By the time the shepherd reached Lorenzo, he was unconscious. The shepherd bandaged Lorenzo's head with his kerchief and went off to fetch the doctor, leaving another shepherd to stand and watch. Lorenzo never regained consciousness. When the doctor arrived, he recognized Lorenzo. The doctor said he must have died immediately on impact. The wound was so deep.

Anna cannot speak. She is beset by sobs.

He didn't suffer long, Mario says. Take some comfort in that.

Anna is beyond comfort. How could Lorenzo be dead and she alive? The difference was too great to bear.

Mario says the funeral will be that afternoon.

I need to see him again, Anna says. I need to see him.

They go back in the mortuary and Anna stops crying for a time, but then the grief returns like waves crashing in on her.

Oh, my poor precious daughter, Mother says, trying to calm her daughter.

Let me be, Anna says.

When Anna has cried all she can, a cold numbness settles in. Mother and Mario walk her home, half carrying her down the road. Along the way, neighbors come up to them and inquire out of concern. Some girls burst into tears at the news.

Nearing home, her sisters hear the cries from the street and come out in alarm. Soon everyone in the family is crying. Mother sets Anna down on the sofa and fetches the calming pills the doctor once prescribed for her husband. Aunt Marie from next door comes in and sits down beside Anna and strokes her hair. Her aunt says it will take some time for her to be able to handle the tragedy. It will take time for her to grasp the pain. Her aunt is considered a wise woman in the family, and her words carry weight. Soon the sedative takes effect and Mother takes Anna to her bedroom to lie down. Mother sits beside her, holding her hand. Sleep finally comes to her like a blessing.

Hours later, Mother carefully wakes her. The funeral will be in an hour. What does Anna want to do? Mario has come to escort her to the funeral. Anna tries to get up from the bed but can't. Mother tells Mario she is unable to go, she is too grief stricken, the shock is too great, but that her husband and her son will go to represent the family. When Mother returns to the bedroom, Anna is shaking badly. Mother asks her if she would like another sedative. Anna says yes, she would. Mother patiently waits for the calm to descend. Her sisters come in the room to be with her and sit round the bed.

Later, Mother makes her some warm broth and begs—no, pleads with tears—for her to eat, even a few sips, and Anna, not wanting to distress Mother any further, submits. She can see the anxiety in Mother's face, in the voices of her sisters, and particularly in the welling eyes of Maria Teresa. Anna is broken, horribly broken, but she cannot break those who love her. As awful as it is, she cannot put her family through another death.

When the sun has set and Anna hears her father and brother return from the funeral, she realizes how exhausted Mother is— her face is so lined and tired. Anna tells her that she can sleep through the night. There is no need to stay. Mother needs her own rest. Anna needs to be alone now. She needs not to be a worry to anyone, at least for the night. Mother sighs, taking some comfort in her words, and leaves her alone,

Anna falls into a profound sleep. Her anxiety and grief dissipate into the deepness of the pillow. Lorenzo comes to her in a dream. He is sitting atop Bella, the white plume in his hat glowing like a votive candle. He is smiling that kind gentlemen's smile, and he is looking right at her. He has never looked more handsome. He bends the long elegance of his neck to speak to her.

"You came to see me today, but you didn't even give me a kiss."

Anna awakes with a start. Her heart is pounding and the blood is rushing to her face. It was a dream, she says to herself. It was a dream.

The family is asleep and the house completely quiet. She has to get to the cemetery. She puts on her slippers and robe. She missed the funeral of the only man she would ever love. She has to go to the grave. She hopes beyond hope that his death isn't real, she hopes he is alive, alive as he was in the dream—so present, so real.

No one in Martina Franca is up. If anyone were to see her at this hour in her robe and slippers they would think her mad, but she doesn't care. She can't care.

It is predawn—the dark blue sky is lightening. The stars are disappearing from the sky. She stumbles her way along the cobblestone walks and up the trail, up the hill to Our Lady of Sorrows. Trickles of sun are breaking over gravestones, over stone angels and cherubs. There is Lorenzo's family plot—a mound of earth covered with roses—white and red—white for his eternal absence, red for the love of his heart. And there, standing over his grave, is Bella, the long chestnut brown neck bowed down to the grave. There is nothing wild about her now, only the hushed deepness of the deepest melancholy. Anna goes up to her.

Come on now, my girl, Anna says, stroking that beautiful elegant neck. I know, I know. We've lost him, you and I. But you can't stay out here in the chill of the morning. You must be terribly hungry, out all night lost in the hills. What a terrible night you've had, a long, terrible night. Come now, my girl. Come now.

Anna takes hold of the rein and slowly leads her away from the grave. Anna walks her down the hill—gently, steadily, so as not to frighten her. She doesn't resist—she wants to go home, to Lorenzo's home. Anna leads her where she wants to go. She kisses the loveliness of her long neck, the mane still tied and pleated, the coat wet from morning dew. She leads her into the farmyard and bids her goodbye with another kiss. And then she shuts the gate and walks the way back to her house of grief.

Aunt Marie said Anna would recover in time and with patience, and her words proved prophetic. She did go on, and when America presented itself like a long, lost promise, she left with her sisters. Anna did love again, but not in the same way. And although she discovered all manner of things in the new country that were good and better, she did not find the happiness that seemed part and parcel of America. She did find, however, much that gave her pleasure and gave her days music and meaning. She always loved opera and Caruso.

I own the remastered recording of Caruso singing *E Lucevan Le Stelle*. The record is dusty, but I wipe it clean with a soft linen cloth. I set it on the old turntable and carefully place the stylus on the record. And as I listen to that voice, that song, those crackles that evaded erasure, I can hear beyond the datedness of the recording and the dated style of singing. I can hear the beauty, and in that beauty I can hear that love is passing and may not come again.

E Lucevan Le Stelle. And the stars were shining.

◆

Simon Perchik

FIVE POEMS

*

You whisper as if smoke
still follows some plane
that left it behind

–mourners understand this
wave goodbye to your words
by leaning closer

the way fires start
though each stone left here
will collide with the sun

–no one would notice
it's two in the afternoon
and all Earth is warming itself

lighting up the sky
no more than ever
hears you talk louder

say where in your mouth
a kiss can be found
came for you and stayed.

SIMON PERCHIK

*

How could a moon so dim
see the room being taken away
–the door was closed from behind

as if nothing will return
except to light the stars
with evenings though the bed

stays empty, was uprooted
pulled further from the wall
no mined for its darkness

where each night pours sand
little by little through the blanket
over a room that died.

SIMON PERCHIK

*

To not hear her leaving
and though this snapshot is wrinkled
it's carried off in a shirt pocket

that never closes, stays with you
by reaching out as eyes
waiting for tears and emptiness

–you remember who filled the camera
except there was sunlight –a shadow
must say something, must want

to be lifted, brought back, caressed
the way a well is dug for the dead
who want only water and each other

–you try, pull the corners closer
over and over folded till you are facing
the ground, the dry grass, her.

SIMON PERCHIK

*

To the dirt that no longer moves
you offer a mask the way a flower
over and over is readied for mornings

where time begins again as stars
sensing honey and more darkness
–by evening your death

will be used to footsteps one by one
broken off a great loneliness
returning row by row as the small stones

cut out for the mouth and eyes
to sweeten it, ask
where you are going by yourself.

*

Though there's no sea nearby
this sidewalk smell from sand
no longer struggling –you point

where the crack will come
when you take your hand away
letting it lie in the street

–what drips from your fingertip
is one wound bathing another
with evenings and shores

covered with the inhuman cries
from small shells still in pain
scattered and not moving

♦

Beth Oast Williams

JUST BENEATH THE SURFACE

The cemetery carries bones
in its pockets,
and you trapeze its perimeter
head down, afraid
of what pulls your swing.

Your grip, even tighter
over cold blocks of granite,
their careful carvings failing
to explain why your father
stopped and you did not.

You once arranged silk flowers
to stand at attention
above his head, a salute
to manmade permanence, as if God
never knew forever.

Forget what the ground
feels like on your knees.
The sole of your loafer,
like a coffin's seal,
protects you from rain.

Crepe myrtles in their pushback
to death drop notes in your path,
softly, and too quietly for you
to hear the rattle of change
just beyond your grasp.

◆

Daun Daemon

REGRETS

With regards to Kate Chopin

Fiction

I.

For almost 13 years, Allie had dug her hands in the rich Sampson County dirt, coaxing her gardens into evermore impressive scope and production. When she bought the flat, uninspired land in 1991 and moved from an apartment in Fayetteville, she knew little about gardening, and the land had shown her its displeasure by drying up.

But she taught herself—through books, magazines, TV shows, agriculture brochures—how to mulch and rotate plantings. She built a potting shed and a greenhouse and started her own seeds in winter's deep gloom. If she didn't have a necessary skill, she learned it. If she needed help with building, she hired one of the Mexican farm laborers up the road.

She had no close friends in this part of North Carolina, and all her family were either dead or living in California. She had three cats for companionship, and they were all she needed. Her life was fine.

II.

On this late July morning, the telephone kept ringing and ringing. Allie could hear its insistent trilling through the kitchen window as she weeded her thickly planted herb garden. Whoever was calling could wait, she thought. The herbs and weeds were thriving, and she couldn't be swayed from her assault on them.

The first spring she owned the farm, she had only enough energy to plot out and plant the herbs: basil, thyme, oregano, lavender, rosemary, parsley, chives, dill, sage, savory, and catmint. She tried cilantro only once, but it went to seed so quickly she could never get much use out of it. She often yearned for fresh cilantro when making a salsa but didn't care to drive the 14 miles to the store just for an herb. She had a special fondness for her herb garden, as it had grown in nicely over the years.

The rosemary was a hardy bush now. Its deep, aromatic fragrance filled the yard after heavy rains, and she rubbed her hands on the leaves whenever she passed by. The lavender was spreading into a pleasing, colorful border. She clipped the buds when they were past blooming to save for sachets she'd sew in the winter. The catmint had conquered an entire quadrant, which was just fine with the cats—they rolled in it and emerged giddy.

"Well hello, Soldier." Allie smiled at her 17-year-old gray cat, whose muzzle was stippled with white. He lazed near the corner of her wraparound porch, stretched beneath the stems of a white hydrangea with ponderous flower heads that drooped toward the ground. "Aren't you a cozy boy?"

The cat raised his head and pointed it in the direction of the long gravel drive that wound to the house from the dirt road. He rose, twitched his whiskers, yawned, and curled deeper into the coolness beneath the bush.

An old Ford sedan was churning up dust as it came too quickly toward Allie's house. The car, a faded dark blue and covered in rust spots and dents, stopped ten feet from where Allie knelt in the dirt. A woman so pregnant that she had to pull herself up by clutching the top of the car door emerged. Her face was wet from crying.

"Lupita?" Allie recognized the woman from the county farmers' market. She sold handmade dolls on Saturdays, but Allie hadn't seen her there this year. Now she realized why. She knew that Lupita lived with her family in a rented house a few miles up the dirt road, but she knew nothing else about her.

REGRETS

"*Hola, senorita.*" Lupita looked into the car, her tone changing to one less cordial. "*Ana Maria, ahora! Dige ella sobre tu padre. Ahora!*"

A young girl with very large eyes and long dark hair pushed open the car door and stepped out. She sucked her lower lip into her mouth and twisted her hands together in front of her body. Lupita slapped the top of the car to get her attention.

The girl quickly stepped forward and recited in a rush, "Mama needs to go to the hospital in Fayetteville. Papa was injured at the chicken plant and was taken there. She is afraid Papa is going to die. She doesn't understand what has happened. Mama thinks that if we go to the hospital with her, we will be too sad and she will not be able to see Papa for long."

The girl stopped speaking and looked across the car's hood at her mother, who slapped the car's roof again with her hand. Allie saw movement inside the car, in the back seat. "Mama has nowhere else to leave us. All the other women she knows work in the chicken plant with their men, and our only relatives here are her two cousins in Duplin County. She will call them later and tell them to come here for us tonight."

Lupita clasped her hands together in front of her heart. "*Por favor?*"

Allie wiped the sweat from her forehead with the back of her hand.

"Mama says, 'please,'" the child stated to Allie. The little girl's accent was slight, as if her native tongue were nothing more than a ghost. Clearly, though, she spoke both languages, whereas her mother did not.

"I know. I know what '*por favor*' means. How many of you are there?"

"Me and my sisters. Bonita is 7 and Carla is 5. I'm Ana Maria – I'm 10. We can stay outside on the porch and wait. I will keep the young ones quiet."

Allie had never kept children before, having never babysat as a teenager and having no nieces and nephews to lavish attention upon. Once, when she lived with her husband near the base, she had helped the other army wives with birthday parties— but that had been long ago.

"All right." Allie nodded curtly at Lupita, then looked back to the child. "You can play in the gardens or on the porch."

"*Gracias! Gracias, senorita!*" Lupita shooed the other girls out of the car. These two, with their luminous large eyes and broad faces, looked like younger versions of Ana Maria.

Lupita drove away, again churning up dust and leaving the three girls standing in silence before Allie.

III.

She assumed they had eaten lunch before Lupita dropped them off, but Ana Maria told her early in the afternoon that they were hungry. Allie served them peanut butter and homemade strawberry jam sandwiches on the porch, where they had been sitting together for almost two hours. The girls gobbled them down in an eerie silence.

Allie gathered their plates and said, "You don't have to be quiet. You can play in the gardens if you want." As Allie turned to go into the house, Soldier emerged from his nap beneath the hydrangea.

The smallest girl gasped. "Kitty!" All three girls flung themselves at the porch railing and peered over at the startled cat, who jumped and then began to lick his shoulder furiously.

"No, that's Soldier." Allie laughed. "I have two more cats. One is a small brown tiger cat named Kitty. The other cat is so orange he looks red. That's why I named him Tomato. I call him Tommy."

"How old are your kitties?" These were Bonita's first words since arriving. Allie felt a brief surge of tenderness for the obviously reserved little girl.

"Well, Soldier there is 17. I brought him here from Fayetteville after, well, I brought him from an apartment. Kitty is 12. She showed up here on the farm about a year after I moved in. She was so tiny, and I don't know where she came from. She's certainly a survivor." Allie smiled at this thought. "And Tommy, well, I couldn't resist a cat so brightly colored, with such vivid fur. I picked him up two years ago from a lady who was giving away kittens outside the Piggly Wiggly."

As if on cue, Tommy sped around the side of the house and up the porch steps. When he spotted the girls, he raised his hackles and danced sideways, sending the children into musical giggles. Once they began to pet him and talk to him, he flopped onto his side and began purring.

"His head is so round–like a tomato!" Ana Maria looked up at Allie. "That's a very smart name for him."

"Thank you, Ana Maria." Allie left the girls on the porch while she canned eight quarts of green beans and baked a peach pie. All three girls knocked on the screen door and asked politely before entering to use the bathroom. They would leave quietly and return to petting the cats—Soldier had eventually joined the party—and chattering away. From Allie's point of view, the cats and girls spent the afternoon in rapture.

By six o'clock that evening, no one had come for the girls. Allie called the hospitals in Fayetteville, but none had any record of a Jorge de los Rios as a patient.

That night, as a full moon rose to illuminate Allie's white garden surrounding the back patio, she served the girls peach pie and ice cream while telling them about the flowers. She pointed out impatiens, climbing roses, gardenia bushes that no longer were in bloom.

"That's a moon vine," she said, pointing to an eight-foot tall tepee structure covered thickly in leaves and white buds. "As we sit here, the flowers will open very quickly, and their perfume will call the moths from the trees. In the morning, the flowers will wilt and die."

"That's very sad," said Ana Maria. "Something so beautiful should live forever."

As she spoke, one of the flower buds popped open and began to unfurl, its creamy whiteness glowing in the moonlight.

"Yes," Allie said. "Yes."

The cousins had not arrived by ten o'clock, so Allie pulled two old sleeping bags from the attic and made up her sofa as a bed for the third child. The girls' soft breathing, which Allie strained to hear from across the hall in her own bedroom, kept her awake most of the night.

IV.

The cautious, reserved girls from the day before had disappeared by the time Allie awoke. Instead of the usual moments of quiet Allie spent lying in bed, thinking of all she needed to do in the day ahead, blinking her eyes at the early morning rays streaming through her bare window, and trying so hard to push away the heaviness she still carried in her heart—instead of this, Allie was greeted with shrill laughter, squeals, thumps, racing footsteps, and finally a crash. After a second of complete quiet, a sorrowful wail broke loose, attended by shushes and soft voices.

In her kitchen, Allie found Bonita picking shards of pottery off the floor and young Carla standing by her with quivery lips and a wet face. The broken pottery was once a lovely bowl, given to Allie as a wedding gift, glazed in fanciful shades of purple, blue, and turquoise. She had used it as a fruit bowl these 20 years.

"Carla wanted a banana, but she is too little to reach the bowl. She didn't mean to pull it off the table," Ana Maria explained. "Please don't smack her."

"Smack her? Why would I do that?"

"Because she did a bad thing," Bonita said. She gathered the pieces of pottery and began to arrange them in a circle on the table. Some of the pieces were quite large and uneven, so these she put aside. The rest she configured into eyes and a sad mouth. "There. I made a picture."

"Bonita likes to find pieces of things and make them into something new. She has done this since she was a baby." Ana

Maria wrinkled her nose at her sister. "Mama says that maybe Bonita will sew one day and work in a factory.

"Seems to me that she could be an artist," Allie said as she poured orange juice and began to make toast for the girls and herself.

"Mama says that we will all need to work when we are 16. She says that we will all have babies to take care of." Ana Maria sipped her juice. "What can we do today?"

"We can garden," Allie said. She thought to herself, *and I will call the county social services.*

"I hope we don't have to pick tobacco like at home sometimes," Carla said. "It stings."

Allie laughed and then showed the girls what she meant by gardening. She taught little Carla how to pull plump green beans from the vines and Ana Maria how to properly water the flowerbeds, though Carla chewed on the beans and Ana Maria more than once tried to water a cat. Bonita, though, took very seriously her duty of cutting a variety of flowers and herbs for an arrangement. Allie, surprised at how cooperative the children were, forgot to call social services.

The phone rang while they all sat on the porch eating egg salad sandwiches and fat red grapes for lunch, the girls slipping bits of egg to the begging Kitty. Allie, always startled by the sound of the phone, paused before standing to go inside.

The nurse on the other end of the line sounded irritated, having tried numerous variations of Allie's phone number before getting it right. Lupita de los Rios, she explained, didn't know that Allie's phone number was unlisted and had lost the slip of paper with the number. Her husband hadn't known it, either, and Lupita had tried to remember the numbers, but—*you know how these Mexicans are*, the woman said—she got them all turned around.

Anyway, said the nurse, Lupita was still in labor and, no, she didn't know anything about any cousins. All she knew was that Lupita's husband was released after treatment in the ER yesterday and that he had stayed with his wife through the night. He would call Allie about the children later. Or so the nurse told Allie. When Allie asked the nurse why the hospital hadn't known that Jorge de los Rios had been admitted into the ER, the nurse stated flatly that the husband's last name was Contreras—and she had had a fine time getting that out of him.

When Allie replaced the receiver in its cradle, she stood for a moment taking slow, deep breaths. The girls would have to stay with her until their father came, and she would have to wait to find out when that would be.

V.

The telephone did not ring that evening, nor the next morning, as three freshly bathed little girls sat naked in Allie's living room playing with some old marbles she had found stashed in an attic trunk. The girls' clothing—every stitch of it—was tumbling in the dryer.

"Whose marbles are these?" asked Ana Maria, ever curious, Allie realized by now.

"They belonged to my husband," Allie said, "when he was a little boy."

Bonita, who had quietly been arranging the smaller marbles into geometrical shapes, looked up. "Carla has some in her mouth."

"Spit!" Ana Maria yelled at her baby sister, who obliged. Saliva flowed, and marbles tumbled from her laughing mouth. "Seven marbles. Wait until Mama hears about this. I think that is a record."

All of them giggled together, but Allie said, "Carla, please don't put any more marbles in your mouth. They're dirty, and you could choke on them."

"Where is he?" Ana Maria asked.

"Who?"

"Your husband. What is his name?"

Allie hadn't spoken the full name aloud in many years. After cutting herself off from her life before, she had kept his name as much a secret thing, as much her very own possession as possible, expressing it only when necessary for whatever bureaucratic reasons arose. Three sets of innocent, expectant brown eyes gazed at her now.

"Tom White. Sergeant Thomas Michael White." There. She had said it, and now the little girls were smiling at her as if a great mystery had been revealed.

"That is a very nice name. Can we see a picture of him?" Ana Maria asked.

Allie walked into her bedroom, which had been off limits to the girls, and took the only framed photograph of Tom in the house from her bedside table. In the photo, he is out of uniform, wearing faded jeans and an NC State University sweatshirt, lounging on a sofa with Soldier cradled in his arms like a sleeping child, the cat's four paws curled in feline ecstasy. Tom is looking into the camera, through the camera at her. He had just said, "I can't wait until I'm holding our baby."

Two weeks later, he was deployed. Three days after that, she miscarried. A month later, without knowing about the miscarriage, he was killed by friendly fire.

She took the photo to the girls.

"Oh, that's Soldier!" Bonita said.

"Yes, it is." Allie stroked Bonita's hair. "He was a young cat then."

"But he still liked to sleep, huh?" Carla said. She ran out to find the cat and cried for Bonita to come with her. When they realized they were outside naked, they squealed, ran into the house and retrieved their clothes from the dryer.

"His hair is as bright as Tomato's!" Ana Maria exclaimed after her sisters were gone. She touched the photograph with her fingertips, a frown creasing her brow. She looked at Allie. "Where is he now?"

Allie wondered if she should tell this child the truth. Did Ana Maria need to know, really? Wouldn't Allie have to explain to her about Iraq and Kuwait? Wouldn't she have to feel the anger and the pain all over again?

"Did he die in a war?" Ana Maria whispered the question, gazing up at Allie's eyes.

Allie nodded.

"Well, he was very brave." Ana Maria placed the photograph on the coffee table and then scurried to find her own clothes.

Allie left the photograph exactly where the child had put it.

VI.

For the remainder of that day, Allie played with the girls. Gardening could wait until another day. They played hide-and-seek outside, Bonita hiding behind the potting shed while Allie pretended not to see her. Little Carla took her cue from Soldier and slipped into the darkness beneath the hydrangea bush. Ana Maria disappeared completely and later would not tell the rest of them where her good hiding spot had been. Allie also taught the girls to play hopscotch and tic-tac-toe, drawing in the red Carolina dirt with a sturdy stick.

Ana Maria helped Allie make cornbread while the two younger girls played outside with the marbles or played their own version of hide-and-seek with the cats.

For dinner, they ate the cornbread drizzled with honey—in a glass of milk. Allie's freshly harvested vegetables — zucchini, tomatoes, corn, peppers, beans—sat ignored on the kitchen counter.

In the evening, when the moonflowers began to open and the night birds to sing, they caught lightning bugs and put them in a canning jar with holes poked in the lid. The girls had never done this before, and they were delighted by the living, pulsing lights. They sat around the patio table, their small faces held close to the glass jar. Allie thought that their skin glowing amber in the luminescence was the most beautiful thing she had ever seen.

The next day began much the same, Allie making blueberry muffins for breakfast and sandwiches for lunch and nothing but play in between. Early in the afternoon, she proposed that they write a skit and act it out together. She told the excited girls that they could even dress up in some of her old clothes, but then the brazen blare of a car horn broke through their chatter.

A car approached the house slowly, silent now that the driver could see them watching. It was Lupita's car. The girls began to jump up and down and shout, "Mama! Papa!" They swarmed the car when it pulled to a gentle stop.

Jorge emerged with a soft blue bundle in his arms. "This is Diego, your baby brother."

He handed the baby to Lupita, who had pulled herself gingerly out of the car, smiled, and waved quickly at Allie. She chattered in Spanish to the girls, lovingly stroking the baby's head.

Jorge stepped closer to Allie, sincere gratitude and warmth in his eyes. "Thank you, ma'am. I am sorry that no one came, but Lupita's stupid cousins heard of work in Virginia and left before we told them to come here. I worked double shift at the chicken plant yesterday to make up for the time. I'll have to do it again tomorrow, too."

Allie only looked at the car, at the children there.

"Do you want to see Diego?" Jorge asked, turning to call Lupita over.

"No," Allie said quickly. "Don't take him away from the girls."

Lupita waved at Allie and got back into the car. Carla and Bonita, clinging to their mother like vines, disappeared into its interior as well. As Jorge started the car, Allie thought they would all be fine. They would all go back home and be fine. But then Ana Maria ran to her and threw her arms around Allie's waist, hugging her tightly, pressing her dark head into Allie's belly, pressing and hugging her so hard that Allie thought she could feel the child's heartbeat.

VII.

After they had gone, Allie said out loud, "Well, there's work to be done."

The words seemed to echo through her gardens, around the porch, and back to her. When the words died away, all that remained in the still air were the sounds of insects and birds and distant farm machinery.

She picked up her garden shears and a basket and headed to her tomato plants, heavy with ripe fruit. As she worked her way to the back of the first row, she noticed that her neglect these past two days had allowed several beautiful tomatoes, some the size of a softball, to begin rotting. She sighed and cut their stems, wondering what she could salvage from them.

Beyond the tomato plants were her cantaloupe vines, and Allie knew that several of the melons were almost ripe. She was startled to find that the vines had been disturbed, rearranged actually so that a bare patch of ground was exposed. Except that the ground wasn't bare.

Allie dropped the shears and basket, scattering tomatoes. She fell to her knees and placed her hands on the mosaic, lingering over each shard of her fruit bowl that formed a large outer heart, then caressing each marble that made up the three smaller hearts held within before burying her face in her hands and weeping like a child.

She didn't notice that Soldier lay napping beneath a squash plant or that Kitty stalked a beetle in the herb garden or that Tommy had followed her into the cantaloupe vines and now leaned into her leg, purring and waiting to be loved.

◆

Christine Higgins

A YEAR OF MOURNING

A small miracle—
this morning, this visit.
I'm still in bed, in my pajamas,
but I can hear them talking downstairs.
I imagine they're sitting
at the dining room table:
my husband and a young woman
we met at the college library—
she's come to help him with a video project.
Ashley's almost the exact age
our daughter would be
had she survived her car accident.

Every now and then I hear them chuckle.
I can smell the coffee brewing.
I hear her get up to let our dog out—
she feels that much at home—
there's pattering of the dog's feet,
then the hinge squeak of the screen door.

Everything's normal for a few minutes.
Everything's as it should be.
From under the covers, I eavesdrop
on their conversation about a new camera.
I imagine a big bouquet of yellow roses on the table—
even though I know that's not so.

MY MOTHER'S VOICE

Oh, Mr. Moon, Moon,
Pretty silvery moon, hiding
behind that tree.

I don't know if she sang it once
and I remember it well, or
if the child I was
begged her to sing it again and again.

It was the soprano voice
I only heard in church, never
as she cleaned house or
cooked dinner or folded laundry.

.

Oh, bright and silvery moon, hiding
behind that tree. My life's in danger
And I'm on the run, there's a man out
there with a Gatling gun.

The danger was depression
that wouldn't quit, inherited
from her drunk father, though probably
not his alone to give.

CHRISTINE HIGGINS

I see her profile in the darkness
dependent on the full moon's electric light.
She's singing, so no threats to beat me
with a brush. No blood rushing
to my forearm where she would
pinch me with her thumb, desperate
for some peace. My father driving,
always driving, for she was too scared
to navigate alone.

Her voice silvery like the song,
notes strung like a pearl necklace.
White against black, the soprano
voice piercing the dark.

◆

Scott Bradfield

ADVENTURES IN RESPONSIBLE LIVING

Fiction

The first time Erica Summerfield left her husband and three children was on a Thursday morning in May while standing in her recently renovated oak-veneer kitchen, spreading mayonnaise on several slices of wheat toast and sprinkling bottled capers on the mayonnaise. It began as a slight decrescendoing of sensation, as if somebody was reducing the volume on the various radio chat shows playing discordantly throughout the house. Everything grew less vibrant and impressionable: the aromas of wildflowers in a glass vase, the textures of wooden cooking implements suspended from a chrome ceiling rack, the shimmer of thickly resined cabinets, and even the scowling, deeply frustrated expressions of Erica's three daughters, who stood observing her like a set of miniature interns being guided through the exhumation of a cadaver.

"I don't like capers," Molly said. It didn't sound like Molly, or the voice of any five-year-old Erica had ever met. For a moment, Erica suspected the words were being beamed into her head by some fugitive radio satellite in outer space.

"Shut up, stupid," another child said.

"Don't call me stupid," Molly said.

"Dad, do you want capers on your sandwich?"

"Dad doesn't like capers. Dad doesn't like anything green."

The more they spoke, the less Erica heard, as if her consciousness were expanding to the point that nothing registered outside it. The only body of determination that existed for Erica right now was the jar of Hellman's mayonnaise on the countertop.

It was one-third full. It contained an indifferent quantity of whiteness, thickness, coherency, and determination.

Then her bubble of awareness diminished again and Erica felt herself descending through thick regions of temperature. It was like the time she went skiing: everything was so white and unremitting that the whiteness eventually grew indistinguishable from itself.

The other voices continued speaking.

"Honey? Can you hear me? Are you all right? Sit down—let me take that. Sally, get your mother a glass of water. Molly, stop crying. Go upstairs and get ready for school. Stepahanie, go with her."

It was definitely his voice, Erica thought. But she wasn't entirely certain what she meant by his "voice," or who he was when he used it.

"Honey? Please let go of my hand and sit down. That's my good girl. You've gone as pale as a sheet. Let's get a blanket around you. Do you know where you are, honey? Just nod to indicate if you hear me. That's my girl. Okay, you can stop nodding now. I'm going to call a doctor, but I won't be gone long. Give me a few seconds to find the phone and I'll be right back."

As if she were responding to some long-buried hypnotic suggestion from the pre-conscious past, Erica found herself regarding the broad bulkhead-like freezer, clean and white and immaculate with silver trim and blinking green indicators. Then someone was helping her to stand on her inflexible feet, turn her face away from the indicators, and proceed in a direction she didn't understand. There was a car, and then another car, and then a parking lot. There were big glass doors and black men in white jackets. Elevator doors opening and closing, pinging like submarines in a movie. Sometimes Erica was inside the elevator; sometimes she wasn't.

Eventually she was sitting in a room somewhere. Someone was speaking to her, either a man or a woman. She didn't care if she recognized them; being recognized was their problem. She just needed to carry on with this thing happening inside her. "I'm going to ask you a few questions," the unrecognizable person said. "Can you feel my hand when I do this? Clench your fist to say yes. To indicate no, just leave it. Understand?"

Of course she understood. Her fist could speak for itself.

"Good. Now, is your name Erica?"

Yes.

"Do you live on the moon?"

No.

"Is your oldest daughter named Molly?"

Yes.

"Is Molly forty-seven years old?"

No.

"Can we make you more comfortable? Maybe tea or coffee? Or something to eat?"

No.

"Would you like to be left alone? Think about that for a moment, Erica. There's no hurry. Just tell us what you want."

Yes, she told them. The answer is yes.

After a moment, something changed in the way his hand rested in her lap. It stopped visiting. It started to reside.

"We need to know if you're in any pain, Erica. Or if you feel disoriented or frightened. If you're trying to speak to us and can't move your lips or articulate what you're trying to say, then I need to know that right now. Maybe you'd like something to help you sleep. Or a small television. All you need to do is ask."

You had to stop answering questions sometimes. Otherwise they never went away.

"I'm taking that as a no, Erica. I need a really firm squeeze if you want me to leave the room. Good. Yes. A firm hard squeeze like that one. You've made your point. You can let go of my hand now. That's a good girl. I'll leave."

For the next several days, she measured time as a sequence of interrogations. How was she feeling, did she need anything, did she want to see her children, was the soup too hot or too cold, how many fingers were they holding up, how much was four plus four. She was asked if she wanted to listen to music. (She didn't.) She was asked if she wanted to watch TV. (She didn't.) She was asked if she wanted to see her children. (She thought about it for a while, but eventually decided that she might actually prefer TV.) She was asked if she wanted to be left alone. This was the only question that answered itself.

Then one morning she awoke and it was over. The room was dark; in the hall outside, the overhead fluorescents glowed dully, like the glimmering corridors of a spaceship in a seventies science fiction movie. She heard thrumming machines in distant rooms, someone shouting in Spanish, a squeaky wheel on a gurney. She sat up in a hard bed, surrounded by a web work of tubes, steel winches, levers, trays and bird-like feeding devices, as if she were some sort of human excavation, an old building being broken down to its foundations and transformed into a taller, more energy-efficient one.

"What does she respond to?"

"Light. Changes in temperature. Voices. It's not a tumor or a stroke. Her blood's fine. She's self-sedating. It's like she's totally relaxed."

"Should we take her home?"

"There's nothing we can do for her here."

"What do I tell the girls?"

"Mommy's resting?"

"How long will the resting continue? What about her bones and muscles? Won't she start to, I don't know, disintegrate? Go soft? What happens to your muscles when you lie around in bed all day? Deliquesce?"

"Yesterday, she sat up and ate the cheeseburger and fries. You'd be surprised how many comatose patients get all randy when it comes to a simple cheeseburger and fries."

"I have so many questions. I don't know which ones to ask first."

"This will definitely be a bitch when it comes to your insurance. Are you with Blue Cross or Standard? It probably doesn't matter. They'll both be a bitch."

"Her skin feels like bread dough."

"Maybe you should take her home, put her in her favorite stuffed chair, and offer her a big bowl of ice cream. She needs to remember who she is and where she's from. Remind her of her responsibilities. Impress upon her that there's only so much freedom that can be allowed for a person in her condition. Tell her, in no uncertain terms, 'Hey, wake up! You've got a house and family to look after. There's no such thing as a free ride. Especially in times like these.'"

And so they took her back to East Windsor in the Range Rover, and she tried to re-establish her familiarity with furniture. There was the cherry veneer Cascade china cabinet, displaying various primary school art projects that had accumulated over the years: a thickly painted green egg-carton caterpillar with pipe-cleaner antennae and pearl-button eyes; a lumpy, imperfectly glazed ceramic ashtray; a macramé of seagulls on a blue ocean framed by popsicle sticks. Or, next to it, the Louis Philippe-style six-drawer sideboard, on which boxes of crayons and water-soluble paint sticks had established residence like trilobite etchings in a Dead Sea bed. Bookshelves filled with everything but books; closets filled with everything but clothes. And finally, the only furniture that mattered anymore: a king-size four-poster bed in the master bedroom, where Erica lay each afternoon watching daytime television programs while her youngest daughter Stephanie played with dolls on the floor.

"You mustn't wake mother," Stephanie whispered, speaking for one weirdly attired doll after another. And then, in another, harsher voice: "What do you mean, 'Don't wake mother? I wasn't waking Mother. You were waking mother."

It was like every conversation Erica had overheard in her entire life. One person filled with several little persons. And none of them got along.

Meanwhile, daytime television delivered images of flat-screen women in various stages of attractiveness trying to relate to one another about their failures as mothers, daughters, wives, or promoters of "hope" and "change." "I just sat up in bed one day," confessed the third highest-paid over-fifty movie actress in America, "and it hit me like a truck. Just because I made lots of money, and drove around in big fancy cars, it didn't make me happy. At the end of the day, I was just a normal middle-aged woman looking for love, and I wanted that love from somebody other than myself." Often the same people appeared on the same show for several days and weeks at a time—so predictably, in fact, that Erica grew afraid of the TV, as if she were reliving the same irresolvable scenario over and over again. It was like transcendence in reverse.

"I don't know why she can't drive me to school," Molly said. "I don't want you to keep driving me, Daddy. I want Mom to do it. Just like always."

Sometimes Erica sat in the living room and ate her meals off a folding aluminum TV tray that, after every meal, she wiped down with a damp white dishcloth and stored behind the sofa. On something called the DAB display of the console radio, she found a classical station that featured broad sweeping arrangements of strings and reeds, and frequent vocal interruptions by men with foreign accents discussing concepts like "timbre," "melodic control," and "tonal technique."

"Your mom will start driving you to school again very soon," the man who was her husband said. "But you need to be patient. She's taking more time to recover than we'd hoped. Now go in there and ask if she'd like more juice. Then let's all drive out to Friendly's for ice cream. That should perk everybody up."

Back when Sally was born, Erica had driven her around the winding two-lane highways of eastern Connecticut every afternoon until she fell asleep in the car seat, her fat little head slumped brokenly to one side, as if she had been drained of animation. It was the best part of each day—that brief period of inertia that occurred whenever Sally stopped crying, and soft roads unreeled freely beneath the car's tires like a memory of the forgotten life.

"I would just continue driving up and down the same roads, talking to myself about my stupid job, or old friends. And you'd be fast asleep in the back seat, Sal, and it was like you were the best friend I ever had. I could tell you anything and you wouldn't judge me, or take me too seriously, or hold it against me later, like you probably do now. I almost hoped you wouldn't wake up, you'd just carry on sleeping, and I could carry on driving and we'd never go home, just you and me driving down that same road forever."

Since Erica was the only one in the car not shoveling chocolate sauce and ice cream into her mouth with a plastic spoon, she could talk as much as she wanted and they had to listen.

"But why did you tell me those things when I was asleep?" Sally asked. "Why didn't you tell Daddy? Isn't he your partner? Isn't he the person who's supposed to help you overcome personal issues like those you were going through then, or the ones you're going through now?"

"Because Daddy was at work," Erica replied simply. "And when he was home, for some funny reason, I'd forget all the things I wanted to tell him. It was like living two separate lives. The life I lived with your daddy and the life I didn't."

Molly, her face smeared with butterscotch sauce like one of her finger paintings from school, said: "But Daddy's here now. You could tell him what's bothering you now. And why you went to the hospital and came back and didn't seem any better than when you went in. Then you could have ice cream too, Mom, instead of just sitting there, you know. And just talking. Like you don't care what we say back. Like those women you're always watching on TV."

Their car proceeded through arcs of light and smatterings of shadow, as if they were journeying through the frames of an old black-and-white movie. Her husband steered with one hand and, with the other, took occasional succinct bites of his mint chocolate chip cone.

Erica hadn't trusted ice cream since she went away, but the idea of mint chocolate chip was starting to look pretty good about now.

"It's not always that simple," Erica said softly, already losing interest in the explanation she was trying to give. "You'll grow up and understand someday, honey. Or maybe someday I'll grow up enough to explain what I'm trying to say."

She thought about joining a support group, but she didn't know what she needed support for. She had never taken narcotics; her alcohol consumption never extended beyond maybe two glasses of wine per month; she didn't gamble; and, so far as she knew, she had never been abused as a child, not even emotionally. In fact, the worst thing that had ever happened to her, she recalled one morning while browsing through the Yellow Pages for any concept that might snag her attention (Home Decor, Physical Therapy, Pest Control) was the divorce of her parents and her mother's subsequent illness, degeneration, and death from a late-diagnosed breast tumor. But even while the memory of those events still filled Erica's mind with a sense of vacancy and indetermination, they didn't feel like impediments to well-being; they just added up to a flat sequence of disparate memories: administering medication to a hollowed-out woman in a damp bed, fixing prescribed meals, performing awkward back rubs and foot rubs, and driving an increasingly gray and thin woman in her "housecoat" back and forth to radiotherapy in Hartford.

"You're probably right, Erica," Dr. Robinson told her during a free introductory self-assessment at the Wellness Center in Manchester, even though Erica couldn't recall putting forward any proposition that required his approval. "People put too much emphasis on 'overcoming' adversity in our culture—it's very American. Often, we just need the time, commitment, and guidance to explore personal issues on a no-win, no-fee basis. I promise, Erica, that if you want to explore any of these well-being issues, I won't attempt to cure you, or convert you to any pre-existing standards of my own. I don't want to make you better, or improve you; you're already perfect as you are. If things work out, Erica, I'll probably learn as much from these discussions as you will. In fact, I may learn a whole lot more."

On the way home from her first "therapy session" (though Dr. Robinson encouraged her to think of it as a "wellness appreciation interlude"), Erica felt so good she pulled out of the parking lot and went straight to the Buckland Hills Mall, where she purchased jeans and shoes for her daughters, shirts and socks for her husband, and a set of matching palomino white terrycloth towels for the guest bathroom. Everything seemed new, precious, monumental, and preternaturally useful at the mall, as if it had been scrubbed free of the most minute human affinities. The high vaulted ceilings were cathedral-like in their importunity; and the streams of multiracial people in new clothes parading across the wide tessellated concourse all smiled to themselves as they passed, as if they were reflecting on a strangely satisfying dream. I could stay here forever, she thought, standing in front of the huge gaping mouth of Dick's Sporting Goods with her plastic sacks of clothes and home furnishings. I could eat Chinese food every night in the international cafe. The children could visit me on weekends, and I could dress them in brand-new clothes three times a day and put them to bed in those huge inflated goose down-stuffed mattresses at Sears. And the best part would be that I'd never have to cook or clean for any of us ever again.

Everything that needed to be done would be done for me by other people.

For the next two weeks, Erica felt reborn and replenished, inhabited by a soft consonantal glow that wasn't hers, so she didn't have to feel guilty about it. She was just the visitant, the person to whom this sense of satisfaction happened. She couldn't control or regulate or summon it. And she couldn't make it stop, even if she wanted to.

"We need to spend more time together as a family," she announced one morning at a full cooked breakfast—bacon and eggs and pancakes and onion-fried potatoes, just like she cooked for her husband before they were married. "That means eating breakfast and dinner together, and not just running off to our various appointed stations in front of our computers or televisions. It means good, open healthy conversations about what we're looking forward to each day and what we hope to achieve. So, let's start with you, Molly. What are you most looking forward to today? Does it have anything to do with that art project you were working on last night? Or do you mainly look forward to spending time with your friends at recess?"

Molly's mouth was filled with fractured toast and orange marmalade. She looked at her father and then at her sister. By the time she looked at her mother again she was slowly, thoughtfully ingesting the secret laryngeal bolus like a python with a rat.

"I'd like more toast, please," she said. "And more marmalade."

Sally, who sat slightly apart from everyone, laughed inwardly. It was a really annoying habit of Sally's since she turned eleven.

"You can have more toast," Erica said coyly, lifting the plate of buttery toast in one hand and the jar of orange marmalade in the other. "But let's finish the conversation we started—and we started with you, Molly. What's your favorite part about

Thursdays? You don't have to be certain—it's not a quiz. Just say the first thing that pops into your mind."

Molly tested the inside of her mouth with her tongue, as if seeking a button that might produce the flavor of more food.

"Thursdays are like every other day," she said. "Math sciences. Volleyball. English. Most of us don't have any choice in the matter."

Erica smiled at her husband, who was popping a shard of crisp bacon into his mouth.

"Help me, honey," she said.

He kissed the tips of his fingers with mock insouciance, as if he had just tasted the world's best veal at a five-star restaurant. Erica hardly noticed the fragment of muesli on his lapel. He was that confident.

"For example," he said, placing his arm around Molly, "I'm looking forward to our big marketing pow-wow this afternoon, when I get to unveil my strategy for monitoring calls to our customer relations center. I'll emphasize the importance of making every customer's call to our service center a satisfactory experience in the otherwise humdrum monotony of their day." He smiled at Erica, as if they were sharing a double entendre. "And we will do this for all our callers indiscriminately. No matter how nutty some of those callers happen to be.

"What were you thinking the next time it happened?" Dr. Robinson asked. He was taking a long swallow from a tall, opaque stippled plastic drinking glass, and they were sitting in the garden behind his office. Bees drifted around his head like a dubious mobile. The garden boasted several tall glazed ceramic lawn ornaments—a pair of long-beaked amorous storks and a lime green Dutch windmill as tall as Molly. "Can you recreate the scene in your mind? Pretend you're watching yourself in a movie. What's happening in that movie? Do you enjoy watching it?"

It was the easiest thing anybody had ever asked her. It simply meant doing what she had wanted to do for months.

"I was waiting at this red light at this big confusing intersection in Vernon. On one side of me was a huge CVS with a full parking lot; on the other side was this almost derelict-looking Taco Bell. And while I'm waiting, I'm trying to think three steps ahead—one, two, three, the way I do whenever I have to make choices. Like what happens next, and what do I do after that, and after that. First thing, the BP station, high-octane fill up, I need to get into the right-hand lane; unless I don't go to the BP station, which means I have to hit the Shell station on my way home, which means making a left turn at a left-turn signal, and that's always more confusing than simply turning right. Sometimes, I try to think several steps ahead, anticipating multiple-choice possibilities, and I'm concentrating so hard on what to do next that I forget what I'm supposed to be doing now, and then the cars start honking, and eventually I realize they're honking at me. Normally, this is when I panic. I've forgotten something, like maybe even the whole world; and now I have to please that world, but I don't know how. Then I find myself staring again at the big revolving CVS sign on my right, listening to some news bulletin on the radio about an airplane crashing, or a ten-car pile-up on 84. And I just let that person keep honking— maybe they're honking at me, maybe they aren't. I let them keep honking for so long that I don't even notice when they've stopped. I'm just vaguely aware that cars are pulling around to my right and left, like I'm this log in the middle of a busy stream. Meanwhile, I'm still staring at the CVS sign. The CVS sign is still there, and I'm still here. And eventually someone comes over to my window and starts to ask questions, like would you please roll down the window, Ma'am, and can I help you with anything, Ma'am, are you okay, and when I don't answer, they go away for a while and come back and then they're helping me out of the car, I feel like an old woman after a stroke, and they're helping me into the back of an ambulance, all these lights and sirens everywhere. And suddenly I'm somewhere else. And a lot of different things happen that I can't remember. And eventually here I am talking to you, even though I hadn't intended to see you ever again."

Dr. Robinson wore brand-new shoes—pale calfskin with leather tassels. A bit faggy, Erica thought. But they pleased her.

He didn't say anything for a while; it was his method.

"So what happened then?" he asked softly. It was like the softest car horn on the smallest, least-threatening car on the road—a gloaming little VW Beetle, perhaps, or one of those so-called Smart Cars.

"I started to imagine," she continued, "what if I wasn't waiting at this specific intersection anymore, on this specific street corner, staring at this specific CVS. What if this specific place opened up onto somewhere else, like it wasn't any single intersection anymore, but turned into every intersection that ever existed. I found it sort of comforting, like I didn't have to make decisions; I could just go along with these things that happened to me. Like I wasn't this specific woman named Erica Summerfield anymore. I was suddenly a lot bigger and more interesting than myself."

It became impossible for Erica to consider what the words "getting better" meant. Perhaps they were being used ironically, or in an admonishing tone. Sometimes it felt as if they were being dangled in front of her like a carrot in front of a mule, but other times they just seemed like the sort of words people used when they couldn't think of anything else to say. "You have to get better," the man called her husband kept saying. "The girls need their mother." Or the girls might say, "You're getting better, Mom. You look so much better than yesterday." And the doctors—there seemed to be several doctors, and they seemed to agree on almost everything—used the words in so many different contexts that it was hard to keep track of what they meant, or to know if they knew what they meant when they used them. "You won't get better overnight, Erica." "If you want to get better then you have to give this new medication a try." Or: "Getting better" doesn't mean taking a wonder drug or finding a magic bullet, Erica. 'Getting better' is a continual holistic process of maintaining the continually escalating failures of our minds and bodies." Or even: "I know you want to 'get better,' Erica. I know you don't want to make your family suffer when they see you getting worse and worse. And you will 'get better' if you *think* you'll 'get better.' 'Getting better' has a lot to do with how you see yourself and how you see yourself in relation to others."

She wasn't entirely sure when she actually forgot what was happening to her and when she simply stopped paying attention. Sometimes she often found herself lying face down on a sheet of thin white paper in a fluorescent white doctor's office while someone inserted something into her ear or rectum. Or she might find herself in her husband's car being driven home by someone who wasn't her husband, but who seemed to know a lot about him. "Your husband wants you to get a lot of rest," the man or woman might tell her. "Your husband will be home soon." Her children seemed to come and go from various locations with a sort of errant willfulness, wearing bright backpacks and plastic shoes that sparkled with cartoonish fairy-dust, or newly acquired cosmetics and spiky hair. Sometimes, being around other people felt like lying at the bottom of a swimming pool gazing up at figures moving back and forth across the blue surface of water. Sometimes those figures noticed her and pointed and said things to her through the warping melody of water. If Erica held her breath for a while and focused all her attention on the faces gazing down at her, she could even speak back.

"It's all just a period of reflection and rest that my mind's telling me I need," she told them. "I really do want to 'get better,' and I will 'get better' very soon. I don't like being a burden to everyone. I really will start pulling my weight. Now look at me, I'm getting out of bed, I'm putting on my slippers and robe. Pass me my brush there; and I'll even wear a little lipstick today, something simple and not too colorful. Why don't you help me into the kitchen and I'll fix everyone grilled cheese sandwiches and glasses of cold milk. It just takes a little bit more effort these days. The way I see it, our lives go on and on, and every day it takes a little bit more effort to get out of bed and fix grilled cheese sandwiches. But we have to get up and make those grilled cheese sandwiches or we forget everything about ourselves. We develop unhealthy mental outlooks. We start to go away."

The third and final time she left her family it was almost December. They were finishing their McDonald's in the parking lot of the Christmas Tree Shop on a hill overlooking I-84, and the low afternoon winter sun reflected off cars and hood ornaments spread out in the parking lot like an aluminum lake. It hadn't snowed that winter, and the cold, bright air was like a realization. The girls were getting milkshakes and secret sauce was all over their best school blouses while they argued about priorities. One of them was supposed to go first but the other one hadn't gone first because she had gone first the previous time. Just ask Daddy. Slow-moving elderly white couples cascaded past their windows in time-lapse photography. Latin-looking couples, and pale Anglo-looking couples and Asian-looking couples pushing huge steel shopping carts loaded with bushy green artificial fir trees, cardboard cases of broken cookies, dented boxes of plastic-sealed pound cakes and pancake mixes, spools of copper wire, and green garden hoses. It was like the desultory tail end of some organized looting expedition at the end of the world. All that stuff coming out and nothing going in except people with wallets and credit cards and children bickering over chocolates.

"Bed sheets for the guest room," her husband said, dabbing the corners of his mouth with the little finger of his left hand. He loved McDonald's, but he hated getting it on his face. "Christmas cards, a school lunch box for Molly, plastic forks for the party, and then get the hell out. If there's one place I hate, it's the goddamn Christmas Tree Shop."

Erica didn't hate it; it helped her identify the passing of time. She had witnessed its many incarnations over the decades as a gigantic furniture outlet, a gigantic remaindered book outlet, and a gigantic remaindered clothing outlet; one year they had even sold actual Christmas trees in the parking lot, bound like hostages in wire mesh. It was the only place so big and busy that other people didn't stop long enough to recognize her—parents of other children, receptionists at orthodontists and dermatologists, former neighbors and paperboys. You couldn't avoid them, but you didn't have to talk to them, either. Everybody was in a hurry to get out of everybody else's way.

"Just stick together," her husband said. "Don't anybody get lost. Not like last time."

Erica was holding Molly's hand, and Molly was holding onto the right side of the shopping cart.

"Stephanie? Where the hell—oh, there you are. Don't you need a pencil case and art brushes? Look, these are ninety-nine cents."

It felt like entering a crowded harbor in the middle of the night, looming angular stacks of boxes hoving into view and out again, broken objects squealing against the hull like rubber buoys and then swinging sternward into another barely open pathway. Erica spotted huge bins filled with plastic wreaths and frizzly tinsel and afro combs and laundry detergents and fabric softeners and generically labeled beer. It felt like getting lost in an episode of *The Simpsons*. At any moment, she expected to stumble upon croaky Marge with her leaning monument of blue hair.

"Oh, look," her husband said. "Chamomile and Herb Conditioner for Oily Hair." It wasn't the worst thing he had ever said to her, but it was the last thing she had expected.

Time and perception went all diffuse and limp. She watched bins of dented bargain opportunities turn away from her like faces on a bus, and after a while she realized it wasn't *them* turning away from *her*, but *her* turning away from *them*. Something closed up inside her. It wasn't a door or a window; it was a box.

She was putting something away in a box; it was hers and she was putting it away, and suddenly she found herself walking alone past huge glass walls, leather sofas, and weirdly elongated vanity tables, totemic upright rolls of carpeting and linoleum and wallpaper. It was like transecting the weird history of commerce, she thought, moving towards wide windows and vistas of freeways and trees and multiply gleaming waterfall-like cars and hood ornaments. She couldn't see her family, but she could hear them far away across the flat distance. With her and then not with her. Maybe they were closing up boxes inside themselves. Maybe it was like this for everybody.

"I think Mom's having an episode."

"Honey? Where are you going? You have to stop this behavior right now."

"I think we should call Dr. Robinson."

"Who's Dr. Robinson?"

"Some therapist Mom met at the hospital."

Her arms were being scratched by leaves and twigs and branches, and her feet were sliding on something soft and loamy, and something else snagged her shoulder, the sleeve of her sweater, she couldn't make it stop. There were more leaves everywhere, red and amber and gold and riddled with rust and mud and moss, you just couldn't make the world hold together long enough to understand it sometimes. But if you were lucky and persistent and smart, you could hold yourself together long enough for it to understand you. Just keep moving. Carry on through whatever restrains you. Otherwise it might keep you; it might win; it might take you back to the Christmas Tree Shop over and over again. And next time, you wouldn't have any choice. They'd make you stay until it was actually Christmas.

◆

Terence Young

WHAT WE KEEP

The beat,
the faith,
the home fires burning.

The people down,
the good work up,
the undesirables out,
the grass off,
the straight and narrow path to,
all of it under wraps.

The books,
the peace,
the house,
the goal,
certain fish,
bad company,
our heads
when all about us
are losing theirs.

The change, we say,
generous over nothing.

Promises, sometimes, and
secrets even when they no longer matter.

Our opinions to ourselves.

Time, if we understand music,
quiet, if we don't.

Our children safe,
our hands off the money,
our friends close etc.,
a little something on the side.

An eye out for strangers,
a copy for our files,
our shirt on and
our big mouth shut.

Fit, if we can,
our fingers crossed.

Our cards to our chest,
a straight face
when it all goes sideways.

Our cool,
our lips sealed,
an open mind
and our nose
to the grindstone.

The ball rolling,
the wolf from the door.
our powder dry.

◆

BOOK REVIEWS

Review by Gerald F. Sweeney

WHAT ELSE YOU GOT? FREELANCING IN RADIO

By Mary Saner
2019, Head to Wind Publishing, ISBN 978-1-939632-07-4;
135 pages

Some of us grew up under the antenna of Radio, the magic box that reached out of its decorated woodwork and dusty cloth to touch our imaginations. Gathering in the sounds, thanks to Tesla and Marconi, of the world around us.

We remember running home in the winter dusk to hear the latest episode of *I Love A Mystery* or *Jack Armstrong, All-American Boy.* Or spreading out in the living room with our parents to listen to the Jack Benny and Fred Allen comedy hours. [Fred Allen joke – "Most people spend the whole week sewing their oats, and then go to church on Sunday and pray for crop failure."]

Or lying in bed at night in the dark with the radio on listening to the big bands playing live across the country—Glenn Miller in the Café Rouge in the Hotel Pennsylvania, in New York, or Tommy Dorsey from the Aragon Ballroom, in Chicago, or, if really late, for Benny Goodman, at the Mark Hopkins, in San Francisco. Some of us recall listening to the radio that bright Sunday morning in December of 1941, when the Japanese bombed Pearl Harbor. Or Edward R. Murrow's wartime reporting for CBS—*"This is London Calling"*—his voice crackling through the Atlantic storms, describing the burning city of the Blitz.

Today, many of us still rely on National Public Radio to forage through the facts of our complicated world.

Mary Saner's book on broadcasting is like riffling through a rummage sale of old-time pleasures. Picking through a stack of books, you might pass up this hodge-podge castaway—single-page vignettes, homemade family pictures in the middle, pieces on motorcycle etiquette, paeans to Chestertown and Echo Hill. *What else you got?*

If you neglect the urge to take her book home, you might miss a good read.

Trust her. She's a radio pro—the kind you believe in.

Ms. Saner bases her radio stories on clear, clean scripts and a bemused take on human foibles and tribal diversity. She plies the complications of life with NPR-like stories that makes you revel in the eccentric jumble of life.

There are stories about Bill Clinton, mall walking, a dinosaur museum, fireworks, near death experiences—all things considered by a straight-shooting mistress of ceremonies with a wide-eyed, independent view.

In the process, the reader learns about running a radio station, freelancing, learning how to communicate, how to conduct an interview, how to edit tape, how to handle agents and narrating a story. Plus, sample scripts.

Buried beneath the digital age lies the primacy of radio. Mary Saner understands its strength and shares her stories with polish and style.

◆

Review by Harold O. Wilson

SAFELY TO EARTH:
THE MEN AND WOMEN WHO BROUGHT THE ASTRONAUTS HOME

By Jack Clemons
2018, University of Florida Press; ISBN: 978-0-8130-5602-9;
264 pages

July 20, 2019, marked the 50th anniversary of the day Neil Armstrong and Buzz Aldrin became the first humans to land on the moon. In support, Command Module Pilot Mike Collins orbited overhead. Jack Clemons' book, *Safely to Earth: The Men and Women Who Brought the Astronauts Home,* reminds us of the special character, commitment, and intelligence of the men and women who worked to achieve President Kennedy's ten-year goal of putting a man on the moon and bringing him and his two mates home safely. Clemons is a former lead engineer on NASA's Apollo Program. He was also senior engineering software manager on the Space Shuttle Program and part of the mission control backroom team that supported the NASA flight controllers on both the return of the Apollo 11 crew from the first moon landing and the rescue of the Apollo 13 crew.

In this well written technical description of the development of the Apollo and Space Shuttle programs, Clemons has given us a very personal view of the men and women at NASA who developed both programs. "Failure is not an option" was the attitude at NASA when Clemons joined the program in 1968.

Unfortunately, this culture grew out of the tragedy of the Apollo fire in 1967 that killed Gus Grissom, Ed White, and Roger

Chaffee. The independent investigation that was undertaken found that the tragedy could have been prevented. It shouldn't have happened.

NASA worked diligently, Clemons writes, *to change their culture from top to bottom of the organization. No longer would one of their own die because someone who was supposed to be supporting them had lost single-minded focus on safety and meticulous attention to every detail.*

Even though Clemons goes on to describe in brilliant and engaging terms the technical development that made the Apollo and Shuttle programs successful, the subtext of his book is really the commitment to excellence of the thousands of NASA engineers and support staff that mirrored the nation's commitment to achieve Kennedy's goal of a man on the moon before the end of the decade.

Was it all worth it—the huge cost of both programs and the needless loss of fourteen astronauts? Of course, there is no way to put a cost on the loss of human life, but there are values that accrue to the future that are beyond measure.

Clemons tells us: *Beyond all the science and technology research, and placement of numerous commercial, military, and civilian payloads and satellites in orbit, these two achievements alone, ISS [The International Space Station] and Hubble, were realized only because the Space Shuttle was there to bring them into existence. These are marvels never before witnessed, and only barely imagined, in the long history of humanity. How does one place a value on the immeasurable?* These two programs literally opened the door to a future beyond imagination.

Why go to the moon? Beyond the technology, there was also an intangible gift from Kennedy's goal. Even though the nation was being torn apart by the war in Vietnam and in the throes of the civil rights movement, we were still bound together as one people by this common venture. Kennedy himself gave the answer:

"We choose to go to the moon in this decade and do the other things, not because they are easy, but because they are hard, because that goal will serve to organize and measure the best of our energies and skills, because that challenge is one that we are willing to accept, one we are unwilling to postpone, and one which we intend to win..."

In his excellent book, Clemons has caught not only the technological capacity of the nation but the vigor and spirit of that time as well; a time in which the nation dared to dream big dreams and then set itself the improbable task of making them a reality.

◆

Review by Joan Cooper

THE ANIMATORS

By Kayla Rae Whitaker

2017, Random House; ISBN: 978-0-8128-8930-4; 384 pages

The friendship between two creative women throws sparks in *The Animators*, a debut novel by Kayla Rae Whitaker. Reminiscent of the troubled friendship between Phineas and Gene Forrester, in *A Separate Peace*, the reader is thrust into the perspective through the first-person narration of a misfit college freshman, Sharon Kay Kisses. Sharon is an insecure Southerner from Kentucky who earned an art scholarship at a second-tier northern college filled with snobby white-privilege and oddballs. Enter the mad genius of the art department—white trash Mel Vaught— talented, rebellious, and impulsive. Together, they become partner animators.

The initial meeting sets a pattern between them—creative bursts, lots of alcohol, pot, other drugs, and carousing. Sharon's total acceptance of her partner's behavior, including the self-destructive, is unnerving but realistic. Sharon is enthralled with Mel's daring and talent. Like in *A Separate Peace*, Mel's doomed character is built for immolation—a brilliant flare like the fireworks she loves. A self-described dyke, Mel dresses in suits instead of cocktail dresses like Sharon. She cuts off her hair, drinks *tussin* (cough syrup) shakes and chain smokes. Yes, it's a bit overdone, but Mel offers a foil for Sharon's insecure femininity as she serial dates or obsesses over lackluster guys.

Whitaker fast forwards ten years after college. Mel and Sharon have created a number of animated shorts, done some edgy advertising work, and produced a movie that earns them a sizable grant. Success flings them into disaster. Whitaker takes her time building each foreshadowing moment with binge drinking, sloppy public appearances, and an onslaught of drugs and sex.

Sharon experiences a stroke on the way to a conference in Florida. Whitaker's depiction of a subarachnoid hemorrhagic stroke through Sharon's eyes is genius—each painful stage is raw and told in short bursts of rich imagery. Thrusting aside their estrangement, Mel sticks with Sharon throughout the ordeal including rehabilitation. The event provides a healing time between the brilliance of their first movie and the damage it unleashed on Mel.

As partners, Sharon and Mel are self-absorbed by their exfoliation of the past that they do not pause to worry about the collateral damage they inflict. Mel's mother is killed after the release of their movie *Nashville Combat,* which features her. Yet, they use the most painful part of Sharon's life as a focal point for the second movie, *Irrefutable Love.*

Written in a fast-action, jumpy rhythm, the plot moves like the animated films that dominate the thoughts of the main characters. Told through the perspective of the seemingly more stable of the two, the reader rides on Sharon Kisses' hyperawareness and insecurity. The duo is self-contained creatively and professionally—more like an old married couple—but there is no sexual relationship. The drive for sex breaks them apart—Mel into destructive and fleeting hook-ups and Sharon into unfulfilling surface relationships.

Like Fitzgerald's *The Great Gatsby,* Whitaker encapsulates her generation and exposes the hedonism of the millennials. Whitaker immerses the reader into the world of the artist who is forced out of the comfortable interior world into the public world. The foibles of brilliant misfits of the same generation, such as Elon Musk or Mark Zuckerberg, fuel social media feeding frenzies. Whitaker depicts the struggle of an introverted intellectual exposed to public scrutiny. Overexposure strips away the sensitivity needed for art. Sharon Kisses is decimated by the end of the novel—she loses Mel, her other relationships, and her health. Whitaker's debut novel delivers a warning about the dangers of self-absorption and the danger of excess.

◆

Review by Suzi Peel

ELIZABETH GILMAN, CRUSADER FOR JUSTICE

By Ross Jones

2018, Secant Publishing; ISBN:978-1-944962-53-1; 265 pages

It is fitting to review *Elisabeth Gilman, Crusader for Justice* for the *Delmarva Review*: a biography of a little-known Marylander, by an author from Baltimore, and published on Maryland's Eastern Shore.

Ross Jones found his sources at Johns Hopkins where he was VP and Secretary of the University. Quotes from Elisabeth Gilman's early writings, and photographs, enliven our sense of her presence.

It speaks to her times (1867-1950) that sources—and therefore the author—ascribe to the men in her life the formation of Elisabeth's progressive ideas, her enduring commitments and skilled interventions. Yet she was a pioneer and leader in all she undertook.

Jones first explores Gilman's personal life in her formative years: her father figures prominently in her childhood, informal education in overseas travel and attendance at his engagements as the first president of JHU. The reader is eager to learn more of the exploits that make Gilman's life the worthy subject of this biography.

Thereafter the author makes much of Elisabeth Gilman's relationship with the charismatic Reverend Mercer Green Johnston. Beyond a meeting of the minds and a melding of engagement as American and world citizens working daily for the greater good, there are intimations of an emotional bond between Green, a married man, and Gilman, the woman who never married.

"She is at the forefront of every worth-while cause in our community."[1]

This reader finds it more important to note that Gilman is clearly portrayed as anchored in her family and in the Episcopal Church, wedded to "advocacy for economic and social justice for America's working people." On that solid base she built her career.

In the war effort in France from 1917 to 1919 in her fifties, she served thousands of meals to men arriving from the front; she was soon given more responsibility in the YMCA using her organizational and leadership skills to great advantage.

Returning to the United States, she found her level in the national Committee of Forty-Eight. It aimed high: creating a new political party centered on social needs, eschewing both parties' growing conservatism and also the rise of communism.

Her sympathies lay with Socialism, but she never joined the party, working steadfastly within the powerful Social Gospel. She planted numerous seeds: advocating for strikers and raising funds for them, condemning child labor, supporting Social Security, promoting peace and more.

Indefatigable, she ran for office several times in Baltimore starting in 1935: for Governor, Senator, Sheriff and Mayor. This enabled her to speak widely about the need for social reforms and improvements in governance.

She described her platform as

---

[1] P. 210 S.B. Charles letter to *The Baltimore Sun*

... A workable peace within the present framework of the United Nations cooperation, a peace with a primary economic basis.

... Emphasis on Civil Liberties.

... Full employment.

... Equal rights for Negroes.

In 1938 the Socialists nominated her as their candidate for the U.S. Senate.

In 1942 the press dismissed her run for Sheriff describing her as "a small woman of 75."

1945, when she ran for Governor, she knew the purpose was to keep a Socialist on the ballot.

She was never returned to office, but her campaigns maintained the focus on solidarity for labor and for democracy.

The *Sun* in a 1945 editorial wrote of Gilman, "Unwearied and undiscouraged" she canvasses "with a hopefulness in which there is no atom of self-seeking or self-deception".

As we highlight achievements of strong women fostering equality and justice, Jones's biography introducing us to Elisabeth Gilman makes a timely contribution with the story of a bold activist.

◆

Review by Crystal Brandt

LISTENING IN: ECHOES AND ARTIFACTS OF MARYLAND'S MOTHER COUNTY

By Meredith Taylor
2018, George F. Thompson Publishing;
ISBN: 978-1-938086-55-7; 265 pages

Merideth Taylor's stunning new book about St. Mary's County opens with Lucille Clifton's "mulberry fields" gently turning our attention to curiosity about what we think we see. With *Listening In: Echoes and Artifacts from Maryland's Mother County* (GFT Publishing, 2018*)*, Taylor reimagines the lives of others and gives voice to walls that talk in a lost language.

The subject may be fading lives and falling structures, but Taylor's form is distinctly alive and modern -- equal parts photo essay, fiction, and oral history -- reminiscent of social media but without the ego. Taylor provides the image, story, and dialogue that work together to satisfy our shrinking attention span and growing appetite for information. Before we know it, we are engaged, our memories enhancing and underscoring what's on the page.

If the images of decay seem foreign and obsolete, Taylor's skillful dialogue feels familiar and necessary, like we've heard it before but need to hear it again. The houses are more than the sum of wood and plaster; they are part of the fabric of historical context surrounding what it means to be human, to establish one's self here, in this place, at that time. This subject and structure of *Listening In* also remind us of our role in the plod of creation and destruction: we rally and sweat to clear the ground; nature, with its slow comfort, reclaims space with grace and ease. No instant gratification here; nature and Taylor both work in nuance and subtlety.

Taylor weaves a regional history of personal narratives using threads real and imagined, and her treatment radiates respect for her subjects and their honesty. While the stories themselves are fabrications, Taylor based them on actual incidents that she learned about from oral histories and her research in St. Mary's County history.

Taylor's flourishes of precise detail—references to stuffed ham, spearing tobacco, maritime life, wisteria and kudzu – never cross into sentimentality or nostalgia. Instead, these details hint at the points where we intersect and divide, where race, class, gender, and more whisper about family, spirit, and identity, about time, change, and what it means to grow, thrive, survive, and die.

The cinematic structure of the book suggests a historical arc, fading in before Emancipation, fading out sometime today or is it last year, perhaps next week. By the last page, we almost have a sense of progress past its prime and on the verge of wearing out its welcome. Almost: the final scene of baptism offers a promise hope and continuity.

Listening In dovetails what *is* with what *was* and makes the past present. Within these pages, we are more than readers -- we observe and participate. We feel as if these stories could go on forever even as each scene closes.

"You folks aren't put off by those old ghost stories, are you," the book asks. On the contrary, Ms. Taylor—we can't put them down.

◆

Review by James O'Sullivan

CHESAPEAKE REQUIEM:
A YEAR WITH THE WATERMEN OF VANISHING TANGIER ISLAND

By Earl Swift
2018, Day St, a William Morrow imprint,
ISBN: 978-0-06-266139-5; 434 pages

As a reporter for the Virginian-Pilot, Earl Swift first visited and wrote about Tangier Island in 1999. From 2015 to 2017, he visited Tangier frequently, taking up an extended full-time residence during the crab and oyster seasons in 2016. Swift reports on this experience in "Chesapeake Requiem," a beautifully written and prophetic story of the people of Tangier, their town, their way of life, their history, and their imperiled future.

Tangier Island, a 789-acre speck of land and marsh, rises only a few feet out of Chesapeake Bay. Captain John Smith is said to have "discovered" the island in 1608, and Tangier has been inhabited since 1666. Today, about 480 people live in three neighborhoods. They make their living on the water, producing one of the largest blue crab harvests in Chesapeake country. Many families have called Tangier home for generations.

The island is sinking and, without intervention, will soon disappear, as have other formerly inhabited Bay islands. James Island is abandoned and reduced to a shoal. Sharps Island vanished in 1963. The last house on Holland Island collapsed into the Bay in 2010. Tangier Island and Smith Island are the only remaining offshore inhabited islands in Chesapeake Bay.

Swift captures the life and pulse of the community as he visits homes, joins church services, celebrates a high school graduation, witnesses a wedding, and attends a funeral. He tours abandoned houses and discovers bones in a cemetery uprooted by storms. He becomes a fly on the wall in the Situation Room, a gathering spot for watermen, where he listens to conversations about storms, crabbing and politics. The mayor of Tangier, a lifelong waterman, becomes his guide to the inner workings of the crab and oyster businesses and to the complex beauty of the Tangier Sound ecosystem.

What are the people of Tangier like? They are at work on the water before the sun rises. They speak a distinct dialect. "Hard" sounds like "howard," "island" like "oyalind." Their story telling and humor is by indirection, something they refer to as talking backwards, as in the following conversation in the Situation Room: "'I know some people who never take a pill,' he said. 'I think they're the only thing keeping me *alive*.' He shook his head. 'Pills, I ain't took none of them.'"

They are well aware that they are literally "losing ground" every day, but they attribute this loss to natural forces of erosion rather than human-driven climate change. Their bond with the island is so deep that Swift refers to them as "creatures of place." Swift acknowledges that "[t]hey can be harshly judgmental, contemptuous of authority, dismissive of book learning..." "But," he adds, "they're also remarkably resilient, hardworking, and courageous. They are willing to die for one another. Their faith is unshakable, and their optimism, wondrous."

Tangier Island is a harbinger of things to come for coastal communities. As Swift puts it: "Tangier Island is not alone in its struggle with the sea. It's just further along in the battle and the worst for it." Given finite resources, Swift raises the question of how we decide which places are worth saving.

In the end, Swift takes a stand with Tangier. "[A]s one who has been allowed, for however brief a time, to pretend he's a Tangierman, it would pain me deeply to see the place disappear.

I'd hate to see its people forced to the mainland. I'd mourn losing this direct connection to the past. The world would be a little less interesting without it."

Swift came to live on Tangier in order to discover what would be lost if the island were to sink beneath the rising waters of Chesapeake Bay. The residents welcomed him and gave him intimate access to their community. Earl Swift has repaid their generous hospitality with a realistic, empathetic and elegiac rendering of their world.

◆

CONTRIBUTING WRITERS

Jacob M. Appel (New York) is the author of three literary novels including *Millard Salter's Last Day* (Simon & Schuster/Gallery, 2017), seven short story collections, an essay collection, a cozy mystery, a thriller, and a volume of poems. He teaches at the Mount Sinai School of Medicine.
Website: www.jacobmappel.com.

Cameron Blais (Rhode Island and Massachusetts) is a fiction writer from Lincoln, Rhode Island. Currently, he studies at Harvard Divinity School and lives in Allston-Brighton, Massachusetts. He has worked alternatively as a bouncer, an aquarium assistant, and a pediatric mental health counselor. *Was*, his flash fiction in this issue, is his first published story.

Ace Boggess (West Virginia) is the author of four books of poetry, most recently *I Have Lost the Art of Dreaming It So* (Unsolicited Press, 2018) and *Ultra Deep Field* (Brick Road, 2017). His work appears in *Notre Dame Review, River Styx, Rattle, Bellingham Review*, and other journals. He lives in Charleston, West Virginia.

Judith Bowles (District of Columbia) is a poet and her poetry collections include *The Gatherer* (Turning Point, 2014), and *Unlocatable Source* (Turning Point 2019). She has an MFA from American University where she taught creative writing. Bowles was a poet in residence at the Bloedel Reserve (August 2019). Her poems have appeared in *Delmarva Review, Gargoyle,*

Ekphrastic Review, Innisfree Journal of Poetry, Better than Starbucks, and *Cobalt Review.* Her current poetry workshop, guided by David Keplinger, of the Creative Writing Program at American University, has published an anthology, *Such Friends as These.*

Scott Bradfield (California and UK) is a novelist, short story writer, and critic. His works include *The History of Luminous Motion, Dazzle Resplendent: Adventures of a Misanthropic Dog,* and *The People Who Watched Her Pass By.* His writing has appeared in *Triquarterly, The Magazine of Fantasy & Science Fiction, The New York Times Book Review, The Los Angeles Times Book Review, The Baffler,* and numerous "best of" anthologies. His stories and essays are forthcoming in *The Weird Fiction Review, The New Statesman,* and *Flash Fiction Magazine.* Bradfield lives in California and London.

Crystal Brandt (Maryland) is a poet and songwriter in Southern Maryland. She teaches writing at St. Mary's College of Maryland and serves as the poetry editor of *EcoTheo Review,* a journal that explores the crossroads of ecology and faith. Website: www.crystal-brandt.com.

Sherry Chappelle (Delaware) won the 2011 Dogfish Head Poetry Prize. In 2016, she was named an Emerging Artist in Literature: Poetry by the Delaware Division of the Arts. She writes from her home in Rehoboth Beach, sings soprano in choruses of the Messiah with the Southern Delaware Chorale, but she says she never developed the ability to play the guitar with her teeth.

Roberto Christiano (Virginia) won the 2010 Fiction Prize from *The Northern Virginia Review.* He received a Pushcart Prize nomination for poetry in *Prairie Schooner.* His poetry is anthologized in the *Gavea-Brown Book of Portuguese-American*

Poetry (Brown University). His chapbook, *Port of Leaving,* was published by Finishing Line Press. In addition to the *Delmarva Review*, his writing is forthcoming in *The Northern Virginia Review*. Website: robertochristiano.weebly.com.

Anne Colwell (Delaware) is the Delmarva Review Poetry Editor and associate professor of English at University of Delaware. She writes poetry, fiction, and nonfiction and teaches all three genres in her classes. She is also a staff member of the Bread Loaf Writer's Workshop. Her poetry collections include *Believing Their Shadows* (2011) and *Mother's Maiden Name* (2013). In addition to *Delmarva Review*, her writing has been published in *Bellevue Literary Review, California Quarterly, Southern Poetry Review, The Madison Review*, and other publications.

Gail Braune Comorat (Delaware) is a founding member of Rehoboth Beach Writers' Guild. She is the author of *Phases of the Moon* (Finishing Line Press) and a collaborating poet for *Walking the Sunken Boards* (2019, Pond Road Press). Her work has appeared in *Gargoyle, Grist, Mudfish, Philadelphia Stories*, and *The Widows' Handbook*. She has been an active member of several writing groups in Lewes, Delaware.

Joan Drescher Cooper (Maryland) is a novelist, teacher, and poet. Her collection of poetry, published by Finishing Line Press, *Birds Like Me* debuted in October 2019. Her novels include *Finding Home at Lilac Hill, Return to Lilac Hill*, and *Lilac Hill Folly* (Salt Water Media). She is a member of Salisbury Rabbit Gnaw Writers, Maryland Writers' Association, and the Eastern Shore Writers Association.

Daun Daemon's (North Carolina) stories have appeared in *Fiction Fix, Southern Women's Review, The Dead Mule, Literally Stories,* and other publications. She has published poetry most recently in *Typishly, Dime Show Review, Third*

Wednesday, and *Remington Review.* She teaches scientific communication at North Carolina State University and lives in Raleigh with her husband and four cats.

Barbara Westwood Diehl (Maryland) is founding editor of *The Baltimore Review.* Her fiction and poetry have been published in a variety of journals, including *Delmarva Review, Quiddity, Potomac Review* (Best of the 50), *Measure, Little Patuxent Review, SmokeLong Quarterly, Gargoyle, Superstition Review, Rivet, Per Contra, Thrush Poetry Journal, Tishman Review, The MacGuffin,* and *Ellery Queen Mystery Magazine.*

Max Roland Ekstrom's (Vermont) poetry has appeared recently in *Hubbub* and *Confrontation,* among other journals. His work is anthologized in *Except for Love: New England Poets Inspired by Donald Hall.* He holds an MFA in Creative Writing from Emerson College. He lives in Vermont with his wife and three children.

R. H. Emmers (Pennsylvania) has worked as a journalist, private investigator and a crisis communications consultant. But he says he finally succumbed to his first love, fiction writing. His stories have appeared in a number of literary magazines, and he's writing a novel. He lives in the northern Pennsylvania woods with his wife Rosetta and dog Casey.

Irene Fick's (Delaware) second collection of poetry, *The Wild Side of the Window,* was published by Main Street Rag (2018). Her first, *The Stories We Tell* (The Broadkill Press), received a first-place award from the National Federation of Press Women. Her poems have been published in *Poet Lore, Gargoyle* and *The Broadkill Review.*

Charlene Fischer-Jehle (Delaware) taught physical education and health in Bethesda for thirty-five years before retiring to the

Delaware shore. She began writing a book of letters to her daughter before she was born and continued until her 21st birthday. Now, she says she is pursuing writing more seriously and has published in the *Washington Post*.

Marvin Jonathan Flores (Virginia) is a first generation American whose parents emigrated from El Salvador during the Salvadoran civil war. He began writing at the age of nineteen, shortly after his best friend died in a car accident. Flores currently resides near Washington D.C. in Falls Church, Virginia, where many of his stories and poems take place.

Katherine Gekker's (Virginia) poems have been published in *Delmarva Review, Little Patuxent Review, Broadkill Review, Poetry South, Apple Valley Review*, and other journals. Two composers have set her poems to music: "…to Cast a Shadow Again" by Eric Ewazen, and "Chasing the Moon Down" by Carson Cooman. Her collection *In Search of Warm* was published by Glass Lyre Press (2019).

Meredith Davies Hadaway (Maryland) is a featured writer in this issue of *Delmarva Review*. She is the author of three poetry collections: *Fishing Secrets of the Dead, The River is a Reason*, and *At The Narrows* (winner of the 2015 Delmarva Book Prize for Creative Writing). She holds an MFA in Poetry from Vermont College of Fine Arts. Hadaway is a former Rose O'Neill Writer-in-Residence and chief marketing officer at Washington College.

Alamgir Hashmi (New York) has published numerous books of poetry and literary criticism and has taught as a university professor in North America, Europe, and Asia. In addition to *Delmarva Review*, his work has appeared in anthologies and journals including *Poetry Review, New Letters, Prairie Schooner, Oxford Poetry, The New Quarterly, New Statesman, Chicago Review, Contemporary Review, Edinburgh Review, Paris Voices*, and *Connecticut Review*. He is a Pushcart Prize nominee and a Rockefeller Fellow.

Christine Higgins (Maryland) has been the recipient of a Maryland State Arts Council award for both poetry and non-fiction. Her work has appeared in *Poetry East, Earth's Daughters* and *Naugatuck River Review*. She is co-author of *In the Margins* (Cherry Grove, 2017). Her new poetry collection, *Hallow*, is set for publication in March 2020 (Cherry Grove).

Mark Jacobs (Virginia) has published five books and more than 130 stories in magazines including *The Atlantic, Playboy, The Baffler, The Iowa Review, Evergreen Review,* and *Delmarva Review*. His stories are forthcoming in *The Hudson Review* and several other publications. Website: markjacobsauthor.com.

Chris Jansen (Georgia) says he has been a nursing home janitor, a paramedic, an IT guy, and, up until recently, a very dedicated heroin addict. He currently lives in Athens, Georgia, where he teaches boxing and cares for a disinterested guinea pig named Poozybear. He has a degree in molecular biology from the University of Georgia.

Marilyn R. Janus (Delaware) was raised on the New Jersey shore and now lives on the Delaware shore. Words and music have guided her life as a church musician, a traveler and a writer of memoirs and poems. *Firewalking*, in this edition of *Delmarva Review*, is her first published short story.

Sylvia Karman (Maryland) is a writer in Ellicott City who hikes whenever and wherever possible. She says that like the loons, she and her husband return every spring to the Adirondacks to hike and kayak until mid-autumn. Retired from a career in public policy, she is completing her first novel. Her poems in this edition of *Delmarva Review* are her first poems in publication.

Kerry Leddy (Maryland) is co-chair of *New Directions in Writing*. Her essays have appeared in: *The New York Times, The Washington Post, Zone 3, Washingtonian Magazine, Voice, Intima, The Account Magazine*. She is co-author of psychology books: *Wearing my Tutu to Analysis and Other Stories* (2011) and *The Therapist in Mourning: From the Faraway Nearby* (2013) both from Columbia University Press, and *Who's Behind the Couch* (2017, Routledge). She is currently writing a novel, *Ghostmother*. Website: www.drkerrymalawista.com.

Christopher Linforth (Oklahoma) has published nonfiction in *The Millions, Whiskey Island, The Dallas Review, South Dakota Review*, and other literary magazines.

Barbara Lockhart (Maryland) received her MFA from Vermont College and is the recipient of two Maryland State Arts Council awards for excerpts from her novel, *Requiem for a Summer Cottage,* and her short stories. Her historical novel, *Elizabeth's Field*, received an Independent Publishers Book Silver Medal Award, and her collection of short stories, *The Night is Young*, won finalist in the National Indie Excellence Awards. She is the author of four children's books as well as a manual on children's literature used nationwide, *Read to me, Talk with me.*

Caroline Maun (Michigan) is associate professor of English at Wayne State University, in Detroit. She teaches creative writing and American literature and is the Interim Chair. Her poetry publications include *The Sleeping* (Marick Press, 2006), *What Remains* (Main Street Rag, 2013), and two chapbooks, *Cures and Poisons* and *Greatest Hits*, both published by Puddinghouse Press. Her poetry has appeared in *The Bear River Review, The MacGuffin, Third Wednesday, Peninsula Poets,* and *Eleven*. Website: www.carolinemaun.com.

CONTRIBUTING WRITERS

Kristina Morgan (Arizona) received an MFA in creative writing and poetry from Arizona State University. Her creative nonfiction essay *Hospital Visit Number 19* appeared in *Delmarva Review* in 2017 and was nominated for a Pushcart Prize. Her poetry has appeared in *LocustPoint, Open Minds*, and *The Awakening Review*. Her book-length memoir *Mind Without a Home: A Memoir of Schizophrenia* was published by Hazelden in 2013. She lives in Scottsdale with her two cats, Grams and Annie.

James Norcliffe (New Zealand) has published nine collections of poetry including *Shadow Play* (2013) and *Dark Days at the Oxygen Café* (VUP, 2016). Recent work has appeared in *Landfall, Spillway, The Cincinnati Review, Salamander, Gargoyle* and *Flash Fiction International* (Norton, 2015). A new collection *Deadpan* (Otago University Press) will be published in 2019.

James O'Sullivan (Maryland) is Fiction Co-Editor of the *Delmarva Review*. He received an M.A. in writing from Johns Hopkins University and a Ph.D. in English literature from the University of Connecticut. He has worked as an attorney, teacher, and science writer. His fiction and poetry have appeared in *Sheepshead Review, Regardie's Magazine*, and the *Laurel Review*.

Brice Particelli (New York) is a 2017 NYSCA/NYFA Artist Fellow in Nonfiction with the New York Foundation for the Arts and the co-editor of *America Street: A Multicultural Anthology of Stories* (Persea Books, 2019). He is currently writing his first novel, *Nakimoa*, a love story set in Kiribati. He earned his Ph.D. from Columbia University and teaches at Pace University. Website: www.briceparticelli.com.

Suzi Peel (Maryland) is an editor on the Eastern Shore, following careers in education and global public health in Europe, Africa and the USA. As a collaborative editor, she assists local poets, authors, and researchers in gaining a greater mastery of craft and creativity in developing their work. She has edited several award-winning books and looks forward to new collaborations.

Simon Perchik (New York) is an attorney whose poetry has appeared in *The New Yorker, The Nation, Partisan Review, Delmarva Review,* and elsewhere. His writing is known for his highly personal, non-narrative style. His poetry collection *Hands Collected* was long listed for the 2000 National Book Award for Poetry. Website: http://www.simonperchik.com.

Ron Riekki's (California) books in 2019 include: *Posttraumatic: A Memoir* (Hoot 'n' Waddle), *Undocumented: Great Lakes Poets Laureate on Social Justice* (Michigan State University Press, with Andrea Scarpino), and *The Many Lives of The Evil Dead: Essays on the Cult Film Franchise* (McFarland, with Jeff Sartain).

Kim Roberts (District of Columbia) is the author of *A Literary Guide to Washington, DC: Walking in the Footsteps of American Writers from Francis Scott Key to Zora Neale Hurston* (University of Virginia Press, 2018) and five books of poems, most recently *The Scientific Method* (WordTech Editions). She is founding editor of *Beltway Poetry Quarterly* and is featured in podcasts sponsored by the Library of Congress and the National Endowment for the Arts. Her website is: www.kimroberts.org.

David Salner's (Delaware) writing appears in recent issues of *Threepenny Review, Ploughshares, Salmagundi, Beloit Poetry Journal, Prairie Schooner, North American Review,* and previously in *Delmarva Review*. His fourth book, *The Stillness of Certain Valleys* (2019, Broadstone Books), includes two poems

first published in *Delmarva Review*. His third book is *Blue Morning Light* (2016, Pond Road Press). Salner has worked as an iron ore miner, steelworker, machinist, and longshoreman. He has a MFA from the University of Iowa and is working on a novel about the sandhogs who built the Holland Tunnel.
Website: www.DSalner.wix.com/salner.

Martin Shapiro (Maryland) is the Humanities Librarian at American University, in Washington, D.C. He has lived in Kansas City, Pittsburgh, and New York City. Currently, he resides in Chevy Chase, Maryland.

Allen Stein (North Carolina) was born in the Bronx and teaches in the English department at North Carolina State University. His poems have been published in over twenty journals, among them *Salmagundi, Delmarva Review, Poet Lore, Willow Springs, New Ohio Review*, and *The South Carolina Review*. His short fiction has also been published in literary journals.

Catherine Stratton (New Jersey) is a writer and filmmaker living in Hoboken. She says she is submitting work to literary journals for the first time and plans to continue working on her craft until she takes her last breath.

Richard Stuecker (Kentucky) is a poet, essayist, playwright, and teacher. Presently, he is also a student at the Bluegrass Writer's Studio MFA program at Eastern Kentucky University. His poems have appeared in *Pegasus* and *Thinker;* essays in *Crambo* and *Louisville Magazine;* and his book reviews in *The Courier-Journal*. A collection of essays on aging, *Vibrant Emeritus,* was published in 2014 by John Hunt Publishing (London).

Gerald F. Sweeney (Maryland) is the *Review's* Book Section Editor. He is past president of the Eastern Shore Writers Association. Sweeney is a veteran and a graduate of Michigan. A retired NY magazine executive, he has just completed the final novel in a seven-book series called *The Columbiad* that follows one family through the 20th Century. The novels include: *Eagles Rising, First Lights, Crashing into Sunrise, A Tournament of a Distinguished White Order, Comes the Electric Circus, Yo Columbia!* and *Wizard Ho!*

Merideth M. Taylor (Maryland) is professor emerita of theater and dance at St. Mary's College of Maryland. She has received awards in directing, playwriting, screenwriting, and historical documentation, and her plays have been produced in Washington, DC, New York, and Valdez, Alaska. *Listening In: Echoes and Artifacts of Maryland's Mother County*, her book of photos and stories, was released in June, 2018.

Alison Thompson (New South Wales, Australia) is an award-winning Australian writer whose poems and stories have been published internationally. She was selected for an Art Omi: Writers Residency (Spring 2019). Alison is a member of the Kitchen Table Poets, based in the Shoalhaven region of NSW. Her chapbooks *Slow Skipping* (2008) and *In A Day It Changes* (2018) were published by PressPress.
Website: alisonthompsonpoetry.wordpress.com.

Sam VanNest (Maryland) graduated from St. Mary's College of Maryland and has a MA in English from University of Oregon. He likes to laugh without guilt, doesn't like nostalgia, likes open mics, and doesn't like podiums. He loves the Chesapeake artists' community, has never liked Ferris wheels, likes certain kitsch, doesn't like assumptions, and likes being. He lives on the Eastern Shore.

Beth Oast Williams (Virginia) is a student with the Muse Writers Center, in Norfolk, Virginia. Her poetry has appeared in or is upcoming in *Lou Lit, West Texas Literary Review,*

Wisconsin Review and *Glass Mountain*. Her poetry was nominated for a Pushcart Prize in 2019.

Harold O. Wilson (Maryland) is Fiction Co-Editor of the *Delmarva Review*. He is the author of *The Night Blooming Cereus and Other Stories* and publishes short stories, literary criticism and poetry on his website: www.haroldowilson.com. In addition, he hosts Delmarva Public Radio's "Writer's Edition" and "Delmarva Radio Theatre." He and his wife Marilyn live on Kent Island, on the Eastern Shore.

David H. Xiang (Missouri) is a poet and student of history and science at Harvard College where he has taken workshops from poets Jorie Graham and Josh Bell. He serves on the poetry board at *The Harvard Advocate*, the oldest continuously published college art and literary magazine in the United States. He started writing poetry as a freshman in high school, after attending the *Kenyon Review* Young Writers Workshop. In 2015, he was selected as a National Student Poet. His inaugural poetry reading was at the White House, at the invitation of former First Lady Michelle Obama.

Terence Young (British Columbia, Canada) is a co-founder and former editor of *The Claremont Review*, a literary magazine for young writers. His most recent book is a collection of short fiction, *The End of the Ice Age* (Biblioasis, 2010). He lives in Victoria, British Columbia.

Sepideh Zamani's (Maryland and Iran) essays, short stories, and novels focus on immigration and exile, gender inequality, and the life of ethnic and religious minorities under forced assimilation. Her first collection of short stories, *Barbuda*, was published in Farsi, in 2016. Two of her books are forthcoming in 2019. She was born in Iran, in 1973, graduated from law school in 1999, and moved to United States a year later.

Andrena Zawinski's (California) poetry has received accolades for lyricism, form, spirituality, and social concern. Her latest collection is *Landings* (Kelsay Books). Other books include *Something About* and *Traveling in Reflected Light*. A long-time feminist and teacher of writing, she founded and runs the San Francisco Bay Area Women's Poetry Salon and is features editor at PoetryMagazine.com.

♦

Delmarva Review

Evocative Prose & Poetry

ORDERS & SUBSCRIPTIONS

Order your own copy of *Delmarva Review* today!

Single copies (trade paperback) are available on Amazon and other online retailers for $15, and eBook copies can be purchased for $3.99. Please visit delmarvareview.org for back issues and much more.

If you're interested in bulk orders or a subscription, please email editor@delmarvareview.org or write Editor at Delmarva Review, PO Box 544, St. Michaels, MD 21663 to let us know.